ABANDONED TO THE STATE
CRUELTY AND NEGLECT IN RUSSIAN ORPHANAGES

Human Rights Watch

New York ·Washington · London · Brussels

ISBN: 1-56432-191-6
Library of Congress Catalog Card Number: 98-88715

Cover photograph © Kate Brooks, 1998. Russian orphans confined to barren day room of *Internat* X, reaching for candies.

Addresses for Human Rights Watch
350 Fifth Avenue, 34th Floor, New York, NY 10118-3299
Tel: (212) 290-4700, Fax: (212) 736-1300, E-mail: hrwnyc@hrw.org

1522 K Street, N.W., #910, Washington, DC 20005-1202
Tel: (202) 371-6592, Fax: (202) 371-0124, E-mail: hrwdc@hrw.org

33 Islington High Street, N1 9LH London, UK
Tel: (171) 713-1995, Fax: (171) 713-1800, E-mail: hrwatchuk@gn.apc.org

15 Rue Van Campenhout, 1000 Brussels, Belgium
Tel: (2) 732-2009, Fax: (2) 732-0471, E-mail:hrwatcheu@skynet.be

Web Site Address: http://www.hrw.org

Listserv address: To subscribe to the list, send an e-mail message to majordomo@igc.apc.org with "subscribe hrw-news" in the body of the message (leave the subject line blank).

Human Rights Watch is dedicated to
protecting the human rights of people around the world.

We stand with victims and activists to prevent
discrimination, to uphold political freedom, to protect people from inhumane
conduct in wartime, and to bring offenders to justice.

We investigate and expose
human rights violations and hold abusers accountable.

We challenge governments and those who hold power to end abusive practices
and respect international human rights law.

We enlist the public and the international
community to support the cause of human rights for all.

HUMAN RIGHTS WATCH

Human Rights Watch conducts regular, systematic investigations of human rights abuses in some seventy countries around the world. Our reputation for timely, reliable disclosures has made us an essential source of information for those concerned with human rights. We address the human rights practices of governments of all political stripes, of all geopolitical alignments, and of all ethnic and religious persuasions. Human Rights Watch defends freedom of thought and expression, due process and equal protection of the law, and a vigorous civil society; we document and denounce murders, disappearances, torture, arbitrary imprisonment, discrimination, and other abuses of internationally recognized human rights. Our goal is to hold governments accountable if they transgress the rights of their people.

Human Rights Watch began in 1978 with the founding of Helsinki Watch, what is now its Europe and Central Asia division. Today, it also includes divisions covering Africa, the Americas, Asia, and the Middle East and North Africa. In addition, it includes three thematic divisions on arms, children's rights, and women's rights. It maintains offices in New York, Washington, Los Angeles, London, Brussels, Moscow, Dushanbe, Rio de Janeiro, and Hong Kong. Human Rights Watch is an independent, nongovernmental organization, supported by contributions from private individuals and foundations worldwide. It accepts no government funds, directly or indirectly.

The staff includes Kenneth Roth, executive director; Michele Alexander, development director; Reed Brody, advocacy director; Carroll Bogert, communications director; Cynthia Brown, program director; Barbara Guglielmo, finance and administration director; Jeri Laber, special advisor; Lotte Leicht, Brussels office director; Patrick Minges, publications director; Susan Osnos, associate director; Jemera Rone, counsel; Wilder Tayler, general counsel; and Joanna Weschler, United Nations representative. Jonathan Fanton is the chair of the board. Robert L. Bernstein is the founding chair.

The regional directors of Human Rights Watch are Peter Takirambudde, Africa; José Miguel Vivanco, Americas; Sidney Jones, Asia; Holly Cartner, Europe and Central Asia; and Hanny Megally, Middle East and North Africa. The thematic division directors are Joost R. Hiltermann, arms; Lois Whitman, children's rights; and Regan Ralph, women's rights.

The members of the board of directors are Jonathan Fanton, chair; Lisa Anderson, Robert L. Bernstein, William Carmichael, Dorothy Cullman, Gina Despres, Irene Diamond, Adrian W. DeWind, Fiona Druckenmiller, Edith Everett, James C. Goodale, Jack Greenberg, Vartan Gregorian, Alice H. Henkin, Stephen L. Kass, Marina Pinto Kaufman, Bruce Klatsky, Harold Hongju Koh, Alexander MacGregor, Josh Mailman, Samuel K. Murumba, Andrew Nathan, Jane Olson, Peter Osnos, Kathleen Peratis, Bruce Rabb, Sigrid Rausing, Anita Roddick, Orville Schell, Sid Sheinberg, Gary G. Sick, Malcolm Smith, Domna Stanton, Maureen White, and Maya Wiley. Robert L. Bernstein is the founding chair of Human Rights Watch.

ACKNOWLEDGMENTS

This is a joint report by two divisions of Human Rights Watch: the Children's Rights and the Europe and Central Asia Divisions. It was researched and written by Kathleen Hunt, a consultant to Human Rights Watch, who as a journalist investigated the orphanages in post-Ceausescu Romania for the New York *Times* Sunday Magazine and covered the break-up of the Soviet Union from 1991-1994 for National Public Radio.

The bulk of the investigation was conducted by Ms. Hunt in Russia, from February 10 to March 9, 1998. Considerable preparatory research was undertaken during January, and follow-up since her return from Russia. The Human Rights Watch Moscow office provided invaluable research and administrative backup throughout this period, and we are particularly grateful to Lyuda Alpern for her full-time assistance.

The report was edited by Lois Whitman from the Children's Rights Division and Rachel Denber of the Europe and Central Asia Division. Michael McClintock, deputy program director and Dinah PoKempner, deputy general counsel, provided additional comments on the manuscript, and Shalu Rozario of the Children's Rights Division and Alex Frangos of the Europe and Central Asia Division provided production assistance.

It is a pity that a vise of secrecy and fear, reminiscent of Soviet times, has tightened around the isolated world of Russia's state orphanages. Many dedicated orphanage staff and foreign volunteers begged us not to reveal their names, or the institutions in which they worked. Russian workers, they said, would be fired for talking to an outsider. Foreign charity workers would be expelled from the institutions and the doors slammed on humanitarian assistance. This would further isolate the system which they felt a desperate need to improve. We have respected these requests.

This report, nevertheless, would not have been possible without the assistance of many who did take the risk to share what they knew about state-run institutions for abandoned children. Of those in Moscow who wish to be named, we especially thank Sergei Koloskov, father of a Down syndrome child and president of the Down Syndrome Association for families with Down syndrome children, Sarah Philips, a former volunteer with the charity organization Action for Russia's Children, and Boris Altshuler, Lyubov Kushnir and Lyudmilla Alexeeva of Rights of the Child, Russia's leading nongovernmental organization dedicated to defending children's rights.

Also in Moscow, we wish to express our gratitude to Dr. Anatoly Severny, of the Independent Association of Child Psychiatrists and Psychologists, Marina Rodman, and Sergei A. Levin. Olga Alexeeva of Charities Aid Foundation shared her expertise and the bounty of her research archives, and Karina A. Moskalenko provided invaluable help with our legal research. Further information and insights were provided by Equilibre, Médécins sans Frontières, and Alexander Ogorodnikov, who runs an independent shelter for runaway children.

Several translators labored over the raft of legal documentation assembled, and assisted with lengthy interviews with orphans. We especially thank Lena Sheveleva, Irina Savelyeva, Tanya Morschakova, Maria Armand, and Alexander Bogdanov.

On our two missions outside of Moscow, Human Rights Watch was generously assisted in St. Petersburg by Médécins du Monde/Doctors of the World; Alexander Rodin, a former deputy in the city council and now independent advocate for children in orphanages, juvenile detention, and the streets; and Alexander Bogdanov, who assisted in the research gathered from a group of teenaged orphans. Our research outside of Moscow would not have been possible without the help of Eduard A. Alexeyev. Further thanks go to Doctor Mikhail M. Airumyan, president of the independent Russian Association of Baby Houses, and Dr. Olga Y. Vassilieva, deputy director of one Russian baby house in a region north of Moscow.

Across the vast territory of the Russian Federation, we would like to extend our appreciation for the time given by dozens of people whom we interviewed extensively by telephone, gathering background information on institutions in rural and remote regions. There are far too many to mention here, but we especially wish to thank Vera Strebizh of Shans, a children's rights group, and Anna Pastukhova of Memorial Society, both of Ekaterinburg.

For the photographs in this report, we are deeply grateful to freelance photographer Kate Brooks, Sergei Koloskov, Natasha Fairweather, and to the British company Independent Television News for permitting us to view the tape of their cameraman's visit to a shocking psychoneurological *internat*. Valuable background information was provided by other journalists, including Zoya Trounova, and Sam Hutchinson, who described the inhuman conditions in the orphanages they had visited during the past two years.

Finally, our heartfelt thanks go to the many Russian orphans who talked freely with us. To protect their privacy, the names of all children in this report have been changed as indicated in the footnotes. Our sincerest hopes go to those who spoke with us as well as to those who are too young, or too neglected, to have yet learned to speak. We call on the international community to hasten the day when they can unlock their minds and develop their full human potential.

CONTENTS

GLOSSARY OF TERMS

Aminazine: Big tranquilizer (neuroleptic) commonly administered in Russian orphanages.

CAT: The United Nations Convention against Torture and other Cruel, Inhuman or Degrading Treatment or Punishment.

CIDE: Comité International pour la Dignité de l'Enfant (International Committee for the Dignity of the Child). Swiss-based organization that published a report on several orphanages and juvenile detention centers in St.Petersburg, 1995.

The Commission: Shorthand reference to the state-run Psychological-Medical-Pedagogical Commission, an interdisciplinary board that evaluates the developmental progress of all orphans in institutions around the age of four. The commission's controversial diagnosis effectively channels abandoned children and children with disabilities into state institutions for the "educable" or asylums for the "ineducable."

CRC: U.N. Convention on the Rights of the Child.

CSI: Christian Solidarity International, a British charity that produced a report in 1991 based on an expert investigation into orphanages and *internaty* in Russia.

Debil: One who is mildly mentally retarded. According to Russian medical references, *debily* tend to imitate, and can master primary school skills. But they do not develop more subtle intellectual feelings such as duty, and their behavior is often determined by chance and unregulated feelings.

Dom rebyonka: Baby house. Orphanage for infants 0-4 years old, run by the Russian Ministry of Health.

DRMRP: United Nations Declaration on the Rights of Mentally Retarded Persons.

DSA: Down Syndrome Association (of Russia), an independent nongovernmental organization.

Dyetskii dom: (plural: *dyetskiye doma*) Children's home, literally. Often used interchangeably with *internat* to refer to state orphanages in general. The nickname "*dyet' dom*," and the adjective "*dyet-domovskii*" are often used pejoratively.

ICCPR: International Covenant on Civil and Political Rights.

ICESCR: International Covenant on Economic, Social, and Cultural Rights.

Idiot: One who has the most profound degree of mental retardation. Russian medical references describe *idioty* as "helpless and requir[ing] care and supervision. Speech is absent." They are considered "ineducable." Diagnosis is "*idiotia*."

Imbetsil: One who has a severe degree of mental retardation (between *debil* and *idiot*). Russian medical references say the hallmark of *imbetsily* is their "inability to engage in abstract thought and to be taught in school. Their feelings are extremely primitive." Thus, they are ineducable. Diagnosis is "*imbetsil'nost*."

Internat: (plural: *internaty*) Boarding institution. Often used interchangeably with *dyetskii dom*, to refer to orphanages for children five to eighteen years. In this report, unless indicated otherwise, "*internat*" refers to the institutions for "ineducable" children run by the Russian Ministry of Labor and Social Development.

ISM: International Standards for Medical Treatment, Including Care of the Disabled and Terminally Ill (from the U.N. and the World Medical Association).

Lying-down room: Room(s) in baby houses and psycho-neurological *internaty* for bedridden children.

NGO: Nongovernmental organization.

Nurse: Training is generally equivalent to nurse's aide in Western medical systems.

Oligophrenia: Mental retardation (from the Greek, "small brain"). Russian medical references indicate that true *oligophrenia* is hereditary, congenital, or acquired early in life. There are three categories, from mild to severe: *debil*, *imbetsil*, and *idiot*. Applied with a broad interpretation to abandoned infants and young children.

Orphan: Also, "social orphan." Used broadly to include abandoned children with one or both living parents, which is the case for roughly 95 percent of children in state institutions. Some parents have relinquished or been denied parental rights, but a substantial number of children who have run away or been abandoned, have parents who still have legal rights.

Pedagogue: Professional educator, included as personnel category in all state institutions. Some specialize in speech and reading, but the level of skill varies widely.

PME: Principles of Medical Ethics Relevant to the Role of Health Personnel, particularly Physicians, in the Protection of Prisoners and Detainees against Torture and Other Cruel, Inhuman or Degrading Treatment or Punishment. (United Nations document.)

Psikhushka: Ironic diminutive for "psychiatric hospital," to which misbehaving orphans can be sent for discipline or treatment.

PTU: Pedagogical Technical Directorate (Ministry of Education system). This is a system of vocational training institutions with dormitory accommodation, for school-aged children who have completed at least six years of standard schooling, and left their children's home.

Psychoneurological Internat: Boarding institution for children five to eighteen years of age, deemed mentally retarded, or *oligophrenic* at the level of *imbetsil* and *idiot*, and thus, ineducable. Run by Ministry of Labor and Social Development.

RFC: Russian Family Code.

Rights of the Child: Independent local nongovernmental organization based in Moscow which advocates human rights protection for children.

Rod dom: Maternity ward in a general hospital in larger towns and cities. Many Russian orphans are abandoned in the *rod dom* shortly after birth.

Sanitarka: (plural: *sanitarki*) Cleaning person or orderly. Although they are trained mainly as orderlies, they are often the only institutional staff who are responsible for the day-to-day care of children in baby houses and *internaty*.

Spets-internat: Special boarding institution. The generic term for institutions housing children with a various categories of physical and mental disabilities. Can refer to *spets-internaty* for "*debil*," or lightly retarded children (Ministry of Education), and the psychoneurological *spets-internaty* for children labeled "*imbetsil*" and "*idiot*" (Ministry of Labor and Social Development).

U.N. Rules: U.N. Rules for the Protection of Juveniles Deprived of their Liberty

Vospitatel': (plural: *vospitateli*) General caretaker of children. Personnel category includes non-academic teachers in children's homes and vocational training dormitories. Education level of a *vospitatel'* is usually equivalent to a primary school teacher.

Ukol beznorme: Injection. Colloquial term used by children in *internaty* to refer to medication, such as tranquilizers, administered without orders from a physician.

WHO: World Health Organization. U.N. agency based in Geneva.

I. SUMMARY AND RECOMMENDATIONS

"It took me a while to realize when I went to the baby houses that they only show you all the healthy ones. Then there are the rooms where the others are just lying there. They're all dying, lying on their backs, staring at the ceiling, generally fed on their backs. I've seen them putting the bottle of boiling hot food into children's mouths. It must be burning, but they're too hungry and just swallow it."

- Sarah Philips, long-time orphanage volunteer
February 23, 1998

"When I was little, Svetlana Petrovna put my head in the toilet and beat me on the behind, hips, and arms. At first she would hit me on my hand—that was while I was small, until I was nine years old. After that she could take a slipper and slap us on the lips. Of course, a kid couldn't do anything or say anything. We were so afraid of her."

"They could put you in the bedroom and make you stay there. They also kept food from you to punish you, too. Right now it's the staff that's the worst thing about life here—especially Svetlana Petrovna....There are about six or seven staff who are about the same."

- Kirina G., fifteen, Moscow orphan
February 20, 1998

"They're called children with no prospects, not trainable, not treatable. A colleague called these psychoneurological internaty "death camps." The situation there is terrible."

- Dr. Anatoly Severny, President
Independent Association of Child Psychiatrists and Psychologists, Moscow,
February 12, 1998

"I could not say that I am proud of [that psychoneurological internat], ...but in general I believe that everything that can possibly be done in the current conditions is being done...And for these [Down syndrome] children [who may come from alcoholic homes], life in an internat is a paradise."

- Natalia Tsibisova, Director of Residential Institutions, Moscow Committee for the Social Defense of the Population, quoted in the Moscow Times, February 7, 1998

It is seven years since the declining Soviet Union released the last of its most renowned political dissidents, and closed a chapter of notorious human rights abuse in psychiatric hospitals and GULAG prisons. Yet today, in another archipelago of grim state institutions, the authorities of the Russian Federation are violating the fundamental rights of tens of thousands of innocent citizens: children abandoned to state orphanages.

Human Rights Watch has found that from the moment the state assumes their care, orphans in Russia—of whom 95 percent still have a living parent—are exposed to shocking levels of cruelty and neglect. Infants classified as disabled are segregated into "lying-down" rooms, where they are changed and fed but are bereft of stimulation and lacking in medical care.

Once officially labelled as retarded, Russian orphans face another grave and consequential violation of their rights around the age of four, when they are deemed "ineducable," and warehoused for life in psychoneurological *internaty*. In addition to receiving little to no education in such *internaty*, these orphans may be restrained in cloth sacks, tethered by a limb to furniture, denied stimulation, and sometimes left to lie half-naked in their own filth. Bedridden children aged five to seventeen are confined to understaffed lying-down rooms as in the baby houses, and in some cases are neglected to the point of death. Those who grow to adulthood are then interned in another "total institution," where they are permanently denied opportunities to know and enjoy their civil and political rights.

The "normal" abandoned children—those whom the state evaluates as intellectually capable of functioning on a higher level—are subjected to cruel, inhuman and degrading treatment by institution staff. They may be beaten, locked in freezing rooms for days at a time, abused physically and sexually. They may be humiliated, insulted and degraded, and provided inadequate education and training.

Staff members may also instigate or condone brutality by older orphans against younger and weaker ones, incidents such as beatings and humiliation. Some children describe treatment as outrageous as being thrown out a window while nailed in a small wooden chest. When orphans finally leave their institutions, they suffer its damaging effects and the second-class status as orphans for the rest of their lives.

It is ironic and deplorable that the very state that is charged with the care and nurture of these vulnerable children condemns them to a life of deprivation and cruelty. Moreover, far too many children are consigned to Russian institutions in the first place. Of a total of more than 600,000 children classified as being "without parental care," as many as one-third reside in institutions, while the rest are placed with a variety of guardians. Thousands more are temporarily quartered in various public shelters and institutions under police jurisdiction simply waiting for an available space in an orphanage.

Humane alternatives to institutions exist and should be used, such as sending children with moderate disabilities home with their parents at birth; providing help for families to cope with their children's disabilities; and providing foster care for children who cannot return to their families. As Russian experts told Human Rights Watch in the body of this report, these alternatives do not require additional resources, but rather a reallocation of existing funds now devoted almost exclusively to expensive institutional care.

Abandoned Children as an Underclass

Human Rights Watch has found that from the moment Russian children are left in state institutions, they become victims of long-held prejudices that all abandoned children are in some way "defective." One source of this discriminatory assumption is the tradition that infants born with severe congenital defects have been abandoned in local maternity wards under pressure and warnings from the medical staff that the family will be ostracized for raising a disabled child.

Even if abandoned infants do not display severe physical or mental disabilities, however, they often come from families with chronic social, financial and health problems—including alcoholism—and they cannot escape the stigma applied to that past. A clear summary of this point appeared in an article in the *Moscow Times* of November 2, 1996, which explored the biases against adopting a baby abandoned by a stranger:

> The fear that the child will in some way be "damaged goods" stems from the knowledge that mothers of mentally and physically handicapped children are routinely advised by doctors to put their baby in an orphanage and "try again." Consequently, healthy babies who are given up for financial or domestic reasons are unfairly branded "defective."

The result is that abandoned children are consigned to the status of "orphan," and further labelled in their medical charts with physical and psychological "risk factors" in their medical charts owing to their background. Testimonies collected by Human Rights Watch are corroborated by the findings of expert investigators from the Swiss-based Comité pour la Dignité de l'Enfant (C.I.D.E.), published in 1995. They found that while Russian professionals used strict criteria in performing psychological evaluations, they also recorded factors in the child's medical history which would be considered as "risk" factors in the West, but commonly become labels of illness for an abandoned Russian child. According to the C.I.D.E. report, these include:

- babies born to alcoholic parents or whose mothers suffered depression during pregnancy will be labelled encephalopathic and remain so until they come of age.
- orphans will be classed as being mentally deficient.
- children with a single physical malformation (a harelip or speech defect...) become subnormal in the eyes of Russian doctors.

International human rights law forbids discrimination on a variety of grounds, including "birth or other status." Under the United Nations' "Principles for the Protection of Persons with Mental Illness and the Improvement of Mental Health Care," Principle number 4 provides that, "A determination of mental illness shall never be made on the basis of political, economic or social status, or membership of a cultural, racial or religious group, or any other reason not directly relevant to mental health status."

In practice, however, the Russian system violates this principle as well as the fundamental tenets of the International Covenant on Economic, Social and Cultural Rights, by branding children of lower socioeconomic origins and children with genetic abnormalities as a class apart.

It does so by attributing to them a propensity for social deviance stemming from their background, and by imposing upon them a life-long stigma and formal restrictions on participation in society. Abandoned children who are diagnosed as "*oligophrenic*," or mentally retarded, carry that label in their official dossier from institution to institution. They have virtually no channels through which to seek a reassessment or reversal of this diagnosis, and even "mild" *oligophrenics* who graduate from technical training schools told Human Rights Watch that they had difficulty appealing for the word to be removed from their file.

Human Rights Watch concludes that the Russian state fails to provide sufficient protection and opportunities to thousands of children who are abandoned to the state at a rate of 113,000 a year for the past two years, up dramatically from 67,286 in 1992. The evidence gathered reveals several systematic disadvantages imposed on young Russian orphans, which violate their fundamental rights to survival and development, and place them in an underclass.

Children abandoned at birth are more likely to be smaller and less developed over time than others, due in part to the significant lack of developmental care in state institutions during the crucial phase of early infancy.

Orphans in Russia have no one to appeal the state's special medical-developmental evaluation, which is performed on virtually all institutionalized children approaching the first year of school and older children at the time of abandonment. As described in greater detail in Chapters IV and V of this report, a diagnosis of severe *oligophrenia* for orphans means a greater likelihood of premature death in an institution that is little more than a warehouse.

According to this "diagnosis," which is delivered by a state-run commission of doctors, psychologists, and educators based at the Chief Psychiatric Hospital No.6 in Moscow, children in Russian institutions face a *"triage"* into one of two tunnel-like systems apart from Russian society at large. As explained in Chapter II of this report, in the best case, they are deemed educable, and proceed to a *dyetskii dom* run by the Ministry of Education, and attend regular Russian schools. In the worst case, they are deemed severely oligophrenic—either *imbetsil* or *idiot*—and condemned to a system of "total institutions" run by the Ministry of Labor and Social Development. There they receive little to no education and only a minimum of maintenance until they reach the age of eighteen, when they move on to an adult institution of the same kind. As the later chapters of this report show, independent child welfare experts in Russia denounce these institutions, claiming that the death rate for children is twice that of children living at home.

The comparatively fortunate orphans who make it into the educable group are still more likely to receive harsher discipline than children whose parents have left them only temporarily in state custody and continue to have contact with the orphanage.

Orphans in state institutions are less likely to be referred for needed medical services than are children with parents. Should orphans happen to be transferred to a hospital for services, they are less likely to receive proper medical treatment than children whose families can cajole and bribe hospital staff to carry out their work appropriately.

Failure to Live Up to National Commitments
The Russian government and its predecessor, the USSR, have long taken pride in the education and upbringing of their children. Its separate world of giant

orphanages reflects the Soviet philosophy of collective action and discipline that guided the institutions erected to house millions of war orphans during the first half of the 20th century.

Since the break-up of the Soviet Union in 1991, however, the increased access to orphanages by journalists and charitable volunteers has unveiled a tableau of horrific conditions and malign neglect in institutions from the heart of Moscow to remote rural provinces. The Russian and international media have widely disseminated the shocking images from the orphanages during the past few years, and at least two international human rights delegations have issued damning reports of their findings, which are cited in the body of this report. Yet deplorable conditions still persist.

Officially, the Russian authorities, starting with President Boris Yeltsin, have repeatedly declared the rights of children a high national priority. The Russian Federation was among the first nations to sign and ratify the U.N. Convention on the Rights of the Child in 1990, the full text of which is presented in the Appendix to this report. Russia has subsequently submitted two periodic reports of its implementation of the Convention on the Rights of the Child, in 1992 and late 1997.

Also during the 1990s, Russia passed a raft of legislation and decrees affirming children's rights to education, health, and special protection against the hardships and upheaval wrought by economic reform. By mid-decade, President Yeltsin had launched two federal programs, "Children of Russia," and "Fundamental Directions of State Social Policy for Improving the Position of Children in the Russian Federation to the Year 2000." These programs are aimed at increasing the efficiency of state programs for children at the federal and local levels, and helping poorer families to provide a stable environment in which a child may develop.

In practice, however, the reaction of the Russian authorities to the critique of their orphanages has been to block access to the institutions; punish or threaten to fire workers if they speak about abuses; and, in some instances, pardon those who are responsible for the wrongdoing.

Senior officials of the three ministries charged with maintaining the orphanages have impeded the efforts of Russian human rights organizations to investigate reports of neglect and malfeasance. Members of such groups and child welfare experts told Human Rights Watch that senior officials flatly rejected their requests to visit the particularly degrading and unhealthy psychoneurological *internaty* run by the Ministry of Labor and Social Development for orphans diagnosed as *imbetsily* and *idioty*.

Failure to Comply with International Obligations

Although the Russian government has signed the Convention on the Rights of the Child, the evidence gathered and presented in this report shows that Russian policies toward abandoned children violate as many as twenty of the convention's first forty-one articles, which comprise a sweeping array of basic rights. More significantly, our evidence reinforces the concerns recorded in 1993 by the U.N. Committee on the Rights of the Child, in its letter replying to the Russian Federation's first periodic implementation report.

- The U.N. Committee featured as a "principal subject of concern," the "practice of the institutionalization in boarding schools of children who are deprived of a family environment, particularly in cases of abandonment or where children are orphaned."

- Another "principal subject of concern" highlighted by the U.N. Committee was the dire situation of disabled children. Human Rights Watch has learned that severely disabled babies are routinely abandoned at the state-run maternity wards, under pressure from medical personnel who warn the recuperating mothers of a life as social pariahs if they keep a "defective" child.

- Finally, the violence against orphans by institution staff and older children, which Human Rights Watch also documents in this report, gives heightened cause to the U.N. Committee's concern about the "occurrence of maltreatment and cruelty towards children in and outside the family." Now, more than ever, the facts substantiate the committee's 1993 suggestion that "procedures and mechanisms be developed to deal with complaints by children of the maltreatment or of cruelty towards them."

Next spring (1999), the second Convention on the Rights of the Child implementation report of the Russian Federation will come up for review by the U.N. Committee; Human Rights Watch urges the committee to place the systematic violations of orphans' rights at the top of its agenda.

To that end, we call attention to several of the more egregious violations of the Convention on the Rights of the Child, among other international documents that are abrogated on a daily basis in Russian custodial institutions.

Contrary to the precepts set forth in Article 23 of the Convention on the Rights of the Child, specifically concerning children with mental and physical disabilities, Russian orphans with severe disabilities are denied virtually every right to medical care, education, and individual development.

Such orphans are officially classified as "ineducable," and are excluded from opportunities to learn to read, write, and in some cases, to walk. In addition, abandoned babies and children of sound mind, but with physical disabilities, are routinely confined to areas in state institutions known as "lying-down" rooms. They are passed over for corrective surgery of conditions such as cleft palate as a result of the compound stigma of being abandoned and being diagnosed as "*oligophrenic*" (mentally retarded).

During a visit to the lying-down room of one psychoneurological *internat*, Human Rights Watch noticed a beaming blond, five-year-old boy walking on the callused sides of his club feet. We asked the *sanitarka* who was playing with him what his diagnosis was. "*Oligophrenia*," she replied. But when we asked specifically about his feet, she replied, "Well, it's the same... *imbetsilnost*."

In addition to the appalling violation of the rights of orphans with severe congenital disabilities, critics of the state's diagnostic procedure also expressed their concerns time and again to Human Rights Watch that too many children were, in fact, wrongly diagnosed. Even the staff at two institutions told Human Rights Watch that they believed that nine to ten percent of the children transferred to them as *imbetsily* and *idioty*, actually had the ability to enjoy productive lives.

The percentage of diagnostic errors was shown to be strikingly higher in a more in-depth clinical assessment of *oligophrenic* orphans published in 1991 by the British charity organization, Christian Solidarity International (CSI).   CSI concluded that in one group of fifty children they studied, more than one-third were within "normal" limits of standard intelligence tests.   On more thorough examination of thirty-four children, the team gathered the startling results that "two-thirds of these '*oligophrenic*' children showed evidence of average or better ability."

In view of the known and suspected cases of misdiagnosis among orphans, Human Rights Watch finds the violation of Article 27 of the Convention on the Rights of the Child particularly relevant. It accords children undergoing medical care the right to periodic review of their treatment and surrounding conditions. In practice, however, Russian orphans with diagnoses of *oligophrenia* have extreme difficulty seeking a re-assessment of their status, which is also a violation of Russian law. Even those classified as "lightly" *oligophrenic* (*debil*) carry the burden of that classification in their official file when they embark on their search for jobs and homes.

The most severe discrimination faced by Russian orphans is suffered by children interned in psychoneurological *internaty* for children with disabilities who are aged five to seventeen years. Article 39 of the convention calls for the promotion of "physical and psychological recovery and social reintegration following neglect, exploitation or abuse...or any other form of cruel, inhuman or degrading treatment or punishment."

Far from receiving treatment towards recovery or rehabilitation, however, Russian orphans consigned to lying-down rooms suffer further deterioration from neglect. Agitated orphans are confined to barren day-rooms where they are tethered, restrained, and given powerful sedatives without medical supervision.

Such examples of inhuman and degrading treatment and punishment are all too common features of Russian orphanages, both for children with severe disabilities, and as well for those diagnosed as "educable." In the latter case, Human Rights Watch discovered elaborate patterns of dehumanizing discipline in the *dyetskiye doma* of the Education Ministry, in which the orphanage directors and staff strove to humiliate children in front of their peers, and at times encouraged their peers to take part in the demeaning punishment.

Such choreography of cruelty by orphanage staff is often devised for the purpose of punishment-by-proxy, through which older or stronger children are delegated to maintain order. The resulting disciplinary pattern alarmingly resembles that found in the Russian military and prisons, both state institutions notorious for their elaborate systems of violence and debasement. Whether for punishment or for simple sadism, this practice amounts to a training module in physical and mental violence.

Moreover, the common practice of interning older children in psychiatric hospitals for rule-breaking behavior such as running away from the orphanage is a perversion of medical ethics and an alarming throwback to the gross misconduct of the Soviet psychiatric profession. Children returning from two weeks to several months in the *psykhushka* report the use of heavy tranquilizers, and appear disoriented and confused to their peers.

These preeminent uses of violence against Russian orphans violate the Convention against Torture and Other Cruel, Inhuman or Degrading Treatment or Punishment, as well as other international standards pertaining to medical ethics and the treatment of persons with mental illness.

This report is based on a month-long fact-finding mission in Russia, during which Human Rights Watch met with more than thirty-one orphans, from some seventeen institutions; six doctors specializing in child development, either working within or outside institutions, four *vospitateli* working with older orphans and ones with disabilities, three children's rights activists, several journalists, and five Western volunteers who have worked extensively in institutions.

Several of these volunteers were among the first outsiders to enter children's institutions in Russia during the early 1990s, and they undertook a survey of orphans' needs for a new charitable assistance program. As a result of their research, and their in-depth work in a number of institutions, the volunteers interviewed for this report hold the most comprehensive information on the system as a whole, outside government officials.

Some of these volunteers and others interviewed by Human Rights Watch were willing to be named in this report. They requested, however, that we not identify the institutions they described, for fear of being banned from them after the publication of this report.

To protect the orphans and others who fear reprisals by officials, we have changed the names of all locations and people in this report, and indicated in the footnotes. Testimonies have been lightly edited for clarity, but otherwise represent interviews Human Rights Watch conducted either directly or with the help of an interpreter.

Following the discussion of relevant international and Russian laws in Chapter III, each chapter takes a phase of an orphan's life in a Russian institution, and introduces the genre of human rights violations they suffer at that stage. The prejudicial stereotype of abandonment is common to all stages, for example, while some abuses, such as malicious and degrading punishment, are more specific to the context of the Education Ministry's *dyetskii dom*.

Recommendations

The only way to bring a halt the cycle of discrimination, violence and impunity that endangers abandoned children in Russia is through a joint campaign by the international community, Russian authorities, and children's advocates to abolish all prejudicial practices and investigate reports of wrongdoing.

Human Rights Watch recommends the following reforms:

To the Russian Government
On reducing the number of children consigned to state institutions:

- Stop medical personnel from pressing parents to institutionalize newborns with severe disabilities;

- Develop and implement a plan for the gradual deinstitutionalization of abandoned children and children with disabilities, and reallocate resources now used for institutional care to develop alternative humane, non-discriminatory alternatives;

- Provide assistance to families in caring for children with disabilities—for example, home helpers, day training and education programs;

- Make utmost efforts to locate other relatives who are willing and capable of assuring care for children when it is not in the best interests of the children to remain with their parents, and provide such relatives with assistance where necessary;

- Provide and supervise foster care for children who cannot remain with their families; and

- Make utmost efforts to seek out appropriate opportunities for adoption when it is in the best interests of the child. Human Rights Watch takes no position on the Russian debate over the advisability of foreign adoption, but urges that in seeking alternatives to institutional life, the best interests of the child always be paramount, and that foreign adoption should not be ruled out as an alternative preferable to institutionalization.

On the matter of discriminatory status

- Ensure that all abandoned and orphaned children, whether disabled or otherwise, receive full respect for their human rights and protection against discrimination;

- Immediately stop applying the diagnosis of *oligophrenia* (mentally retarded) to infants or young children until they can be observed and examined adequately over a period of time;

- Commence investigation, with the participation of independent medical, educational, and mental health experts, into the process of evaluation at the age of four, which channels abandoned children almost irreversibly into educable and ineducable worlds. This investigation should aim to reform the evaluation procedure in order to take into consideration the extremely limited experience of instutionalized children;

- Appoint an independent "observer group" including experts in pediatrics, child development, and neuropsychology among others, to take part in the official evaluations conducted by the state Psychological-Medical-Pedagogical Commission, and vested with the power to challenge diagnoses determined by the commission;

- Establish a mechanism for all orphans to exercise their right to appeal the discriminatory diagnosis of *oligophrenia*, and to expunge it from their records, if need be. In conjunction with this action, quickly establish a department staffed with medical, educational, mental health and social work experts to process appeals from older children with completed educations;

- For children too young or otherwise unable to file their own appeals for re-assessment of their diagnoses, enlist independent Russian child welfare experts and attorneys versed in children's advocacy, to assist or represent the child in making the appeal;

- Immediately lift any formal restrictions against appealing the diagnosis of *oligophrenia*;

- Immediately cease to inscribe orphans' official identification documents, including passports, with "*dyetskii dom*" (children's home), and list only the street address as place of residence;

- Immediately take steps to end the gross neglect, and the physical and psychological abuse by staff working in the custodial institutions of the three ministries involved: Health, Education and Labor and Social Development;

- Immediately undertake a public education effort at the federal, regional and local levels, to dispel the deep-rooted prejudice against children who have disabilities and children who are abandoned by their parents. This campaign should enlist experts and popular personages throughout the Russian Federation, as well as abandoned children, those with disabilities, their relatives and advocacy groups for such children . Making use of all possible media and school curricula, the campaign must have as its goal to debunk the myth that abandoned children automatically inherit physical and mental abnormalities and behavioral patterns such as criminality. It should also raise awareness as to the rights and potential of disabled children;

- Consistent with the 1993 recommendations of the U.N. Committee on the Rights of the Child, immediately undertake a parallel in-service training program for staff of state orphanages to dispel these same prejudices and emphasize the rights of disabled persons. Such training should also inform orphanage staff of the significant advances made in the education and treatment of children with bona fide disabilities. Many staff are plainly unaware of the clinical profile and developmental potential of children with Down syndrome, cerebral palsy and other conditions; and

• In conjunction with public education in the institutions, initiate a program in the psychoneurological *internaty* to introduce reading to all children. In addition, furnish them with sorely needed children's books and primers, as well as writing paper, crayons and pencils.

On the matter of punishment, abuse and deplorable conditions
• Immediately issue a directive to all ministries and orphanage directors that corporal and psychological punishment of children are strictly prohibited. To end the system of impunity in the institutions, the directive must state that alleged violators will be subjected to investigation. If necessary, they will be disciplined, dismissed or submitted to criminal prosecution;

• In conjunction with the above, commence systematic investigations of conditions in selected baby houses; psychoneurological *internaty*; orphanages run by the Ministry of Education; dormitories for orphans fifteen to seventeen years of age who are attending technical training institutes;

• Immediately furnish children in state institutions with information about their basic rights, including their right to file grievances confidentially. This information should be conveyed through social workers and members of independent NGOs, and should include guarantees for their protection against retribution in the event that the alleged violator is convicted;

• Immediately establish an effective channel through which orphans may make confidential complaints to an independent outside authority about violence and misconduct committed, or instigated, by the institutional director, staff or other children;

• Immediately appoint an independent, standing commission of experts from the fields of pediatrics, neurology, psychology, and early childhood education, vested with full authority to conduct unannounced visits to institutions and to order official sanctions for violations; and

• In the meantime, expert consultants should be enlisted by each ministry to review and revise the standards of institutional care in accordance with the tenets of international and Russian law. Each of the Russian ministries responsible for children's custodial institutions—Health, Education, and especially the Ministry of Labor and Social Development—should make its current standards for institutional conditions and treatment public and transparent.

On the right to health care

- Ensure, in adherence to Russia's national legislation and international law, that all abandoned children in state custody be provided with necessary medical care. A survey should be undertaken immediately to identify children awaiting surgery to correct cleft palates, heart defects and other problems that threaten a child's survival. These children should be provided with the prescribed services as soon as possible.

On reforming the management and treatment of orphans

- All staff at baby houses, children's homes and psychoneurological *internaty* should undertake a course of formal training. The course must impress upon all employees that the protection of the children's well-being is of utmost importance and that babies require visual, auditory and tactile stimulation at from the earliest moment possible;

- Develop, with the cooperation of the U.N. Children's Fund (UNICEF) and the World Health Organization (WHO), new training programs for child-care workers which will incorporate the experience and research findings from various countries. These should demonstrate the critical importance of individual attention and sensory stimulation for infants from their earliest days, in order to enable normal intellectual development;

- Encourage existing independent efforts to provide foster care in families, and pursue a policy for the gradual deinstitutionalization of orphans. But given the alarming rates of widely reported domestic violence in Russia, and the potential for misappropriation of large-scale subsidies, the Russian authorities must proceed with extreme care to develop strict screening and monitoring criteria before launching a national program of foster care and domestic adoption;

- Undertake a comparative analysis of the costs of institutional care versus subsidized home care for families who abandon children for reasons of economic hardship. The authorities must make the maximum effort to discourage poor families from leaving their children in state care, which some experts calculate to be at least twice as expensive as subsidizing the child's care at home;

- Undertake a similar analysis of the relative cost of institutional care and subsidized home care for children with congenital conditions such as Down syndrome, cerebral palsy, and other disabilities. The Health Ministry in particular must immediately cease to advise families to abandon their children in the maternity ward, and instead enable them to raise them at home with the help of re-allocated state funds;

- In the meantime, ensure that adequate salaries are offered to orphanage staff, who should be recruited carefully for their professional competence, integrity, and respect for children's dignity; and

- All institutions for abandoned children or children with disabilities should be required to provide access to their financial records, budget, and staffing data to any member of the public upon request. Ministerial budgets for such institutions, including amounts allocated per institution and per child for housing, medical care, food, and clothing should likewise be public records available on demand.

To the United Nations
- The U.N. Committee on the Rights of the Child and UNICEF should strongly urge the Russian government to begin the process of gradually closing the psychoneurological *internaty* in favor of alternative models such as family sized foster care and adoption;

- The U.N. Committee on the Rights of the Child should investigate conditions in the institutions for Russian orphans run by the Ministries of Health, Labor and Education. This delegation should concentrate on egregious violations of the CRC, including the extreme deprivation of orphans labeled *oligophrenic* as infants; the denial of corrective surgery to orphans labeled *oligophrenic*; and cases of misdiagnosis at the age of four which have resulted in the denial of education to tens of thousands of orphans;

- The U.N. Special Rapporteur on Torture should investigate conditions in Russian institutions, including those run by the Education Ministry for children from five to seventeen years old. Various forms of inhuman and degrading treatment and punishment should be investigated, including excessive use of isolation, restraints, sedatives, and psychiatric hospital stays for children who attempt to run away from the orphanage. For older children, the U.N. Special

Rapporteur should place high priority on investigating patterns of punishment-by-proxy: physical and psychological abuse committed by directors and staff through the instigation of favored children against other ones;

- UNICEF and the U.N. Committee on the Rights of the Child should assist the government to develop its campaign to dispel widespread prejudice and ignorance about abandoned children and children with disabilities; and

- UNICEF should develop an information campaign to inform children in state orphanages about the few emergency "hot lines" available for children in some Russian regions.

To the Council of Europe
- The Parliamentary Assembly should appoint a rapporteur or instruct rapporteurs for the Monitoring Committee to investigate conditions in the institutions for Russian orphans.

- The Committee for the Prevention of Torture should investigate conditions in institutions for Russian orphans. Various forms of inhuman and degrading treatment and punishment should be investigated, including excessive use of isolation, restraints, sedatives, and psychiatric hospital stays for children who attempt to run away from the orphanage. For older children, the Committee should place high priority on investigating patterns of punishment-by-proxy: physical and psychological abuse committed by directors and staff through the instigation of favored children against other ones.

To Donor Governments
- Use all available influence to urge the Russian authorities to undertake an immediate investigation into the violations of children's rights in state-run orphanages and to bring offenders to justice;

- Earmark funds for training of various categories of staff for baby houses, psychoneurological *internaty* and institutions for "educable" children. Projects should include supporting professionals from selected countries with humane child welfare systems to spend several months as resident trainers in Russian institutions;

- Earmark funds to support the work of existing independent treatment centers for children with disabilities, which provide alternative "second opinion" diagnoses and daytime rehabilitation which enables parents to raise their children at home;

- Earmark funds for independent Russian NGOs to work with the government in launching a nationwide public education program to disseminate the U.N. Convention on the Rights of the Child and U.N. standards for persons with disabilities and mental retardation. This program should highlight the equal rights of children who are abandoned and those with disabilities;

- Earmark funds for independent Russian NGOs working in the field of child welfare and children's rights to assist orphans in filing grievances; and

- Establish a strict independent oversight mechanism for monitoring and auditing disbursement of all donated funds to ensure their intended use.

To Nongovernmental Organizations
- Nongovernmental organizations that provide assistance to Russia, including humanitarian groups and adoption agencies, should press for an end to ill-treatment and discrimination against abandoned and orphaned children and for transparency in the management of children's institutions.

II. THE ODYSSEY OF A RUSSIAN ORPHAN[1]

We did a lot of art in the dom rebyonka (baby house). The children were begging us to hang their paintings over their bed. The staff took the paintings and we never saw them again. They said that these children are being raised in state institutions and would always be in groups the rest of their life. No reason to pamper them with personalized things now, because they wouldn't be allowed such things later in life. And that would only make problems. This mentality is so entrenched.[2]

Background[3]

Russian institutions are bursting with abandoned children, who now total more than 600,000 children who are defined by the state as being "without parental care."[4] During each of the last two years, more than 113,000 children have been abandoned, reflecting a breathtaking rise from 67,286 in 1992. Another 30,000 are

---

[1] For purposes of this report, the term "orphan" refers to children who are abandoned to the state, including the vast majority of "social orphans" whose parents are living. It is used interchangeably with the term "abandoned children." Children with severe disabilities are frequently mentioned throughout this report, because they often become abandoned children and thus enter the population of "orphans."

[2] Human Rights watch interview, Theresa Jacobson (not her real name), former volunteer in a Moscow baby house, March 8, 1998.

[3] In this report, the word "children" refers to anyone under the age of eighteen. The U.N. Convention on the Rights of the Child defines a child as "every human being below the age of eighteen years unless, under the law applicable to the child, majority is attained earlier" (Article 1). Convention on the Rights of the Child, G.A. res. 44/25, annex 44 U.N. GAOR Supp.(No.49) 167, U.N. Doc. A/4/49 (1989). The full text of the Convention on the Rights of the Child is set forth in the Appendix.

[4] Ministerstvo truda y sotsal'novo razvitia Rosyskoi Federatsii. *O polozhenii detei v Rosyskoi Federatsii. 1996 god.* (Ministry of labor and social development of the Russian Federation.) *On the Situation of Children in the Russian Federation.* Annual report for 1996 (Moscow: Ministry of Labor and Social Development, 1997), p. 107. Also supplementary statistics from Human Rights Watch interview with Dr. Anatoly Severny, child development expert and president of the Independent Association of Psychiatrists and Psychologists, February 12, 1998.

reported to run away from troubled homes each year, clogging the urban railway stations and metros, sometimes ending up in shelters and orphanages.[5]

Since the collapse of Soviet rule in 1991, these children have become the jetsam in Russia's stormy economic transition. Their families are often poor, jobless, ill, and in trouble with the law; this burgeoning class of abandoned children has come to be called "social orphans"—indicating that ninety-five percent of abandoned children have a living parent.[6]

Official statistics on abandoned children abound, and the figures gathered from various official sources often do not correspond. The institutions that care for children span three government ministries, and the categories listed in statistical tables either overlap or are so vaguely defined as to make a fine breakdown of numbers extremely difficult. [7]

According to compilations published by UNICEF in 1997, some 611, 034 Russian children are "without parental care." Of these, 337,527 are housed in baby houses, children's homes, and homes for children with disabilities.[8] According to

---

[5] *On the Situation of Children in the Russian Federation*, p. 107.

[6] UNICEF, *Children at Risk in Central and Eastern Europe: Perils and Promises*, Regional Monitoring Report No. 4 (Florence: International Child Development Centre, 1997). Hereafter cited as UNICEF, *Children at Risk*.

[7] Government reports on children's welfare services include a variety of institutions called "*internat*" in Russian. This means "boarding" institution, but must not be construed to be equivalent to educational institutions with the same title in other countries. Russian *internaty* may bear specialized prefixes, such as "auxiliary" and "*spets*," which cater to children with various levels of disability and educational need. Some *internaty* combine boarding and education facilities for children; some contain both abandoned children and children whose parents take them home on the weekends. In daily parlance, however, people in Russia often use terms loosely and interchangeably. The Ministry of Education operates a variety of *internaty*, or boarding institutions, for two major categories of orphans from five to eighteen years of age who have been classified as educable.

[8] UNICEF, *Children at Risk*, p. 67. UNICEF underscores the difficulty in obtaining reliable statistics on children in public care, writing that, "Rather than reflecting a problem-oriented approach to meeting children's needs, data are simply collected and published according to administrative categories, even through there are considerable overlaps and variations among the functions of different institutions. For example, children with slight disabilities may be placed in orphanages, while homes for the disabled may host some basically healthy children. In most cases, however, there are no comprehensive data providing an overview of the needs of all children with disabilities in substitute

a Russian expert in their field, the latter figure includes children living part-time at home, and the full-time orphan population in institutions is closer to 200,000. Of these, at least 30,000 are committed to locked psychoneurological *internaty* for "ineducable" children, run by the Ministry of Labor and Social Development.[9]

The remaining number, according to government tables, are placed in alternative custody, including group homes and other guardianship perhaps with members of a child's extended family. Although some tables list foster care as one of the alternative forms of custody, an international child development specialist told Human Rights Watch that there are only several hundred children living in family-sized settings, and that the standard "foster care" involves larger groups.[10] Human Rights Watch commends the few pilot programs in foster care that have begun in Russia and urges speedy development of further projects that provide humane alternatives to large institutions.

It was beyond the scope of this report to conduct a full investigation of the many categories of institutions. But based on reliable sources most familiar with custodial care for abandoned children, Human Rights Watch has focused on three classes of institutions for this report: *dom rebyonka, dyetskii dom,* and psychoneurological *internat.*

Archipelago of closed institutions

Orphans in Russia are herded through a maze of state structures operated by three government ministries, which compete for limited state funds and overlap in their mandates for certain categories of orphans and children with disabilities. The Ministry of Health is charged with the care of abandoned infants from birth to

---

care....Indeed, poor data availability and inadequate statistical reporting are major constraints for effectively tackling, at the national level, the many issues surrounding children in public care. There is an acute need for internationally coordinated action to improve administrative reporting systems and develop specific problem-oriented surveys. Without these, children will continue to be 'lost in state care.'" Ibid, p. 68.

[9] Human Rights Watch interview, Dr. Anatoly Severny, February 12, 1998 and November 14, 1998; UNICEF, *Children at Risk*, p. 70.

[10] Human Rights Watch interview, international child welfare specialist, October 15, 1998.

roughly four years of age, and houses them in 252 baby houses which are called "*dom rebyonka*," housing from 18-20,000 children.[11]

All abandoned infants spend their first three to four years in a baby house, and are then distributed to institutions under the control of either the Ministry of Education or the Ministry of Labor and Social Development.[12] Among those under the Ministry of Education, one group of children is deemed to have no disabilities, and the second group contains children diagnosed as lightly disabled, and officially termed "*debil.*"

The most common institution for the "educable" children is called a *dyetskii dom* (children's home), which generally houses boys and girls. They generally attend regular Russian public schools for the compulsory nine years, where they can earn a secondary school diploma, or they can leave school at the age of fifteen.[13]

Abandoned children may also live in *school-internaty,* where they receive their education inside the institution where they live. Following secondary school, these children in the care of the Ministry of Education may receive two to three years of further training in a trade, which they pursue at another boarding institution under the Pedagogical Technical Directorate (PTU). While studying skills such as carpentry, electricity, masonry, and stuffed-animal making, among others, the children are housed in dormitories staffed by the Ministry of Education.[14]

At the age of five, the second group of orphans under the Education Ministry's purview—the *debily*—is channeled to *spets internaty* (or "auxiliary *internaty*"), where they reside while taking a significantly abbreviated course of education totaling six years, far short of a high school diploma. They are also offered

---

[11] Ministerstvo truda y sotsal'novo razvitia Rosyskoi Federatsii. *O polozhenii detei v Rosyskoi Federatsii. 1996 god.* (Ministry of labor and social development of the Russian Federation.) *On the Situation of Children in the Russian Federation.* Annual report for 1996 (Moscow: Ministry of Labor and Social Development, 1997).

[12] Until a few years ago, children went to a pre-school institution after the baby house until being transferred a second time to the *dyetskii dom* for their school years. This practice is being phased out in order to minimize the number of institutions where children spend their lives.

[13] Though not officially blocked for higher education, it is rare for orphans to achieve a sufficient academic level to qualify for university entry.

[14] Human Rights Watch interview, orphans, St. Petersburg, February 27, 1998.

vocational training, but their program and residence are generally segregated from the non-*debil* orphans.[15]

Under Russian law, the state must provide all orphans leaving the care of the Education Ministry with an initial stipend, housing and employment. But the economic crisis since the introduction of market reforms and privatization of apartments makes this increasingly difficult. Indeed, the prospect of life in the outside world is a source of great worry to the orphans and child welfare experts alike.[16]

The Ministry of Labor and Social Development takes charge of orphans who are diagnosed by a board of state medical and educational reviewers as having heavy physical and mental disabilities at the age of four. Officially labeled "*imbetsil*" or "*idiot*," they are committed to closed institutions which often resemble Dickensian asylums of the nineteenth century. There they remain until the age of eighteen. Those who survive to that age are transferred to adult psychoneurological *internaty*, or asylums, for the duration of their lives. [17]

Fragmentary statistics on the mortality rates in the institutions under the Ministry of Labor and Social Development indicate that these orphans are at significant risk of premature death. One leading child welfare advocate in Moscow told Human Rights Watch that estimates from government figures indicate the death rate in these *internaty* is twice the rate in the general population. He also knows one *internat* where he said that the death rate rose to as high as three and a half times the rate in the society outside its walls.[18]

While we were not able to obtain government statistics to corroborate these estimates in Russia, we noted that UNICEF researchers found higher death rates in these psychoneurological *internaty* across most of the former Soviet bloc.[19] A

---

[15] Human Rights Watch interview, Russian orphanage teacher (*vospitatel'*), March 5, 1998.

[16] Human Rights Watch interviews, orphans in Moscow, St. Petersburg and region north of Moscow, February-March 1998; Dr. Anatoly Severny, Moscow, February 12, 1998.

[17] Human Rights Watch interview, Dr. Anatoly Severny, February 12, 1998.

[18] Ibid. It is not clear if these death rates refer to the total Russian population, to children in general, or to children with disabilities.

[19] UNICEF, *Children at Risk*, p. 89.

1996 national statistic from Ukraine indicated that "approximately thirty percent of all severely disabled children in special homes—a staggering figure—die before they reach eighteen." [20]

While UNICEF acknowledges that many of these children are at increased risk from their underlying conditions, it attributes part of the high mortality figures to crowding, poor hygiene, and low standards of care.[21]

Soviet-era policies and practices persist in Russian institutions. Renowned for its centralized control, the sprawling system of *internaty* for abandoned children was inspired by the Soviet philosophy favoring collective organization over individual care, and the ideal that the state could replace the family.[22] Regimentation and discipline were integral to this philosophy, and restricted access to the institutions apparently permitted the director and staff to operate with impunity.

While most Russians who left their children in state care during the late Soviet period did so for such reasons as poverty, illness, and family problems, a certain proportion of children came from working parents and students who used the orphanages as weekly boarding institutions and retrieved their children during the weekend.

This was considered normal practice, according to the long-time director of a Moscow baby house, who told Human Rights Watch how university students would house their infants with her sometimes for two to three years:

> We had families who had three kids who stayed here, then the parents finished studies and picked up the kids and left to go back home with them. We actually considered it to be fine. They were normal parents. They came and breast-fed them. In only one case the mother threw away (gave up) her child after six months.[23]

---

[20] Ibid.

[21] UNICEF also reports that health standards have fallen in baby houses: "The incidence of malnutrition disorders, rickets and anaemia increased in Russian infants homes by 20, 13 and 75 percent respectively between 1989-1994." UNICEF, *Children at Risk*, p. 83.

[22] Ibid., p. 84.

[23] Human Rights Watch interview, Dr. Elena Petrenko (not her real name), March 2, 1998.

The contrast between the doctor's attitude toward children who had parents to visit them and those who were fully abandoned, illustrated the deep bias against orphans and their parents that endures today.

Orphan care varies broadly across Russia, making it very difficult to draw conclusions about cities, regions, or even classes of institutions. For much of this century, for example, Moscow has been a world apart from anywhere else in the sprawling country, and this gulf has widened dramatically with the lifting of market controls in recent years. In matters of public funding, children's institutions in the capital and several other main cities enjoy higher levels than those in the regions of Mordovia, Tver' and Smolensk.[24]

But even the USSR, in its idiosyncratic way, was a land of exceptions. Orphanage directors, like the bosses of factories and vast collective farms, enjoyed considerable discretion over their domains. The director's personal commitment to children's welfare worked to the favor or to the detriment of the orphans. Human Rights Watch learned of compassionate, energetic directors with imagination and pluck who sought out child welfare information from the West, and took the initiative to improve their institutions by raising money locally and training their staff.

The result today is a hybrid of the former centralized system and low-grade anarchy, which also applies to the uneven enforcement of laws and standards protecting children introduced by the Russian Federation since 1991. This is complicated by the process of decentralization generally unfolding in the government ministries that oversee the institutional care and the diagnosis of children.

Among the positive consequences of the transitional period of the 1990s has been the initial access to institutions by charities and professionals, bringing assistance and information. The most marked improvement in the physical conditions is seen in the baby houses, which have received substantial assistance from international adoption agencies.

But one of the negative effects of this low-grade anarchy is that while abuses in the institutions may be exposed, children's rights advocates report that many more go unreported and there is an absence of accountability between central and local jurisdictions.

For all these reasons the findings from our mission do not apply to every orphanage in Russia. Variations and exceptions abound in every respect, from the circumstances leading to the abandonment of an infant, to the education, health and course of development enjoyed by or denied a child.

---

[24]   UNICEF, *Children at Risk*, p. 87.

There are general contours to this landscape, however, and the following section is offered to help navigate through the tunneled world of Russian orphans. It presents their odyssey in terms of the best and worst prospects that the state offers an abandoned child. It is followed by a discussion of variations, and the prevailing prejudices and attitudes that foster the violation of these children's rights.

Odyssey of a child

Type 1: Best prospects for a child abandoned at birth and healthy

In this case, a child is born at a state-run hospital or maternity ward and is left there in the hands of the Ministry of Health. The staff of the maternity ward will observe the child, giving him or her various medical and developmental diagnoses based on what it known of the family history and birth.

According to Russian medical practice, all risk factors are listed on any infant's chart under the initial diagnosis, and the high risks of many orphans win them a diagnosis of at least "delayed." Within a few weeks, all infants, except those who require immediate hospital care, are transferred to state-run baby houses where they reside for roughly four years.

Even in the best case, children who are closest to normal health at birth become retarded to some degree after these four years of collective living, deprived of individual nurture. An alarming number of less resilient infants seem to succumb to a self-fulfilling diagnosis of retarded.[25] This puts them at a distinct disadvantage at the age of four, when all institutionalized children are evaluated by the state Psychological-Medical-Pedagogical Commission of the Ministry of Education for distribution to institutions for children five years old and up.[26] The evaluation, which becomes an official "diagnosis" entered into an orphan's record, is often based on the visiting commission's one-time session with the child.[27]

It is impossible to overstate the crucial importance of this test to an orphan's future. It is a crossroads which routes the child either to a life of limited

---

[25] Human Rights Watch interviews, Dr. Vsevolod Rybchonok, March 6, 1998; Dr. Anatoly Severny, February 12, 1998.

[27] According to experts interviewed by Human Rights Watch, Russian children living with their families undergo a general developmental evaluation as they approach school age, but this is conducted by a different department of the Ministry of Education. Human Rights Watch interview, Ministry of Education official, October 19, 1998.

opportunities, or to a life of doom. Many Russian experts interviewed by Human Rights Watch sharply criticized this process, and could readily identify children who were certainly misdiagnosed. Although Russian law provides for the child to appeal through his legal guardian, it is almost impossible for a four-year-old in the custody of the orphanage director to lodge a complaint.

In the best case—if the toddlers clear this hurdle—they will be channeled into an orphanage in the Education Ministry system. There they will receive nine years of public education, learn a vocation, and get a job and place to live after the age of eighteen.

In general these children will enter the tunneled domain of state institutions, where they will inhabit a stultifying world apart from society at large. Orphans in Moscow told Human Rights Watch that their public school classmates teased them as *"dyet-domovskii"* kids. [28] Upon returning to their *dyetskii dom* after a school day, the orphans are once again in their separate world, where they find a dubious haven. Teenaged orphans in Moscow and St. Petersburg interviewed by Human Rights Watch reported several categories of abuse they had suffered or witnessed. They said that children with no parents are treated more harshly than those whose parents are in touch with them. Punishment by the director and staff may involve physical assault, verbal abuse, public humiliation (for example forcing children to strip in front of peers), isolation in unheated rooms in winter, or standing naked in front of an open window in winter. Runaways from the orphanage are often regarded as abnormal and sent to psychiatric hospitals.[29]

Brutal treatment is not confined to direct confrontations with adults, however, for they encourage older children to beat up, bully, intimidate and coerce the younger ones.[30] Orphans interviewed by Human Rights Watch had abundant episodes to recount, including punishment by proxy. Not only are they brutalized by this, they are socially stunted, and poorly prepared for a decent life as adults in the outside world.

---

[28] Human Rights Watch interview, Irina V., Masha K. (not their real names), Moscow orphans, February 20, 1998.

[29] Human Rights Watch interviews, orphans, Moscow, February 20, 1998; St. Petersburg, February 27, 28, 29, March 1, 1998. See Chapter VII for a detailed discussion of the children's treatment.

[30] Human Rights Watch interviews orphans in St. Petersburg, February 28, 29 and March 1, 1998.

When the orphans graduate from their world of the *dyetskii dom*, they face a "new Russia" in such social upheaval and economic disarray that it is distressful for those who have grown up in it. Gone is the social safety net of the Soviet era which at least guaranteed orphans housing, employment and a place in the army. Now, as a diplomat in Moscow told Human Rights Watch, "Their passport is marked with "*dyetskii dom*" so that people always know they were from orphanages. They have no one to turn to when they're unleashed at eighteen. Some have never ridden a metro before or been to a store or anything. A lot of them end up on the streets."[31]

Type 2: *Worst prospects for a child abandoned at birth and disabled*

A baby born with physical or mental disabilities in Russia faces the worst prospects if he or she is abandoned at birth. Some of them have only physical disabilities, or minor mental retardation and could learn to walk and talk, read and write. Among these are children with mild Down syndrome, cerebral palsy, and correctable conditions such as club foot and cleft palate.

Numerous parents are routinely pressured at the maternity ward to give up such infants.[32] After initial observation they are transferred to baby houses where the children classified with severe physical and mental disabilities are segregated into lying-down rooms. Confined to cribs, staring at the ceiling, these babies are fed and changed, but they are deprived of one-to-one attention and sensory stimulation and are not encouraged to walk or talk. However tentative their diagnosis of retardation was at birth, particularly for those who have only physical disabilities, it becomes self-fulfilling by the age of four.[33]

In the worst case, these babies fail the diagnostic evaluation of the Psychological-Medical-Pedagogical Commission at the age of four and are handed over to the Labor and Social Development Ministry. There they are interned in closed *internaty* for *imbetsily* and *idioty*, where there is little more than a perfunctory classroom to keep some of the children busy for a few hours a week.

The bedridden children from the baby houses are again confined to cots in lying-down rooms, often laid out on bare rubber mattress covers, unclothed from

---

[31] Human Rights Watch interview, March 3, 1998.

[32] Human Rights Watch interview, two child welfare experts, Moscow, February 20 & 23, 1998.

[33] Ibid.

the waist down and incontinent, as we witnessed in one *internat* and heard in credible reports from volunteers working in many state institutions.[34]

Human Rights Watch saw children who were considered "too active" or "too difficult" being confined to dark or barren rooms with barely a place to sit. The staff tethered them by a limb if they believed they might try to escape, and restrained others in makeshift straitjackets made of dingy cotton sacks pulled over the torso and drawn at the waist and neck.[35]

Children with Down syndrome and other hereditary conditions are regularly passed over for corrective-heart surgery that is routine in the West, based on a long-held bias against spending medical resources on children judged as "socially useless."[36]

The orphans who survive to the age of eighteen move on to an adult *internat*, again removed from public view. Some, however, are housed in huge centers with hundreds of handicapped people across the age spectrum and where older inmates feed and care for younger or more disabled ones.

Variations on these cases
There are scores of variations on the two types of journeys followed by Russian orphans. For instance, some children are abandoned after living several years at home. As one baby house director told Human Rights Watch, this can occur in the case of severe disability, when a family struggles for a while to raise their child themselves:

> If the mother decides to keep the child, after three years, maybe, she loses her job. The state subsidides are minimal. The man might leave her. While the child weighs under twenty-two pounds, she can carry him. But then the baby grows, more care is needed and she has less money, and her physical and moral strength is getting weaker. We know instances where those cases will be found locked in a dark room in an apartment, because the mother had to go

---

[34] Human Rights Watch visit to *Internat X* and interviews with staff, February 15, 1998; interviews, volunteers working in state institutions, February 1998; interviews, two Health Ministry officials who periodically visit *Internat Y* for disabled orphans, March 5, 1998.

[35] Human Rights Watch visit to *Internat X,* February 15, 1998; interviews, volunteers in orphanages, February 1998.

[36] Human Rights Watch interview, Dr. Anatoly Severny, February 12, 1998.

to work to feed her children, because the monthly pension for having a disabled child is really miserable—200,000 rubles (U.S. $30).[37]

Not all variations are so bleak. Volunteers and child development specialists in Russia told us about an increasing number of children who are being kept an extra year or two in the baby houses in order to improve their chances of passing the commission evaluation and avoid banishment to a psychoneurological *internat*. In addition, not all the children in baby houses are neglected equally, as certain children have winning personalities or attractive characteristics that encourage the staff to devote more attention to them.[38]

Finally, all children have their individual constitutions, which miraculously navigate some of them through the harshest circumstances, and help them not only to survive, but thrive.

Prejudice against orphans: a legacy of ignorance and fear

At the heart of the systematic abuse and neglect suffered by orphans in Russia lies a deep tradition of ignorance and fear. Time and again people told us, repeating like a mantra, how the Soviet ideology promoted the quest for the perfect Soviet man. As Dr. Severny explained, "All children and everyone had to meet the standard, and if they did not meet the standard, they had to be kept apart and hidden from the rest."[39] Children with disabilities were not seen in public, and the myths associated with them flourished.

The effort to hide such children from the rest of society reflects a "deep, deep prejudice and fear of handicapped people in general," according to a journalist who has worked extensively on the issue of disabilities and orphans in Moscow.[40] The process begins in the maternity ward, only hours after the infant is delivered: "That's where the doctors tell the parents, who are already in shock from the birth of a child with difficulties, that the child will never walk, will never talk, will drool

---

[37] Human Rights Watch interview, Dr. Mikhail Airumyan, March 5, 1998. Exchange rate as of March 1998. As of November 1998 all dollar values in this report are now halved due to August 1998 ruble devaluation.

[38] Human Rights Watch interview, volunteer, February 23, 1998; journalist, February 11, 1998.

[39] Human Rights Watch interview, Dr. Anatoly Severny, February 21, 1998.

[40] Human Rights Watch interview, Natasha Fairweather, February 20, 1998.

all his life. They encourage them to give the child up. They terrorize them. And they also associate disabilities with moral shortcomings of the parents, and make the parents feel guilty for something they must have done."[41]

One of the most pernicious consequences of this prejudice is that it taints all abandoned children in Russia, despite the fact that the issue has been discussed and debated abundantly in the Russian press for several years. A clear summary of this point appeared in an article exploring local biases against adopting a baby abandoned by a stranger.

> The fear that the child will in some way be "damaged goods" stems from the knowledge that mothers of mentally and physically handicapped children are routinely advised by doctors to put their baby in an orphanage and "try again." Consequently, healthy babies who are given up for financial or domestic reasons are unfairly branded "defective."[42]

That Russians often regard orphans as "not really human" corroborates numerous interviews we had with the *sanitarki* in *Internat* X and with press articles we reviewed for this report, in underscoring the notion of genetic determinism that informs both lay people and orphanage staff.[43]

We found an alarming number of references in the Russian press to disabled orphans as "not really human." A sympathetic explanation was offered to us by a Russian journalist who has followed the problem closely:

> I'm sorry to say, you will hear terrible things about orphanages and they are probably true. It is a really large scale problem. The staff sees them as animals. We saw it. Even the nannies who "love" them, treat them mostly—really like pets. They do not really see that there is a person inside who could think, or learn something.

> Recently there was an article in a Russian paper about a baby house where kids with defects live. A few days later the readers wrote a reply, that these kids

---

[41]   Ibid.

[42]   Juliet Butler, "Someone Else's Baby," *Moscow Times*, November 2, 1996, p. 14.

[43] Human Rights Watch site visit to *internat,* February 15, 1998; interview, Marina Stepanova (not her real name), February 10, 1998, among others.

should be killed. "We don't want to see them," they said. People are not ready to share any money with those that are disabled. They believe they're not really human beings. It's terrible, I know.[44]

Such views are hardly the most shocking to be expressed in the Russian press since the appalling conditions of psychoneurological *internaty* were revealed several years ago. In 1993, an article in a Moscow daily quoted a letter that had appeared in a leading Russian weekly from the mother of a child with Down syndrome. The letter was entitled, "Why Coddle Such Freaks?," and it read, "I am asking the doctor to put my child to sleep. I have been told that we have humaneness in our country," she wrote. "We have humaneness—so we let them live?"[45]

Fear to expose the truth
Reinforcing the legacy of ignorance and fear of orphans is the pervasive fear of exposing abuses of children's rights, all the way from the time that parents are terrorized into leaving their child in that ward, to the years when the children are beaten up and bullied in the *dyetskii dom*. One former charity worker who helped distribute private donations to many baby houses summed up what others told Human Rights Watch:

If you expose everything, they will shut down the institution to outsiders. No one says to open it up to scrutiny, because there's no faith in the justice system. No top heads will roll. So keep quiet.

They have a saying in Russian, "*Tishe yedesh, dal'sho budesh*," which means, "The more quietly you go, the farther you go." The nail that sticks up highest gets hit first. The kids can't talk either; keep them far enough away that nobody knows. These are all stewing grounds for enormous amounts of pathology.[46]

---

[44]   Human Rights Watch interview, Marina Stepanova, journalist, January 22, 1998.

[45]   Andrea Smith, "Don't Give Up: She May be Talking with Angels," *Moscow Tribune*, April 29, 1995, p. 8.

[46]   Human Rights Watch interview, Sandy Marinelli (not her real name) Moscow, February 25, 1998.

In another interview, the Russian journalist Marina Stepanova further illustrated the power of an orphanage director to punish staff who share information with outsiders:

> We were told last time that the nurses who talked with us were fired, but the director stayed on. When we were there in the winter of 1997, the nurse told me that people came with stuffed animals, and the next day they were for sale in the market. It's quite clear that the kids are being deprived of food. We brought five cartons of yogurt, and the best they will get is two. This orphanage system has to be changed at the top.[47]

---

[47] Human Rights Watch interview, Marina Stepanova, February 11, 1998. Based on her earlier visit to *Internat* X.

III. RELEVANT INTERNATIONAL AND RUSSIAN LAWS

States parties shall take all appropriate legislative, administrative,
social and educational measures to protect the child from all forms
of physical and mental violence, injury or abuse, neglect or negligent
treatment...while in the care of legal guardians or any other person
who has the care of the child.

- The Convention on the Rights of the Child. Art. 19 (1)

Starting from their abandonment, Russian children in orphanages are deprived of basic human rights at every stage of their life—from the most fundamental right to survival and development, to their rights to humane treatment, health, education, and full enjoyment of civil rights. These rights are interlocking, and their violation has a compounding effect, consigning these children to truncated lives in a permanent underclass.   This chapter address the legal basis of these rights, in the major international human rights instruments to which Russia is a party, in non-binding international standards pertaining to medical ethics, disability, mental illness and the treatment of juveniles in detention, and in Russian law.

Abandonment and Disability as a Basis for Invidious Discrimination
There is little doubt that the more than half-million children registered as orphans in the Russian Federation suffer acute social discrimination and endemic denial of their civil, political, economic, social and cultural rights, particularly in comparison with children who live with their families. The simple fact of abandonment or orphanage propels children into an institutional system that prejudices their physical, emotional and mental development; it denies them appropriate health care, education, and puts them at serious risk of physical and mental abuse inflicted or tolerated by state employees in the name of discipline. Most significantly, the fact of abandonment and orphanage stigmatizes them for life, a stigma that is memorialized in official identity documents and from which they cannot escape as they seek employment and a normal life in the community.

The stigma of abandonment is reinforced and compounded by the popular assumption that such children must have inherited mental deficiencies and deviant personalities to have caused their parents to abandon them, an assumption particularly likely if they come from poorer or troubled families. Often they are quickly classified as retarded by medical personnel, adding a second burden of discriminatory status as "disabled." Even those considered "normal" graduate into society under a heavy burden of educational and social retardation in comparison to their peers, and suffer the stigma of their childhood origin for life.

Children who have genuine physical or mental disabilities, or who are improperly classified as such, suffer discrimination so intense that they are denied the opportunity to develop to the best of their abilities, and indeed, they are often subjected to such extreme neglect, prejudice or abuse that their very lives may be endangered.

International law specifically prohibits invidious discrimination that denies rights to certain classes of people because of inherent social characteristics. Major international human rights instruments to which Russia is a party, including the International Covenant on Civil and Political Rights, the International Covenant on Economic, Social and Cultural Rights, and the Convention on the Rights of the Child, all prohibit discriminatory denial or abridgment of rights on the basis of race, color, sex, language, religion, political or other opinion, national, ethnic or social origin, property, birth, "or other status."[48] Discrimination against a child because of circumstances such as orphanage or abandonment, depending on the facts, could fall into the category of discrimination on the basis of social origin or even birth. In any event, such circumstances are embraced by the term "other status," which is intended to be construed broadly as applying to qualities of human identity similar to those of race, sex, language, religion, opinion, national or social origin, property, disability or birth. The international bodies that interpret the covenants on civil and political rights and on economic, social and cultural rights have both laid particular emphasis on protection of the rights of abandoned or institutionalized children, highlighting their understanding that this circumstance should never be considered a permissible basis for discrimination. The Human Rights Committee, for example, has specifically required states to report on "the special measures of protection adopted to protect children who are abandoned or deprived of their family environment" with the understanding that economic, social and cultural measures must be taken to ensure that all children develop in such a way as to be able to enjoy their civil and political rights.[49] The Committee on Economic, Social and Cultural Rights and the Committee on the Rights of the

---

[48] See Convention on the Rights of the Child (hereinafter CRC) Article 2(1); International Covenant on Civil and Political Rights (hereinafter ICCPR) Article 2(1); International Covenant on Economic, Social and Cultural Rights (hereinafter ICESCR) Article 2(2).

[49] See Human Rights Committee, General Comment 17 on Article 24 of the International Covenant on Civil and Political Rights (Thirty-fifth session, 1985).

Child have likewise highlighted the state's duty to ensure a minimal level of economic, social and cultural rights to all children, including those who are disabled or institutionalized.[50]

Disability, a quality frequently assumed to be the reason behind parental abandonment in Russia, has been consistently interpreted as an impermissible grounds of discrimination on the basis of "other status." The Committee on Economic, Social and Cultural Rights, a United Nations body which interprets and evaluates state performance under the International Covenant on Economic, Social and Cultural Rights, has concluded that the prohibition of discrimination "clearly applies to discrimination on the grounds of disability." The Human Rights Committee, the body which monitors state parties compliance with respect to the International Covenant on Civil and Political Rights, has enjoined states to provide information specifically on measures of protection for children "who are abandoned or deprived of their family environment." The Convention on the Rights of the Child, of more recent origin than the previous two covenants and the most widely ratified human rights treaty in the world, specifically lists "disability" as a prohibited grounds of discrimination.[51] For the above reasons, Human Rights Watch considers that denial or abridgment of fundamental human rights to children who have been abandoned or orphaned, and who may or may not suffer a mental

---

50 See e.g. CESCR observations on the third periodic report of Ukraine1995, paragraph 21, that "the fulfilment of the right to education involves an obligation for the government to provide free primary education for all, including children with disabilities and children assigned to homes or institutions;" CRC observations on Peru's initial report, 1993, paragraph 10, expressing concern "that stringent budgetary measures .... have adversely affected the rights of the child in Peru. Vulnerable groups of children, including ... orphans, disabled children, children living in poverty and children living in institutions are particularly disadvantaged in their access to adequate health and educational facilities and are the primary victims of various forms of exploitation.... ... [T]he long-term considerations embodied in the structural adjustment policies have not adequately taken into account the specific needs of the children...."

[51] U.N. Convention on the Rights of the Child. GA res. 44/25, annex, 44 U.N. GAOR Supp. (No. 49) at 167, U.N. Doc. A/44/49 (1989). Entered into force September 2, 1990. Ratified by the USSR June 13, 1990. Entered into force in Russia, legal successor to the USSR, September 15, 1990.

or physical disability, is a violation of the most basic tenets of international human rights law.

The Decision to Institutionalize The Child

The right to a family[52]

The starting point for the cycle of abuse these children face is their abandonment by their parents and entry into the closed world of institutional life. The major human rights instruments—The Universal Declaration of Human Rights, and the "international bill of rights" comprising the two covenants on civil and political rights, and economic, social and cultural rights—all recognize the family as "the natural and fundamental group unit of society" which is "entitled to protection by society and the State."[53] The Convention on the Rights of the Child specifically provides that the child has from birth "the right to know and be cared for by his or her parents," the right to "preserve family relations as recognized by law without unlawful interference."[54] The Committee on Economic, Social and Cultural Rights has interpreted the injunction that states render assistance and protection to the family as the fundamental social unit as requiring that states do everything possible to enable disabled persons to live with their families.[55] Two non-binding instruments approved by the U.N. General Assembly, the Declaration on the Rights of Mentally Retarded Persons and the Declaration on the Rights of Disabled Persons, respectively provide that institutionalization of such persons is acceptable only where "necessary" or "indispensable" and otherwise recognize

---

[52] ICESCR, (Articles 12, 13, 6, respectively). Article 2 (2) further stipulates that these rights "will be exercised without discrimination of any kind as to race, colour, sex, language, religion, political or other opinion, national of social origin, property, birth or *other status*" (emphasis added).

[53] Universal Declaration of Human Rights (hereinafter UDHR) Article 16(3); ICCPR Article 23(1), ICESCR Article 10(1).

[54] CRC, Articles 7(1), 8(1).

[55] General comment 5, para. 30.

their right to live with their family or foster parents, who in turn are due assistance and support from the state.[56]

Yet instead of providing support, the norm is for state medical personnel to urge parents to abandon children showing any evidence of disability, even when the disabling condition is relatively manageable or susceptible to therapeutic treatment, such as hare lip (cleft palate) or minor cerebral palsy. Indeed, the rationale generally given by medical personnel to the parents is that parents who undertake to raise a disabled child at home risk becoming social pariahs.

Arbitrary deprivation of liberty

Although institutions may, as a last resort, substitute for the family in the case of orphaned or abandoned children, institutionalization inevitably entails an extra degree of restriction of the child's right to liberty. International instruments recognize that institutionalization is a "least favored" option, below keeping the child with the family or placing the child in a foster family or similar environment or encouraging domestic or international adoption.[57] In all Russian institutions for abandoned children, boys and girls are generally removed from the greater

---

[56] Declaration on the Rights of Mentally Retarded Persons, G.A. resolution 2856 (XXVI) of December 20, 1971, paragraph 4 provides:

Whenever possible, the mentally retarded person should live with his own family or with foster parents and participate in different forms of community life. The family with which he lives should receive assistance. If care in an institution becomes necessary, it should be provided in surroundings and other circumstances as close as possible to those of normal life.

Declaration on the Rights of Disabled Persons, G.A. Resolution 3477 (XXX) of December 9, 1975, paragraph 9, similarly provides:

Disabled persons have the right to live with their families or with foster parents and to participate in all social, creative or recreational activities. (....) If the stay of a disabled person in a specialized establishment is indispensable, the environment and living conditions therein shall be as close as possible to those of the normal life of a person of his or her age.

The meanings of terms such as "necessary" and "indispensable" evolve with advancements in medical and social science. The trend since these declarations were adopted has been to recognize fewer and fewer situations where separation from the community and institutionalization is considered "necessary" or "indispensable" for the welfare of the mentally or physically disabled.

[57] See, e.g., CRC Article 20, providing that a child who is temporarily or permanently deprived of a family environment is entitled to alternative care, including "foster placement, *kalafah* of Islamic law, adoption or *if necessary* placement in suitable institutions for the care of children" (emphasis added); see also, supra, footnotes 6-9.

community and normal social contact; in institutions for the care of moderately to severely disabled children, the restriction of liberty can be extreme, with children locked into rooms, tethered to furniture, or confined to bed until their transition to even more draconian institutions upon adulthood.

The right not to be arbitrarily deprived of liberty is fundamental, recognized in the Universal Declaration of Human Rights,[58] the Convention on the Rights of the Child[59] and the International Covenant on Civil and Political Rights.[60] The right to liberty is derogable under the last treaty only in times of a public emergency declared by the state which threatens the life of the nation;[61] limited financial or technical resources do not alone constitute the conditions for such an emergency.[62] Detention is "arbitrary" even when sanctioned by existing law where it is imposed in a manner that is unjustified, disproportional, capricious, or without due process. Given that institutionalization may be the only means to protect the health and welfare of some children, at least during a transitional period to more humane community-based alternatives, what sort of controls are required under international law to ensure that decisions to confine the child are reasonable, proportional, and subject to periodic and independent evaluation?

With regard to the child who has been placed in institutions for the purpose of care or treatment of physical or mental health, the Convention on the Rights of the Child requires that he or she has the right to "a periodic review of the treatment provided...and all other circumstances relevant to his or her placement." It further provides, "Every child deprived of his or her liberty shall have the right to prompt access to legal and other appropriate assistance, as well as the right to challenge the legality of the deprivation of his or her liberty before a court or other competent, independent and impartial authority, and to a prompt decision on any such

---

[58] UDHR Articles 3 and 9.

[59] CRC Article 37.

[60] ICCPR Article 9.

[61] ICCPR Article 4.

[62] U.N. Economic and Social Council, Commission on Human Rights; study of the Implications for Human Rights of Recent Developments Concerning Situations Known as States of Siege or Emergency, U.N. Doc. E/CN.4/Sub.2/1982/15.

action."[63] For this right to be meaningful, the child must have recourse to adults who can act independently and in the child's interests to initiate review or challenge of a decision of confinement to any particular institution.[64]

The importance of an independent advocate for the child's interest is vividly illustrated by the fact that it is generally only those institutionalized children retaining contact with their families or acquiring a friendly advocate within the system that can challenge either a diagnosis as mentally impaired or their placement within the institutional track. The directors of orphanages, while potentially advocates for improperly confined children, cannot be presumed to act independently and in the child's best interests, given that they receive additional state subsidies for children with disabilities and thus have a direct conflict of interest with the child. Nor is there any evidence that Russian children with disabilities are able to challenge the initial decision to institutionalize them with the help of available medical or social service officials, who appear often to pressure parents into abandonment rather than seek support to enable parents to keep disabled children.

The child's right to development

The Convention on the Rights of the Child recognizes "the right of every child to a standard of living adequate for the child's physical, mental, spiritual, moral and social development" in Article 27(1). While primary responsibility for supporting the child rests with parents, "[s]tates parties, in accordance with national conditions and within their means, shall take appropriate measures to *assist parents and others responsible* for the child to implement this right and shall in case of need provide material assistance and support programmes, particularly with regard to nutrition, clothing and housing" (emphasis added).[65] The right of mentally and physically disabled persons to develop to the full extent of their

---

[63] CRC Article 37(d).

[64] N.B. The Declaration on the Rights of Disabled Persons provides that such persons "shall be able to avail themselves of qualified legal aid when such aid proves indispensable for the protection of their persons and property" (paragraph 11) while the Declaration on the Rights of the Mentally Retarded provides a right for such persons "to a qualified guardian when this is required to protect his personal well-being and interests" (paragraph 5).

[65] Article 27(3) emphasis added.

potential is likewise well-established in international standards.[66] The development of human potential in a physical, mental, spiritual and social sense embraces a wide spectrum of rights, some of which will be briefly discussed below.

The right to life

The child's right to life and survival, recognized by all major human rights instruments,[67] is basic to any notion of development. In the context of civil and political rights, it often implicates the right to be free of cruel and inhuman treatment or other forms of life-threatening persecution, and in the context of economic, social and cultural rights, it often implicates the right to health and to basics such as adequate shelter, nourishment and clothing.

The right to health

The right to "the enjoyment of the highest attainable standard" of health is recognized by both the International Covenant on Economic, Social and Cultural Rights and the Convention on the Rights of the Child.[68] Both instruments provide that economic, social and cultural rights shall be realized progressively, to the maximum extent of the state's available resources.[69] However, there must be no discrimination in the allocation of health care, so that the inferior treatment of abandoned or disabled children is a clear violation of their rights. Moreover, the

---

[66] The Declaration on the Rights of Mentally Retarded Persons, paragraph 2, provides:
The mentally retarded person has a right to proper medical care and physical therapy and to such education, training, rehabilitation and guidance as will enable him to develop his ability and maximum potential.
The Declaration on the Rights of Disabled Persons, paragraph 6, provides:
Disabled persons have the right to medical, psychological and functional treatment, including prosthetic and orthetic appliances, to medical and social rehabilitation, education, vocational training and rehabilitation, aid, counseling, placement services and other services which will enable them to develop their capabilities and skills to the maximum and will hasten the processes of their social integration or reintegration.

[67] See, e.g. ICCPR Article 6(1), CRC Article 6, ICESCR Article 12 (discussing in context of right to health, reduction in infant mortality, and healthy development of child).

[68] ICESCR Article 12(1) (specifying "physical and mental health"), CRC Article 24(1) (specifying "health").

[69] CRC Article 4, ICESCR Article 2(1). N.b. "available resources" includes foreign aid in all its forms.

bodies that monitor implementation of these treaties have time and again drawn attention to the particular care due to vulnerable groups, such as children generally, and abandoned, disabled or institutionalized children in particular.[70] It follows that where the state deprives individuals of liberty and assumes a custodial function, its responsibility to provide the means for basic rights such as food, clothing, medical care and physical security is at its highest.

Abandoned children in Russia's institutions frequently receive minimal or no health care, and scant attention to their basic needs, virtually ensuring they will achieve a debased standard of physical and mental development and health. On

---

[70] CESCR concluding comments on Nicaragua's initial report, 1994: "14. The Committee wishes to bring to the attention of the State party the need to ensure that structural adjustment programmes are so formulated and implemented as to provide adequate safety nets for the vulnerable sectors of society in order to avoid a deterioration of the enjoyment of the economic, social and cultural rights for which the Covenant provides protection."

CRC concluding observations on Peru's initial report, 1993: "19. The Committee urges the Government of Peru to take all the necessary steps to minimize the negative impact of the structural adjustment policies on the situation of children. The authorities should ... undertake all appropriate measures to the maximum extent of their available resources to ensure that sufficient resources are allocated to children. In that regard, particular attention should be paid to the protection of children living in areas affected by internal violence, displaced children, disabled children, children living in poverty and children living in institutions...."

CRC concluding observations on the Russian Federation's initial report, 1993: "9. The Committee is concerned that society is not sufficiently sensitive to the needs and situation of children from particularly vulnerable and disadvantaged groups, such as the disabled, in the light of article 2 of the Convention.

11. ... [T]he Committee is concerned about the practice of the institutionalization in boarding schools of children who are deprived of a family environment, particularly in cases of abandonment or where children are orphaned."

In this regard it is notable that U.N. standards for children institutionalized in a state's juvenile justice system are entitled to very specific rights relating to health care. The U.N. Rules for the Protection of Juveniles Deprived of their Liberty (hereinafter Rules for the Protection of Juveniles) specify that "[e]very juvenile shall receive adequate medical care, both preventive and remedial, including dental, ophthalmological and mental health care, as well as pharmaceutical products and special diets as medically indicated" (Rule 49) and that "[e]very juvenile who is ill, who complains of illness or who demonstrates symptoms of physical or mental difficulties, should be examined promptly by a medical doctor" (Rule 51). U.N. Rules for the Protection of Juveniles Deprived of their Liberty (U.N. Rules) GA Res 45/113. annex, 45 U.N. GAOR Supp. (No.49A at 205), U.N. Doc. A/45/49 (1990).

the rare occasions that they are sent to hospitals for treatment, they are relegated to a lower standard of care and attention for lack of a parental or institutional advocate. Misdiagnosis of mental and physical handicaps ensures that many children will suffer debased mental and physical health. In the most severe situations, children who are bedridden are not encouraged to develop motor skills but confined to "lying down rooms," in some cases left to die.[71] Moreover, these deficiencies in care and treatment are largely remediable without any extraordinary allocation of resources; training and dedication to rehabilitation and nurture for institutional staff, medical personnel and parents would alone cause an immense and immediate improvement in the situation.

The administration of drugs or commitment of children to psychiatric institutions for non-medical purposes such as restraint, discipline or punishment is a particular abuse of medical ethnics and international law that persists in Russian institutions for disabled or abandoned children.[72]

The right to education

The right to education is another universally-recognized right considered fundamental to the development of human personality, and the exercising of civil and political rights.[73] The provisions of the Convention on the Rights of the Child are particularly detailed, requiring that the right be achieved on the basis of equal opportunity, that primary education be made compulsory and free to all, and that secondary and higher education, as well as vocational education, be encouraged.[74] Of particular relevance to Russia's institutionalized children is the Convention's statement that education shall be directed to "[t]he development of the child's

---

[71] Human Rights Watch interview, Sarah Philips, February 23, 1998; interview, Natasha Fairweather, journalist, February 20, 1998.

[72] See below, discussion of the Principles for the Protection of Persons with Medical Handicaps, Principle 10 (Medication).

[73] See UDHR Article 26, ICESCR Article 13, Human Rights Committee, General Comment 17 on Article 24, paragraph 3 ("In the cultural field, every possible measures should be taken to...provide [children] with a level of education that will enable them to enjoy the rights recognized in the Covenant, particularly the right to freedom of opinion and expression.").

[74] CRC Article 28(1).

personality, talents and mental and physical abilities to their fullest potential" and [t]he preparation of the child for responsible life in a free society".[75]

Children in standard Ministry of Education orphanages told Human Rights Watch that their schooling consisted of regular public school courses in mathematics, history, geography, Russian literature and so forth.[76] But further interviews with child welfare advocates indicate that even within the public system, orphans are less likely to receive remedial assistance or private tutoring, and therefore leave school with a sub-standard education.[77]

Although children who are classified as only slightly retarded (debily) may receive vocational training in adolescence, such training inadequately prepares them for employment in adult life because of their reduced course of study, even when they are capable of achieving more. Indeed, this group rarely can earn high school diplomas since they generally receive only five or six years of compulsory education. Another of the concerns most often voiced during our interviews with a cross-section of Russian orphans and their caretakers was that a rigidly sequestered institutional life failed to prepare them to adapt to normal roles in society, let alone support themselves.

Even the little that these children receive is more than those who are officially labeled—accurately or inaccurately—as seriously handicapped or mentally retarded at age four. These children are deemed "ineducable," and warehoused for life in psychoneurological internaty where little or no physical or mental rehabilitation, or effort at basic socialization is attempted despite the clear requirement that these children be given education to maximize their potential.

And prior to this early triage, few infants and toddlers in Russia's baby houses receive the adult attention, stimulation and preparation in basic social skills that lay the critical foundation for all further cognitive development and capacity for education, making "retardation" in some form all but inevitable.[78]

---

[75] CRC Article 29(a) and (d).

[76] Human Rights Watch interview, Moscow, February 20, 1998.

[77] Human Rights Watch interview, juvenile rights lawyer, October 14, 1998.

[78] Studies in the United States and Western Europe have shown that such mental, physical and emotional retardation is a common consequence of keeping very young children of all capabilities in large-scale institutions where they are unlikely to receive the type of intensive, one-on-one personal attention that they would normally get in a family setting See Deborah A. Frank, M.D., Perri Klass, M.D., Felton Earls, M.D. and Leon

Cruel, inhuman or degrading treatment and torture

The prohibition against cruel, inhumane or degrading treatment or torture is a peremptory norm of international law, codified in numerous treaties and not subject to derogation even in times of emergency.[79] The distinction between torture and other cruel, inhuman or degrading treatment or punishment is one of degree and purpose: torture is recognized as an "extreme and deliberate" form of such treatment,[80] and is intentionally inflicted on a person by officials at their instigation or with their acquiescence for reasons such as punishment or "discrimination of any kind."[81] No malevolent intent is required to show perpetration of cruel, inhuman or degrading treatment; it is not a justification that such actions were taken for administrative convenience or lack of appropriate resources.

Children in Russia's institutions for children are subjected to cruel, inhuman or degrading treatment, which in its extreme forms may be described as torture inflicted because of the pariah status that abandonment or disability carry. This sort of abuse can occur in the context of "discipline" in orphanages, or routine administrative practices such as keeping children in isolation, physical restraints, or locked in cold, windowless rooms.

The Convention on the Rights of the Child specifically commands states to take measures to protect children "from all forms of physical or mental violence, injury or abuse, neglect or negligent treatment, maltreatment or exploitation, including sexual abuse, while in the care of parent(s), legal guardian(s) or any other

---

Eisenberg, M.D. "Infants and Young Children in Orphanages: One View from Pediatrics and Child Psychiatry," in *Pediatrics*, Vol. 97 No. 4 (April 4, 1996). With regard to cognitive development, these authors conclude "unless children are placed with families before 4 years of age, they remain at a cognitive disadvantage compared with biologic or foster home-reared children of the same social class." Id. at 572.

[79] See UDHR Article 5; ICCPR Articles 7 and 4(2) (on non-derogability); CRC Article 37(a); and generally the 1984 Convention against Torture and other Cruel, Inhuman or Degrading Treatment or Punishment [hereinafter "Convention against Torture"].

[80] Declaration on the Protection of All Persons from Being Subjected to Torture and Other Cruel, Inhuman or Degrading Treatment or Punishment, adopted by General Assembly resolution 3452 (XXX) of December 9, 1975, Article 1(2).

[81] Convention against Torture, Article 1(1).

person who has the care of the child."[82] Children who become the victims of "any form of neglect, exploitation or abuse; torture or any other form of cruel, inhuman or degrading treatment or punishment" are entitled under the Convention on the Rights of the Child to "appropriate measures to promote physical and psychological recovery and social reintegration".[83] This recovery is expected to take place "in an environment which fosters the health, self-respect and dignity of the child."[84] Far from being institutions for the care, protection and treatment of abandoned children, Russian orphanages and *internaty* are often the locus of further abuse and neglect. The following sections describe a sampling of the treatment we have found violative of international law.

Physical Abuse

Many of the "normal" administrative practices found in institutions for mildly or severely disabled children amount to cruel, inhuman or degrading treatment. Tying children in sacks, tethering them to furniture, confining them needlessly to beds, warehousing them in barren and windowless rooms, denying them available food, keeping them in unsanitary accommodations or in inadequate clothing, denying them appropriate medical treatment—all these practices constitute cruel, inhuman and degrading treatment. Negligent practices that facilitate sexual and physical abuse of children either by other children or by staff also violate the state's duty to protect children in its care from cruel, inhuman or degrading treatment. Commingling of older children with younger, or boys with girls without proper supervision is common in Russian institutions, and sometimes facilitates such abuse.

We received numerous credible accounts of beatings being used as punishment for institutionalized children. In extreme cases, these incidents clearly amount to torture. It is noteworthy that even international standards on juveniles detained in the justice system forbid corporal punishment, placement in

---

[82] CRC Article 19.

[83] CRC Article 39.

[84] Ibid.

dark cells, closed or solitary confinement, or any other type of punishment that may compromise the physical or mental health of the child.[85]

With regard to discipline, the Convention on the Rights of the Child provides that states parties shall "take all appropriate measures to ensure that school discipline is administered in a manner consistent with the child's human dignity and in conformity with the present Convention."[86] That obligation is broader than the requirement that discipline not be "cruel, inhuman or degrading"; discipline must also comport with the Convention's aim to ensure the full development by each child of his or her individual potential and respect for the human rights of others.[87] Yet the abuse of discipline is frequently extreme, involving elaborate orchestrations of humiliation by institutional personnel in ways that enlist other children to participate as abusers.

A signature feature of the violence used against Russian orphans, especially in the homes for "normal" children run by the Education Ministry, is the orchestration of corporal punishment by the director through the agency of older children. Human Rights Watch is deeply alarmed by the patterns of cruelty and malicious violence that orphans described during interviews in Moscow, St. Petersburg and Novgorod region—patterns mirroring the findings of lengthy investigations into the deadly hazing and gang-rule in the Russian military and prisons.[88]

Psychological Abuse

Cruel, inhumane or degrading treatment may consist of verbal as well as physical abuse, or exposure to contempt and ridicule. In this sense, it is closely tied to violations of the individual's right to privacy, honor and reputation, a right

---

[85] See, e.g. U.N. Standard Minimum Rules for the Administration of Juvenile Justice (Beijing Rules) GA Res. 40/33, 40 U.N. GAOR Supp. (No. 53) at 207, U.N. Doc. A/40/53 (1985), Rule 17.3; U.N. Rules for the Protection of Juveniles Deprived of their Liberty (Rules for the Protection of Juveniles) Rules 63-64.

[86] CRC Article 28(2).

[87] CRC Article 29(1).

[88] Kathleen Hunt, "Mothers and Sons," *The Los Angeles Times Sunday Magazine*, April 12, 1992; Kathleen Hunt, feature report on deadly hazing, National Public Radio's "All Things Considered," April 19, 1992; Sergei A. Kovalev, Human Rights Ombudsman of the Russian Federation, report on violence in the Russian military, 1994, 1995.

which pertains to children as well as adults.[89] We encountered numerous instances where institutional staff openly discussed with us, in front of the child concerned, details of parental abandonment or disability in humiliating terms; even though personnel may have meant no harm, this was undoubtably cruel, or degrading for the child concerned. Even more obvious forms of humiliation and violations of privacy were reported by children in institutions under the Ministry of Education, including staff and directors stripping children naked, publicly mocking them, or ridiculing them as homosexuals.[90]

Grievance procedures

Human Rights Watch finds that few children bring formal complaints of physical and psychological violence by institution staff and older children, in part because they are uninformed of their rights and because they have no access to independent sources of legal advice. Given that the perpetrator is often the director or a staff member, the children also have little faith that the system would deliver justice. Those who do file complaints fear the real risk of retribution from the staff either directly, or indirectly through the favored children. Finally, some of the children we interviewed echoed a disturbing version of the famous rationalizations used by relatives of Stalin's victims: if the orphanage staff punished or beat them, there must have been a reason for it.[91] Yet the right to make complaints of ill-treatment and have them addressed is a premise of human rights law, deriving from the state's obligation to "ensure" rights.[92] Directors of institutions in theory should

---

[89] See UDHR Article 12, ICCPR Article 17 and CRC Article 16.

[90] Human Rights Watch interviews, orphans in St. Petersburg, February 27, 1998.

[91] Human Rights Watch interview, adolescent orphan, St. Petersburg, February 27, 1998.

[92] See, e.g. UDHR Article 8 ("Everyone has the right to an effective remedy by the competent national tribunals for acts violating the fundamental rights granted him by the constitution or law"); ICCPR Article 2(1) ("Each State Party...undertakes to respect and to ensure to all individuals within its territory and subject to its jurisdiction the rights recognized in the present Covenant..."); CRC Article 2 ("States Parties shall respect and ensure the rights set forth in the present Convention to each child..."); CRC Article 12(2) ("...the child shall in particular be provided the opportunity to be heard in any judicial and administrative proceedings affecting the child..."); CRC Article 19(states shall take all appropriate measures to protect the child "from all forms of physical or mental violence, injury or abuse, neglect or negligent treatment, maltreatment or exploitation" and such

be able to act in the interests of children with regard to such complaints, yet even if they are not implicated in the abuse, they may have a conflict of interest because of their relatively   autonomous role in hiring and directing all institutional personnel.   This points again to the need for children to have access to an independent advocate, separate from institutional personnel, who can intervene where necessary to protect the child's safety and pursue cases of abuse at all levels of the relevant administrative department and justice system.

Specific standards applicable to children with mental or physical disabilities
      Children with mental or physical disabilities are doubly vulnerable, and thus recognized in international law as entitled to an especially heightened degree of protection.   Some of the standards applicable to this group that are particularly relevant to the abuses discussed in this report are treaty obligations of Russia; others are non-binding standards approved by the U.N. General Assembly, which are nevertheless authoritative in state's duties with regard to the internationally recognized rights of the mentally or physically disabled discussed above.

      The Convention on the Rights of the Child has explicit provisions on children with mental or physical disabilities at Article 23.   It provides that states parties recognize such children "should enjoy a full and decent life, in conditions which ensure dignity, promote self-reliance and facilitate the child's active participation in the community."   Moreover, states are obliged to "ensure the extension, subject to available resources, to the eligible child and those responsible for his or her care, of assistance" and such assistance "shall be provided free of charge, whenever possible".   Assistance "shall be designed to ensure that the disabled child has effective access to and receives education, training, health care services, rehabilitation services, preparation for employment and recreation opportunities in a manner conducive to the child's achieving the fullest possible social integration and individual development, including his or her cultural and spiritual development."   The institutional care that Russia offers children with disabilities is not merely inadequate, but is also not a cost-effective method of delivering services and support to children who could often be better served by remaining in a family setting.[93]

      The Declaration on the Rights of Mentally Retarded Persons and the Declaration on the Rights of Disabled Persons, discussed above, contain important

---

protective measures shall include "reporting, referral, investigation...and, as appropriate, for judicial involvement.")

[93] Human Rights Watch interview, Dr. Anatoly Severny, February 12, 1998.

standards, including the principle that such persons have the right to, wherever possible, live with their families or in foster families and participate in community life;[94] the right to medical treatment, education and rehabilitation to enable them to develop to the maximum their potential and capability;[95] and the right to legal safeguards against abuse, due process and the assistance of a guardian or legal representative.[96]

Another important standard adopted by the U.N. General Assembly in 1990 is the Principles for the Protection of Persons with Mental Illness and the Improvement of Mental Health Care (hereinafter Mental Illness Principles).[97] Diagnosis of the abandoned or disabled child as *imbetsil* and *idiot* is tantamount to a determination of mental illness. These Principles, explicitly founded on the International Covenant on Civil and Political Rights and the International Covenant on Economic, Social and Cultural Rights, set out detailed standards of protection, care, treatment and medication especially relevant to children in psychoneurological *internaty*.

Central to this instrument is the patient's right to be treated "in the least restrictive environment and with the least restrictive or intrusive treatment appropriate to the patient's health and the need to protect the physical safety of others."[98] The mentally ill individual has the right to be treated and cared for, as far as possible, within his or her own community, and if treatment is in a mental health facility, that facility should be located near the patient's home or family,

---

[94] Declaration on the Rights of Mentally Retarded Persons, paragraph 4; Declaration on the Rights of Disabled Persons, paragraph 9.

[95] Declaration on the Rights of Mentally Retarded Persons, paragraph 2; Declaration on the Rights of Disabled Persons, paragraph 6.

[96] Declaration on the Rights of Mentally Retarded Persons, paragraphs 5, 6 and 7; Declaration on the Rights of Disabled Persons, paragraphs 4, 10 and 11.

[97] Principles for the protection of persons with mental illness and the improvement of mental health care, GA Res. 46/119 December 17, 1991 [hereinafter "Mental Illness Principles"]. For an extensive discussion of the origin and scope of these Principles, see Eric Rosenthal and Leonard S. Rubenstein, *International Human Rights Advocacy under the "Principles for the Protection of Persons with Mental Illness,"* International Journal of Law and Psychiatry, vol. 16, pp. 257-300 (1993).

[98] Mental Illness Principles, Principle 9(1).

and the patient has the right to return to the community as soon as possible.[99] "Medication...shall never be administered as a punishment or for the convenience of others."[100]

The Mental Illness Principles address the prejudicial effects of status as abandoned or disabled on the cycle of diagnosis and further discrimination. Under Principle 4(2), "A determination of mental illness shall never be made on the basis of political, economic or social status, or membership of a cultural, racial or religious group, or any other reason not directly relevant to mental health status." With regard to Russia's practice of keeping children institutionalized without further meaningful evaluation after the critical triage at age four, Principle 4(4) states "A background of past treatment or hospitalization as a patient shall not of itself justify any present or future determination of mental illness."

This instrument is also very explicit on the limits of use of physical restraints and involuntary seclusion. Neither may be used except "when it is the only means available to prevent immediate or imminent harm to the patient or others" and restraint and seclusion "shall not be prolonged beyond the period which is strictly necessary for this purpose." A personal representative of the patient must be notified of any incidents of restraint or seclusion; such incidents shall be recorded in the patient's medical record; and patients subject to such measures shall be kept "under humane conditions and be under the care and close and regular supervision of qualified members of the staff".[101] The Mental Illness Principles are especially strong on the right of redress for abuses. Every patient and former patient has a right to make complaints, and states are obliged to provide mechanisms for monitoring compliance with the Principles, submission, investigation and resolution of complaints, and institution of disciplinary or judicial proceedings for professional misconduct or violation of a patient's rights.[102]

One of the most recent standards adopted by the U.N. General Assembly is the Standard Rules on the Equalization of Opportunities for Persons with Disabilities

---

[99] Mental Illness Principles, Principle 7.

[100] Ibid., Principle 10.

[101] Ibid., Principle 11(11).

[102] Ibid., Principles 21 and 22.

(Equalization Rules).[103] These Rules are unique for the particular emphasis they lay on involving the families of persons with physical and mental disabilities in virtually every aspect of public policy, education and treatment, and in recognizing the importance of organizations of persons with disabilities in these functions and in advocacy. Rule 1 emphasizes "awareness-raising" in the sense of public education and education specifically directed at children and teachers to dispel prejudices that impair children with disabilities in enjoying their rights, to inform on the programs and services available to them, to emphasize their equal rights, and to educate the public and professionals on the potential of persons with disabilities. The Rules also provide for equal medical care for infants and children with disabilities in relation to other members of society (Rule 2.3); equal educational opportunities (Rule 6); and the state's duty to enable them to live with their families (Rule 9.1).

Finally, international standards of medical ethics pertaining to the detained are also pertinent to the situation of institutionalized children. The Principles of Medical Ethics relevant to the Role of Health Personnel, Particularly Physicians, in the Protection of Prisoners and Detainees against Torture and Other Cruel, Inhuman or Degrading Treatment or Punishment (hereinafter Principles of Medical Ethics) speak to several of the particular abuses suffered by children in Russia's orphanages. Principle 2 enjoins health personnel from engaging "actively or passively, in acts with constitute participation in, complicity in, incitement to or attempts to commit torture or other cruel, inhuman or degrading treatment or punishment"; and principle 5 bars the use of restraints or drugs if not based on purely medical criteria and not necessary for the health and safety or protection of the person in detention.

Russian Law

Russian law forbids the kind of discrimination that abandoned children face. Its generous entitlements—at least on paper—to children, to children in institutions, and to children with disabilities is at variance with the sordid conditions and neglect in which they often live.

The Constitution of the Russian Federation is the primary document that enshrines the ban on discrimination, which is repeated in relevant laws on education, health care, and the rights of people with disabilities. It also upholds the right of all citizens to such social and economic benefits. Article 19 states unequivocally:

---

[103] Adopted by the General Assembly 85th plenary meeting, December 20, 1993 A/RES/48/96.

(1) Everyone shall be equal before the law.

(2) The state shall guarantee the rights and freedoms of the individual and citizen without regard to gender, race, nationality, language, origins, property or official position, place of residence, religious orientation, convictions, membership in public associations and other circumstances. Any restrictions on the rights of citizens on social, racial, national, linguistic or religious grounds shall be forbidden.

Article 39 of the constitution guarantees the right to social security "in case of disease, disability, loss of a breadwinner [*kormilets*], for the rearing of children and other circumstances established by law"; Article 40 upholds the right to housing and mandates that the underprivileged receive housing free of charge; Article 41 upholds the right to health care free of charge in state and municipal establishments; and article 43 upholds the right to primary and secondary education that is accessible and free of charge.

Article 38 places the family "under the protection of the state."[104] The family code in Article 54 declares the right of the child to be reared in a family "to the degree that this is possible."[105] Article 123 of the family code sets out three forms of caring for abandoned or orphaned children—adoption, wardship (*pod opyeku,* or *popechitel'stvo*), or foster care (*priyemnaya semya*); or, in the absence of these opportunities, care in an institution. The family code does not declare affirmatively that a family environment is the preferred solution for placing and rearing abandoned children. Numerous laws and regulations, however, attempt to support rearing abandoned children or children with disabilities in the family by offering a variety of financial benefits in the form of monthly support payments, extra days off from work, and the like for families caring for children with disabilities and for foster families.

As stated above, Russian law regards education and health care as fundamental human rights, and basic laws on health care and education should

---

[104] Article 38 reads in full: "Motherhood and childhood, and the family shall be under the protection of the state. Care for children and their upbringing shall be equally the right and the obligation of parents. Able-bodied children who have reached the age of eighteen shall care for parents who are not able-bodied."

[105] It also states that the child has the right to live with his or her parents if this does not contradict the interests of the child. The Family Code of the Russian Federation entered into force on March 1, 1996.

serve to protect children with and without disabilities in orphanages from discrimination and poor care in both areas. The Fundamentals of Legislation of the Russian Federation on Health Protection (the Health Protection law)[106] declares unequivocally that health protection is an inalienable right, and forbids discrimination on any grounds in the sphere of health care (Article 17).[107] It specifically bans discrimination based on a person's "illness," and provides for non-specified sanctions for such discrimination. Article 20 of the Health Protection law requires medical care to be free of charge in state and municipal health systems. The law supports single-parent families and families with children with disabilities by opening the door to special entitlements.[108]

---

[106] Its full title is Fundamentals of Legislation of the Russian Federation on Health Protection No. 5487, adopted July 22, 1993 with Additions and Amendments of December 24, 1993 and March 2, 1998.

[107] Article 17 reads:

Citizens of the Russian Federation shall enjoy the inalienable right to health protection. This right shall be guaranteed by environmental protection, the creation of favorable conditions for everyday life, rest, education and instruction of individuals, the production and sale of good-quality foodstuffs , and also by the provision of medico-social aid *accessible to the population* [emphasis added].

The state shall provide its citizens with health protection, regardless of sex, race, nationality, language, social background, official status, place of residence, religion, beliefs, membership of public associations *or other circumstances* [emphasis added].

The state shall guarantee to its citizens protection against any form of discrimination based on disease. Persons guilty of violating this provision shall bear responsibility as stipulated by law.

[108] Article 20 (4) reads: "Families with children (with preference for incomplete families rearing disabled children and children without the care of parents) shall have the right to health protection privileges established by Russian Federation legislation, the Republics within the Federation. . . ." Commentary to Article 20 refers to a Ministry of Labor and Russian Insurance Supervision explanation clarifying how such parents may obtain four additional paid days off per month to care for children with disabilities.

The law also specifies the rights of particular groups, including minors, servicemen, "invalids,"[109] the elderly and the like. The section on the rights of minors (Article 24) enumerates various rights, such as "dispensary observation and treatment" . . . medico-social aid . . . sanitary-hygienic education . . . instruction and labor in conditions meeting their physiological needs . . ." It also establishes that parents or guardians may apply to the state to institutionalize minors with "physical or mental handicaps" at the expense of the state. The section on the rights of invalids generally enumerates the services and medicines to which they must have access free of charge. Of special relevance is Article 27(4), which allocates four extra working days per month to "one of the working parents or person acting *in loco parentis* for taking care of disabled children and invalids from childhood before they reach eighteen years of age."

The Federal Law on Education[110] guarantees "accessible and free" primary and secondary education (Article 5.3). Secondary professional education and higher education are also free, but admission is on a competitive basis. While orphans and "handicapped individuals" can compete, the law makes no provision for supplemental assistance such individuals may need to compete fairly. The law mandates that the government is to provide financial assistance to children for the education of children in impoverished families and those handicapped since birth (Article 40.7).[111]

---

[109] The term "invalid" in Russian parlance can signify a range of things, from a person with a serious high-blood pressure condition, to a person with a serious physical disability, such as blindness, or mental disability. There are three levels of "invalid" status, to which accrue numerous and various entitlements, from discounts on electricity bills to monthly pensions from the state.

[110] Adopted in 1996. Available in *Vsye Nachinaetsya so Shkoly* [Everything Begins with the School] (Moscow: Biblioteka "Rossiyskoi Gazety" 1998), pp. 6-51.

[111] Government regulations and normative acts provide for assistance to families in the education of children with disabilities. For example, a July 1996 resolution mandates the government to cover the cost of educating at home a child with disabilities, should such costs "surpass the norm." This applies to children who "for reasons of the state of their health, either temporarily or permanently cannot attend general education establishments . ..." It is unclear to which empirical circumstances this applies. Resolution of the Government of the Russian Federation No. 861 on Confirming Ways for Rearing and Educating Children with Disabilities at Home and in Nonstate Educational Establishments. Adopted July 18, 1996.

Guarantees to education for people with mental disabilities are weaker than those set out in the U.N. Convention on the Rights of the Child (Article 23) and in the United Nations Declaration on the Rights of Mentally Retarded Persons. Article 5.6 of the education law promises that the state will "create a situation in which they will receive an education based on special pedagogical methods, which will correct their developmental problems and advance their social adaptation." For this purpose, Article 50 .9 envisages "special educational establishments and classes." The Declaration on the Rights of Mentally Retarded Persons emphasizes the rights of people with disabilities to development "to the maximum of their potential and capability," and to "fullest possible social integration."

Children (with and without disabilities) in orphanages should also benefit from Russian laws that protect them as target groups as children, abandoned children, and people with disabilities. In July, the Russian Duma sought to strengthen the protection of children's rights by adopting the Law on Basic Guarantees of the Rights of the Child.[112] Article 4 of this law declares that the aim of state policy on children is to realize their constitutional rights, by, inter alia, not permitting discrimination, and by assisting in the "physical, intellectual, mental, spiritual and moral development of the child." Article 8 of this law mandates "minimal social standards of indicators for a child's quality of life," which relate to social services responsible for guaranteeing accessible free primary and high school education, free medical services, professional orientation, and the like. Notably, Article 8.3 grants children in "establishments" such as health care establishments and educational establishments[113] the right to a periodic review of services—by agencies authorized by the local government—provided to them in these establishments.

The Law on Additional Guarantees for the Social Protection of Child-Orphans and Children without Parental Guardians brings together in one piece of legislation provisions for budget allocations for orphans and abandoned children and a restatement of their rights to education, medical services, housing and judicial protection that were previously enunciated in many different laws. Examples of these include the right to free professional education, to circumvent entrance examinations for professional schools where admissions are on a competitive basis,

---

[112] Adopted July 3, 1998. Published in *Rossiyskaya gazeta* (Moscow), August 5, 1998.

[113] Article 8.3 does not enumerate per se children's homes, internaty, or psycho-neurological internaty, however these would be assumed under 8.3's general reference to "and other establishments."

an annual cash grant to purchase educational materials, and an additional student stipend not lower than 50 percent of the monthly minimum salary.

In its preamble, the Law on Social Protection for Invalids in the Russian Federation[114] defines "social protection as "guaranteeing invalids the same rights and opportunities for realizing civil, economic political, and other rights and freedoms envisaged in the . . . [C]onstitution, and also with universally recognized principles of international law. . ." as other citizens. It further defines social protection as "a system of economic, social, and legal measures by which the state guarantees invalids the conditions for overcoming or compensating for limitations on their abilities and which are directed towards creating opportunities for them to participate in society equally with other citizens." Article 19 of the same law obliges the state to provide invalids free general education and professional training. Much of the law discusses the particular benefits and entitlements that accrue to invalids and the families or guardians who care for them.

Russian law criminalizes the "failure to fulfill obligations in child rearing", if this is combined with cruel treatment. Under Article 156 of the Russian criminal code,[115] this may apply to parents, teachers, or staff of "educational, medical, or other establishment responsible for the care of a minor." Offenders are punished by a fine from fifteen to one hundred minimum monthly salaries or up to two years of imprisonment.

---

[114] Adopted October 20, 1995.

[115] Criminal Code of the Russian Federation, adopted May 24, 1996, entered into force January 1, 1997.

IV. THE "GILDED CAGE" OF THE DOM REBYONKA: INFANCY TO FOUR YEARS[116]

You'll see a child lying on a cot staring at the ceiling, obviously in terrible need of love—I have heard the staff say in all innocence to me, "We told the mother 'don't bother to come to visit.' The child doesn't understand anyway."[117]

Introduction

Of all the institutions for abandoned children in Russia, the 252 baby houses for orphans from zero to four years of age have greatly benefited from a flood of international charity. Yet beyond the playrooms and dormitories brimming with donated toys and bright new furnishings, the minimal care and therapeutic intervention in most baby houses prompted one baby house doctor with decades of experience to describe the average institution as a "gilded cage."[118] The evidence gathered by Human Rights Watch indicates that at this early stage in orphans' lives, their rights are systematically violated by prejudicial stereotypes; segregation and severe neglect of babies with disabilities; denial of medical services; abuse of sedative drugs; and deprivation of the opportunity for individual development.

Lying-down rooms—gross neglect of infants with disabilities

In a world apart from the daily life of Russians, the lying-down rooms of the baby houses are yet another world removed. According to a volunteer who has visited a vast number of baby houses, they all had at least one, lined with fifteen to twenty bedridden children.[119]

Throughout our interviews with volunteers and regular visitors to Russian baby houses, the extreme neglect of those who are segregated away in the lying-down rooms was frequently described. The pattern is captured in the following testimony

---

[116] Human Rights Watch interview, Dr. Olga Vassilieva, March 5, 1998.

[117] Human Rights Watch interview, Sarah Philips, February 23, 1998. Based on four years' experience volunteering in children's custodial institutions and shared experience with fellow volunteers.

[118] Human Rights Watch interview, Dr. Olga Vassilieva, March 5, 1998.

[119] Human Rights Watch interview, Sarah Philips, February 23, 1998.

by a photographer who has visited more than a dozen baby houses and psychoneurological *internaty* since 1997:

> About twenty kids were lined up in cribs. Bottles were propped up against the crib and they were in a vegetative state. In one there was a kid six years old the size of a two-year-old. All this goes on in the same institutions where other kids are running around. They're clearly neglected by comparison.[120]

One volunteer showed Human Rights Watch a photograph of an eight-year-old girl who was allowed to stay unusually long in her baby house while volunteers searched for a home for her:

> This little girl has mild cerebral palsy in her legs and because of this, she's about to be diagnosed as retarded and sent for life in an *internat* of the Ministry of Labor and Social Development. Look at this! They make her sleep sixteen hours a day. She's eight years old and she's made to stay with three-year-olds. She gets no stimulation.[121]

Compounding a stigma with multiple diagnoses

The lying down rooms of the baby houses are only the most ghastly product of a conundrum of stigmatization that begins before the baby opens his or her eyes. First the baby is abandoned and diagnosed with developmental delays. Then, the addition of further diagnoses compounds the original stigma of abandonment. The long-time director of a Moscow baby house succinctly described this conundrum of "abnormality":

> All the babies are problematic, maybe some more or less, but they're all problematic. Because if you understand: take the situation when the mother wants to throw away the baby. If parents are normal they'd never allow it. So that means that the families are not normal. And what can the state do if the children have no mothers? Of course we try to do our best.[122]

---

[120] Human Rights Watch interview, photographer, February 11, 1998.

[121] Human Rights Watch interview, Sarah Philips, February 23, 1998.

[122] Human Rights Watch interview, Dr. Elena Petrenko, baby house director, Moscow, March 2, 1998.

Starting from behind with a provisional diagnosis of *zaderzhka* (delay), Russian infants soon acquire a raft of conditions in their medical charts which they may be unable to shed as they move through the state institutions.

The philosophy of health care in Russia is different from the U.S. It's more like Europe by the way doctors are trained to address relatively minor things more seriously than in U.S. They make a list of diagnoses, but are simply describing "risk factors," to let other doctors know: maternal risk factors, infant risk factors.[123]

But Dr. Rybchonok went on to say that children in Russia are especially put at risk by the ambiguity of the records, because very often the records "are not dated." He explained:

There's a signature of the physician, but there's no date. But what's more important, there's almost never a date when the diagnosis was first given, or a date when the condition was resolved. It's very unclear if the child had problems chronically or just after birth. Mostly they copy the previous list of diagnoses and then don't date it.[124]

Repeatedly Dr. Rybchonok stressed to us, " If this diagnosis is *not* true, it's really a disaster for an individual."[125]

Doctors and the other experts in child development whom we interviewed for this report frequently criticized this diagnostic tradition. We were therefore particularly dismayed to note that a concise critique of this practice of "over-diagnosing" was presented as long as three years ago to the Council of Europe by an expert team who visited Russia in June 1994.[126]

---

[123] Human Rights Watch interview, Dr. Vsevolod Rybchonok, March 6, 1998. Dr. Rybchonok has travelled widely for a western-based charity, and has performed general medical examinations on several thousand institutionalized children.

[124] Human Rights Watch interview, Dr. Vsevolod Rybchonok, September 23, 1998.

[125] Ibid.

[126] "The Children of St. Petersburg" Report by Mrs. Anne Plessz and Mr. Jean-Claude Alt for the Comite International pour la Dignite de l'Enfant (C.I.D.E.) on Children's Rights in Russian Prisons and Orphanages. Council of Europe. "Congress of Local and Regional

The experts reported that Russian psychological norms are based on very strict criteria. Apart from these norms, however, factors that in the West are considered as being simple medical risks, will, in Russia, be labeled as illnesses:

- babies born to alcoholic parents or whose mothers suffered depression during pregnancy will be labelled encephalopathic and remain so until they come of age.
- orphans will be classed as being mentally deficient.
- children with a single physical malformation (a harelip or speech defect...) become subnormal in the eyes of Russian doctors."[127]

Human Rights Watch also found that these early diagnostic practices interfere with a child's right to full development and in certain cases, to life, itself. Moreover, abundant information gathered in Russia indicated several crucial incentives behind "over-diagnosing" that suggest violations of basic medical ethics.

According to a former charity worker who distributed assistance to impoverished baby houses and has travelled widely in Russia since 1991, one legacy of the Soviet medical bureaucracy encourages hospital staff to avoid any risk of sanctions for errors detected under their care. For example, she recalled the case of a child she knew well who had a medical chart with a catalogue of conditions including *oligophrenia* and encephalopathy.

A doctor told me that they have to cover their butt. They could lose their job, so they write many diagnoses. And you know the penal system here. It's a "better safe than sorry" system.[128]

A second factor that encourages exaggerated diagnoses, is the Russian law which until recently, prohibited international adoption of "healthy" children. "The

---

Authorities of Europe." CG/GT Jeunes (1) 5. Strasbourg, Jan 24, 1995. Based on a 1994 June 13-22 visit. Press File. Information document prepared by the Secretariat for the attention of the CLRAE Youth Group.

[127] C.I.D.E., p. 12.

[128] Human Rights Watch interview, Sandy Marinelli, February 25, 1998.

doctors in the system wanted the kids adopted, so they'd say that this child has a tumor and then "wink" at you.[129]

Finally, a widely cited incentive for over-diagnosing is the extra financial subsidy and salary increment that the state grants to institutions that care for children with disabilities. The entitlement to these subsidies was confirmed by children's rights activists as well as by staff of state institutions.[130]

One volunteer who worked in a Moscow baby house for a year and a half recalled to Human Rights Watch,

> Once, in a rare honest moment with the acting director, she told me, 'We are considered as a medical facility because more than half our children are considered to have medical defects.' So they could finagle more money for the place. [131]

Another baby house director told Human Rights Watch, however, that the subsidy does represent the greater burden shouldered by the staff in dealing with disabled children, even though the salary levels remain very low and do not attract specially trained personnel:

> A pedagogue in a baby house who works here, for the Ministry of Health, will get a 20 percent higher salary than from another ministry. Yet what should we be talking about if the salary of a doctor is only $100 a month? Of course, all these places with "problematic kids" get higher pay because we have to deal with all the kids, including the problematic ones.[132]

Debilitating effects of institutional deprivation

It is by no means only the "problematic kids" who suffer setbacks from institutionalization in Russian baby homes. Dr. Rybchonok, who has examined a

---

[129] Ibid.

[130] Human Rights Watch interviews, Dr. Anatoly Severny, February 12, 1998; director of a Moscow baby house, March 2, 1998; volunteers in Moscow baby houses, February-March 1998.

[131] Human Rights Watch interview, Theresa Jacobson, March 8, 1998.

[132] Human Rights Watch interview, Dr. Elena Petrenko, March 2, 1998.

vast number of children from Russian institutions, described the broader impact of deprivation:

> I see children who've been institutionalized after parents lost their parental rights. If the kids lived with their parents even two years, they are very different. They don't look like institutionalized children. They've been loved. *Even* in an alcoholic family, the child could be smaller than normal and could be abused. But the child still looks different.

> Those children who have lived all their time in an institution are really special. Because of being exposed to sensory deprivation after two years, they have no social skills, they don't grow that well, some are off the growth chart. That's the big impact. That's the negative side of the institutions. If someone's trying to find that situation, look at the last century. There's a high risk of disability, attachment disorders. That's just through sensory deprivation.[133]

Recent research on the developmental challenges of children adopted from orphanages in Eastern Europe and the former USSR shows promising evidence that children can make remarkable recoveries from the deprivation of institutional life.[134]

---

[133] Human Rights Watch interview, Dr. Vsevolod Rybchonok, March 6, 1998. For some of the early studies done on the detrimental effects of institutions on children, see John Bowlby, *Maternal Care and Mental Health* (Geneva: World Health Organization, 1951) and *Childcare and the Growth of Love* (Baltimore: Penguin, 1953); D.A. Frank, et. al, "Infants and Young Children in Orphanages: One View from Pediatrics and Child Psychiatry" in *Pediatrics*, vol. 97, no.4, 1996, pp. 569-578. W.A. Mason, "Early deprivation in the biological perspective," in *Education of the Infant and Young Children*, V.H. Denenberg, ed., (New York: Academic Press, 1970); René Spitz, "Hospitalism: An Inquiry into the Genesis of Psychiatric Conditions in Early Childhood," in *The Psychoanalytic Study of the Child*, Volume 1 (New York: International University Press, 1945) 53-74, and "The Role of Ecological Factors in Emotional Development in Infancy," in *Child Development*, vol.20, 1949, pp. 145-155.

[134] E.W. Ames and L. Savoie, "Behaviour Problems of Romanian Orphanage Children Adopted to Canada," presented at the Thirteenth Biennial Meetings of the International Society for the Study of Behavioural Development (June 1994); V. Groze and D. Ileana, "A Follow-up Study of Adopted Children from Romania," in *Child and Adolescent Social Work Journal*, vol. 13, no. 6, 1996, pp. 541-565.; S. Morison et al, "The Development of Children Adopted from Romanian Orphanages, in *Merrill-Palmer Quarterly*, vol. 41, no.

But most of Russia's orphans, including those deemed officially "normal," will never enjoy the opportunity to leave institutional life for a family environment where they can catch up on their time lost. The majority of Russia's orphans will be stuck for all their formative years within the tunnel of state institutions, only to emerge when they reach the age of eighteen. Moreover, those who have been wrongly diagnosed as "ineducable" will lose any opportunity to catch up.

Human Rights Watch asked a long-time director of a baby house to compare specifically the developmental opportunities for orphans reared in Russian institutions with those of children raised in families. She replied:

> There's a big difference. First of all, the deprivation of a mother is the lack of personal love. If you talk about a baby in his mother's hands, touching him, it's been scientifically proved that this influences his development.
>
> However good our conditions are here, we're still like a "gilded cage." The kids are still humiliated—some because they always lived in a "collective" place. Everything is always done altogether in line, never in private, to sit at a table to eat. It's always this public, "grown-up" behavior, and in our point of view, it affects the child's mind. It affects the development of their nervous system.
>
> Also in small "collectives," it becomes a struggle to survive. They become aggressive. It's natural, if someone has to struggle to survive.
>
> They have no attachment. They have nothing of their own—not his toy, or her toy. They don't even have personal clothes. There is no face that a child wants to see all the time. Or even, he constantly has to see a face he doesn't want to!
>
> Of course, we recognize these problems, but it is physically difficult to meet their individual needs. We try to give them individual attention. Some staff take the children home for a few days, so they will see what a home is like.[135]

But while Dr. Vassilieva believes that this brief exposure to family life benefits children by providing them "some kind of 'fresh air,'" it also causes

---

4, 1995, pp. 411-430.

[135] Human Rights Watch interview, Dr. Olga Vassilieva, March 5, 1998.

psychological complications. "Because there's a lot of stress for the child. They see 'home' children and can't answer why they don't have a home, themselves."[136]

The problem for the majority of children is that they will rarely even visit a private home, and this, Dr. Vassilieva believes, impedes these children in their adult life:

> The opportunity for the orphans is much lower. It's very heavy for them. We're now raising the kids of the kids we had before. The grown-up kids don't have the impulse to establish a family. They have a couple of marriages, and then leave their children.[137]

Orphans denied personal possessions

The "collective" philosophy criticized by Dr. Vassilieva is a pillar of Russian institutions, and it contravenes the basic precepts of the Convention on the Rights of the Child protecting the individual development of a child. The following is one volunteer's graphic account of the concerted policy in her Moscow baby house to deprive children of individual possessions. The experience of Theresa Jacobson has been corroborated by a number of others interviewed by Human Rights Watch.

> It was one of the better baby houses, because there were a lot of private aid groups there. But they'd keep a lot of the donations locked up in a storage room downstairs. A lot of stuff we brought, we wouldn't see. "It's not necessary to give out the toys at once," they would say. "Save some for a rainy day." Part of this is this due to the Russian mentality, that they never know what will happen. So they keep huge packages of toys in storage...

> Also, there was a norm of two toys per child. But it was for a child as part of the group. Not for an individual. Toys were kept in a glass case, and brought out when we came. I brought a cassette player for one little boy who was blind and just lying there, out of it. They came up with excuse after excuse for why they never used it. It disappeared.

---

[136] Ibid.

[137] Ibid.

The Anglo-American school gave a toy to each child each year, but then found that the toy only went to the "collective." A child was not allowed to have her own little teddy bear on the bed. The rooms were bare.[138]

Although there has been a deluge of toys donated to baby houses since international charities began to assist them in the early 1990s, the children's beds in many baby houses are still bare. In addition to eyewitness accounts by numerous people interviewed by Human Rights Watch, we observed this irony first hand during a visit to a well supported baby house in Moscow.

Reminiscent of the peculiar practice in Romanian orphanages to display newly acquired developmental toys in places only accessible to the staff, the staff of the Moscow baby house called our attention to their bright array of Montessori toys stacked in the glass cabinet just inside the play room. They stopped our tour briefly to demonstrate how the toys worked, and then put them back and closed the cabinet door.

More significant was the apparent absence of rapport between the toddlers and the staff who stood stiffly at several arms' lengths from the children. This distance contrasted sharply with the rapport Human Rights Watch observed on a visit to another well appointed baby house outside Moscow, where the staff and children played and embraced easily during and after their lunchtime meal.

Another notable feature of the Moscow baby house we visited which confirmed patterns described by regular visitors to state institutions, was the extraordinary silence and orderly atmosphere for a building full of small children. Even as a group of preschoolers was piling on their snow suits for their afternoon recess, there was barely a sound in the cloakroom, either among the children, or between them and the two women from the staff who were supervising them.

The abuse of sedative drugs

There is a high premium placed on orderliness and quiet and we learned that Russian orphans pay a high price for this. Human Rights Watch heard repeated references to the use of strong tranquilizers such as aminazine in the state institutions, and noted the sharply critical findings of an international team of

---

[138] Human Rights Watch interview, Theresa Jacobson, March 8, 1998.

investigators in 1991, who also stressed the high risk of liver damage to the orphans.[139]

We were also told by the staff of an *internat* for disabled orphans that they regularly give the children aminazine when they are agitated and it is time for them to go to sleep.[140]

One former volunteer who regularly worked for a year and a half in a Moscow baby house described most vividly how her suspicions about routine sedation were reinforced when she returned for a visit after giving birth to her own baby:

> They have very clear ideas about children and sleeping. I came in after my baby was born. They asked how much the baby sleeps. And when I answered, "Not much," they told me, "Oh that's very, very bad, the baby needs sleep. We can give you injections that you can give to put the baby to sleep." I'm positive this is what they do to get them to sleep, especially the ones that they call "nervous." The staff was horrified that my child slept so little.[141]

Discrimination against orphan babies requiring medical care

When orphans in a Russian baby house need medical treatment in a hospital, they face a new hurdle of discrimination. Human Rights Watch learned about routine practices regarding orphans from a volunteer, one of whose tasks it has been to arrange for medical care for children in the baby houses:

> The baby house staff put the baby in an ambulance. Sometimes someone will accompany the child, and then drop the child off just inside the hospital door. The child is left completely alone and can languish [in the hospital] for three months. Not even a representative from the baby house will come to see the child. I've been in the hospitals many times, many times, and seen this. They definitely discriminate against the baby house children. They put all the *dom rebyonka* children into one room, so they're given completely second-class treatment.

---

[139] Human Rights Watch interview, Dr. Anatoly Severny February 12, 1998; Caroline Cox et al., *Trajectories of Despair* (Leigh-on-Sea: Christian Solidarity International, 1991) , p. 15. Hereafter cited as Cox, *Trajectories of Despair*.

[140] Human Rights Watch interview, Alla Sergeyeva (not her real name), *sanitarka*, pyschoneurological *Internat* X, February 15, 1998.

[141] Human Rights Watch interview, Theresa Jacobson, Moscow, March 8, 1998.

How was this treatment "second-class?" You know how it is in a Russian hospital. The family of the patient has to bribe the doctor, bribe the nurse, in order to be sure to get what you want done. The staff know that these are only *dom rebyonka* children, so no one's relatives are going to give them anything for their treatment. So they put them aside and deal with the others.[142]

It is crucial to note that some significant variation does exist in the treatment of orphan babies throughout the vast Russian Federation, and the performance standard seems to be set by the director of a given baby house. Human Rights Watch learned of at least two baby houses in Moscow and one in a town in the Volga region where visitors described positive reforms in child care, including the smaller, more intimate children's cottage approach.

But Human Rights Watch also obtained sufficient testimony from Russian and foreign experts to raise serious concerns that discrimination in the health sector against babies and older children in state institutions included being bypassed for corrective surgery—for heart defects, cleft palate—that would improve the child's chances of surviving to adulthood.

Arranging for corrective surgery, like many services in the former Soviet Union, can require a great deal of time for diagnostics, paperwork, and scheduling of the procedure. Financing should not be a problem, as Russian law guarantees the provision of medical care free of charge to children in the custody of the state.

But procedures are increasingly costly, since market reforms have driven up the prices on medical services along with everything else. Without parents who can physically make the rounds to the myriad authorities to pressure them for the procedure within their legal rights, the children are at the mercy of the orphanage director and staff to take up their plight. In unusual cases, a charity volunteer can find the extra time to do the extensive work on the child's behalf. [143] As Dr. Vsevolod Rybchonok explained to Human Rights Watch, "They're just second-class people. That's why those patients are kicked out to the *internaty*. And these kinds of services, like heart surgery, are very expensive now. "[144]

---

[142] Human Rights Watch interview, Sarah Philips, February 23, 1998.

[143] Ibid.

[144] Human Rights Watch interview, Dr. Vsevolod Rybchonok, March 6, 1998.

One of the most egregious cases recalled by volunteers in the orphanages was that of Alina,[145] age five, from one Moscow baby house:

> She was a cleft palate case. A simple cleft palate. It had grown so badly because no one treated it when she was little. Her mouth was a nightmare. She couldn't eat, and of course, she was diagnosed as an *imbetsil* because she couldn't talk.[146]

The director of the baby house in charge of this case did not acknowledge the case in an interview with Human Rights Watch, or that such a potential problem exists. She described the system in positive terms:

> Actually those babies who should be operated on *are* operated on. But actually the kids who are intellectually very bright but have physical problems, they are very well adopted by foreigners. We've had several babies with no legs who were adopted, treated and made prostheses in Sweden.[147]

Rationale of budget and staff limitations

The lack of public funds is a constant lament in Russian institutions for orphans across the board, and the staff and directors we interviewed laid the blame for human rights violations in the institutions on the nation's financial crisis.[148] Salaries, if paid at all, are so low that only the least-skilled people apply for jobs. Also because salaries are so low, Human Rights Watch learned that two or three staff positions will be filled by one person, who will work three strenuous shifts in a row, rather than the single six-hour shifts regulated for those assigned to the most severely disabled.[149]

---

[145] Not her real name.

[146] Human Rights Watch interview, Sarah Philips, February 23, 1998. (See Chapter V for full description of Alina's case.)

[147] Human Rights Watch interview, Dr. Elena Petrenko, March 2, 1998.

[148] Human Rights Watch interviews, Moscow baby house, March 2, 1998; psychoneurological *Internat* X February 15, 1998; psychoneurological *internat* February 16, 1998; volunteers in baby houses, February 13, 23, March 7,8, 1998.

[149] Human Rights Watch interview, Natasha Fairweather, February 20, 1998.

Russian human rights activists and independent child development specialists, however, reject the "financial crisis" claims, insisting that the state provides sufficient funds but the directors allocate too little to the actual care of the children. For instance, in an interview with Human Rights Watch, Dr. Anatoly Severny explained that one government ministry channeled 2,500 rubles ($400) per child per month to one *internat* he knows, but the daily allocation per child is only 17 rubles (three U.S. dollars) for food and 17 rubles (twenty-five cents) for medicine. [150] Furthermore, he and other advocates claim that since institutions do receive higher subsidies for sicker children, there is an incentive to keep as many children in the institutions as possible, despite the child's potential. Some even claim that the funds are plainly misused, allegations that time did not allow us to corroborate. [151]

On the other hand, Human Rights Watch learned that the acute poverty in some regions of Russia can inflict real economic deprivation upon orphans. In one rural region where winter food shortages are acute, one baby house director made desperate calls to the local factories to beg for basic milk and bread to feed the children. [152]

Financial shortages, nevertheless, do not explain the wanton neglect of disabled children left in lying-down rooms. This, according to a wide range of health professionals, orphanage volunteers, human rights advocates and journalists interviewed by Human Rights Watch, goes straight back to the prejudicial stereotype of orphans, and the general attitude of the baby house staff.

Sarah Philps, a volunteer with four years of experience in Russian state institutions, told us:

> It's attitude, more than anything else. Attitude, plus no feeling at all of responsibility by anyone who looks after them. I know this sounds extreme, but I've seen it again and again. So we are not talking about money at all. We are talking about no conscience, no soul.

---

[150] Human Rights Watch interview, Dr. Anatoly Severny, February 12, 1998; exchange rate as of February 1998.

[151] Human Rights Watch interview, human rights advocate, Moscow, February 16, 1998.

[152] Human Rights Watch interview, Sandy Marinelli, Moscow, February 25, 1998. Marinelli is a former volunteer whose charity provided assistance to many poor baby houses.

They'll say there's no staff, no staff. But meanwhile, you're very much aware that fifteen women are sitting in the back having lunch, leaving one person there to feed all the children. In another former Soviet republic, by contrast, they shared the feeding shift and everyone takes turns putting a kid on their knee and feeding him. It's also symptomatic of the terribly rigid adherence to their roles. If there's only one *vospitatel'*, then none of the others will do that work.[153]

Conclusion

Despite the debates over budgets and attitudes, the evidence collected by Human Rights Watch indicated that life in Russian baby houses further retarded orphans' growth, denying them the basic right to develop their full potential. The first clear impact of this deprivation is documented in the following chapter on the controversial state commission that determines the course of an orphan's future.

---

[153] Human Rights Watch interview, Sarah Philps, February 23, 1998.

V. THE POINT OF NO RETURN:
DIAGNOSIS AT AGE FOUR

The diagnosis that's been given by pediatric neurologists sticks to children for the rest of their life. This is a disaster for the children.[154]

This evaluation commission is our greatest shame.[155]

As the linchpin in the life of a Russian orphan, the test by the state-run Psychological-Medical-Pedagogical Commission, with the consequence it carries, is the single policy most criticized by advocates for children abandoned to state institutions in Russia. Just as in the notorious orphanage system of Ceausescu's Romania, which international and Russian child development experts cite for comparative reference, the evaluation of all children at the age of four is the basis for the triage of orphans as they are consigned to state institutions for the rest of their childhood.

Among the flaws in the evaluation procedure most often cited in our interviews with doctors, child development specialists, and human rights advocates were:

- the brevity of the examiners' one-time session with the child;
- the intimidating presence of a panel of strange doctors to a child who has limited exposure to life outside the walls of an institution;
- the inappropriate questions often used to measure the intelligence of such a sheltered child;
- the misdiagnoses and the virtual impossibility of revoking them;
- the dire consequence of a "life sentence" in a psychoneurological *internat*;
- the discrimination against "light" *oligophrenics* seeking higher education, jobs and housing.

The disadvantages confronting the four-year-old orphans are similar to those they face at the moment of abandonment, when they can be given a provisional

---

[154] Human Rights Watch interview, Dr. Vsevolod Rybchonok, Moscow, March 6, 1998.

[155] Human Rights Watch interview, Dr. Tatiana Moroz (not her real name), psychiatrist, Moscow, February 12, 1998.

diagnosis of delayed or retarded.[156] But the evaluation performed at four years of age marks a point of no return. A diagnosis of serious *oligophrenia*—as *imbetsil* or *idiot*—will condemn the child to life in a psychoneurological *internat*, where his or her rights to education, health care, and protection from harm will be permanently denied. Based on independent investigations in into the accuracy of diagnoses, published in 1991, from 30 to 60 percent of orphans diagnosed as *oligophrenic* may be wrongly ascribed.[157] And Human Rights Watch learned from the staff of two *internaty* for severely disabled orphans that perhaps 10 percent of their children could have "useful lives."[158] Conservatively then, at any time in Russia, at least 3,000 of the 30,000 children in *internaty* could be there by mistake, and untold thousands more who have diagnoses of lighter *oligophrenia*—*debil*—may be wrongly marked as well. Neither these children, nor those who have severe congenital disabilities, should be subjected to such violations of their most fundamental rights.

Introduction to Russia's Psychological-Medical-Pedagogical Commission

During its month-long mission to Russia, Human Rights Watch made at least half a dozen attempts to interview a member of the Psychological-Medical-Pedagogical Commission or, at a minimum, to obtain a copy of the clinical and educational standards used to evaluate the children. We never succeeded. The resistance we encountered harkened back to the Soviet protection of even the most innocuous of public documents as state secrets.[159]

Interviews with orphanage staff and others allowed us to piece together information on the composition and procedures followed by the commission.

---

[156] Human Rights Watch received varied information from Moscow experts themselves concerning the rules and actual execution of a diagnosis on infants and children, underscoring the need for transparency in the Psychological-Medical-Pedagogical Commission. One expert told us that the diagnosis of *oligophrenia* (congenital retardation) cannot be made in the maternity ward, but can be made after one year of age. Volunteers working in baby houses and doctors who have examined medical records of institutionalized babies prior to and after adoption, have seen "*oligophrenia*" marked on files of children under the age of four. Human Rights Watch interview, Moscow attorney, October 14, 1998; Carole Hartigan, October 14, 1998; Western pediatrician, October 16, 1998.

[157] Cox, *Trajectories of Despair*, p. 15.

[158] Human Rights Watch interviews, February 15, 1998; March 5, 1998.

[159] Human Rights Watch telephone interviews, Moscow, February-March 1998.

Headquartered at Chief Psychiatric Hospital No. 6 in Moscow, the Russian Psychological-Medical-Pedagogical Commission is an arm of the Institute of Corrective Pedagogy, operated by the Ministry of Education. It is affiliated with the Ministry of Health, which is effectively a partner in the process.

The panel for a given evaluation can vary from two to several members, and should include at least one education specialist and a psychoneurologist. According to a Russian child development expert, the original concept behind the commission was to classify children in order to prepare them for more efficient rehabilitation. The children were all compared at a certain age level, and it was thought that if a child could not be trained, he or she would have to be separated from the rest. There was no interest in integrating them with the mainstream of children.[160]

A Human Rights Watch interview with a Ministry of Labor and Social Development official who had served for many years on the Psychological-Medical-Pedagogical Commission in her previous position with the Ministry of Education corroborated this view. "The Ministry of Education takes care of children who can be trained and the system of the Ministry of Development (sic)—we cover kids who *cannot be trained*," Valentina V. Terekhina told Human Rights Watch.[161] When we asked what happens to children at the time of their important diagnosis at the age of four, if they are classed as imbetsil or idiot, she repeated:

> So it's the same. If you take the children in the baby houses who have potential to be trained, they go to the Ministry of Education. Those who cannot be trained, such as Down syndrome for example, they are transferred to invalid houses of [the] Social Welfare [Ministry] (sic)...We cover the children of very very low intellectual capabilities, and practically speaking, those who cannot take care of themselves—daily care—because their intellectual level is so low, low, they cannot even do that.[162]

---

[160] Human Rights Watch interview, Dr. Anatoly Severny, February 12, 1998.

[161] Human Rights Watch interview, Valentina V. Terekhina, Ministry of Labor and Social Development, Moscow, March 6, 1998. The current Ministry of Labor and Social Development was earlier called the Ministry of Social Welfare.

[162] Ibid.

The very act of judging a wide spectrum of children with correctable disabilities as "ineducable" is a fundamental form of discrimination, and an abrogation of the basic right to education set forth in the International Covenant on Economic, Social and Cultural Rights, and the Convention on the Rights of the Child. Moreover, the hostility of state officials to the mounting criticism of the commission by independent Russian specialists poses a particular obstacle to transparency and reform. In our first attempt to obtain the public standards used for the evaluation, a Ministry of Health official, Valentina B. Chumichova, lambasted Russia's leading children's rights advocates and independent child psychiatrists as people who "need to break the whole system of health and education for orphans."[163]

She also criticized the advocates' goal of transferring disabled orphans to the jurisdiction of the Ministry of Health, which they consider a more appropriate authority than the Ministry of Labor and Social Development for the health, development and dignity of vulnerable children.

Valentina B. Chumichova's comments reveal stark insights into the official attitude toward the neglect and cruelty that is widely documented in state institutions for children. "All the problems in our system are caused by lack of money. If a person gets only 300,000 rubles ($50), he cannot be loving to a child. Because if you get this salary and go out into the street and see a kitten, you're going to kick it when you pass it."[164]

The Ministry of Health official further expressed the deep-rooted cynicism found among many government officials working in social welfare when she questioned the motives of the vocal human rights groups. "They only raise this problem because it's very *modna* [chic] right now, not because they're worried about children."[165]

Human Rights Watch also contacted a Ministry of Health official named Svetlana R. Konova, who is involved with the operation of baby houses. To our request for the standards or tests used to evaluate orphans at the age of four, she

---

[163] Human Rights Watch interview, Valentina B. Chumichova, March 1998.

[164] Ibid. Exchange rate as of March 1998.

[165] Ibid. For further information, we were told to submit a written request to the Health Ministry.

replied, "It's not so secret but I should not give information without the permission of my boss."[166]

Further calls were placed to Chief Psychiatric Hospital No.6 in Moscow, where we reached Lyubov A. Andreeva, a deputy to the head of the commission. She, too, advised Human Rights Watch that she needed permission from her superior before she could meet with us. On the matter of testing standards, however, she went on to say, "We have no standards. We have very professional staff, all good pedagogues and doctors. And they know all about this problem."[167]

As Human Rights Watch requested details, the official answered, "We use three methods—Wechsler, Rubinshtein, clinical *razbor* [classification], and other methods. We use a program designed by a scientist at the Scientific Institute of Psychiatry in Moscow to determine the intellectual level of the kids."[168]

Human Rights Watch obtained a contrasting view of the official testing standards from a child development specialist working with one of Moscow's few innovative foster care programs. "The methods the commission uses are not so modern," she said.[169] Moreover, she criticized the format of the evaluation, which creates an intimidating environment for a four-year-old. "Imagine, many adults come here and sit down. It is frightening to the child. They ask something and the child's scared. What level of development can he show the adults?"[170]

A hazardous turning point: intimidation, inappropriateness and error
It is difficult to overstate the significance of this examination, which for some children, is a matter of life and death. The deterioration of children committed to these *internaty* is of grave concern to doctors who examine them. Dr. Vsevolod Rybchonok, who has conducted general medical examinations on several thousand children during the last few years told us:

> If they're transferred to special institutions [*internaty*], it's like a prison to the brain. There's a total lack of sensory stimulation. There's no input, no

---

[166] Human Rights Watch interview, Svetlana R. Konova, March 1998.

[167] Human Rights Watch interview, Lyubov A. Andreeva, March 3, 1998.

[168] Ibid.

[169] Human Rights Watch interview, child development expert, March 1998.

[170] Human Rights Watch interview, child development expert, March 1998.

competition with other children if the others are even more retarded. It's just a process of slowing down, slowing down, then idling—and then—stop.[171]

It is impossible to know the total number of misdiagnosed Russian orphans who have been warehoused in the fetid psychoneurological *internaty* under the Ministry of Labor and Social Development. According to Dr. Severny,

"About nine to ten years ago some people from Moscow State University surveyed children in auxiliary *internaty* operated by the Ministry of Education for children diagnosed as lightly *debil*. What I was told by the people who did that survey, was that they found 80 percent of the diagnoses were inaccurate—in other words, not *oligophrenic*. That is the only survey I know of and it was not published. Nobody's heard anything from the survey team since."[172]

In 1991, evidence of unfounded diagnoses was again a finding of an investigation conducted by an international team of child development experts in several orphanages in Moscow and St. Petersburg.[173] The team, sponsored by the nongovernmental organization Christian Solidarity International (CSI), found that among fifty children in one group tested in St. Petersburg, "one-third of the children classified as *oligophrenic* scored within normal limits."[174] After doing a more thorough test on some children, the team found the results even more striking and disturbing. Of the thirty-four *oligophrenic* children aged six years and over, two-thirds showed evidence of average or better ability.[175]

The CSI investigators concluded that both of the psychologists on the team were "concerned about the large numbers of children assigned questionable diagnoses. These were usually expressed in negative, denigratory terms such as

---

[171] Human Rights Watch interview, Dr. Vsevolod Rybchonok, March 6, 1998.

[172] Human Rights Watch interview, Dr. Anatoly Severny, February 12, 1998.

[173] Cox, *Trajectories of Despair*, p. 15.

[174] Ibid., p. 15.

[175] Ibid.

'debilitated oligophrene,' 'imbecile,' *idiot.*' Once imposed in early childhood, these labels are seldom reviewed and reversed."[176]

It was clear to the director of a large baby house in a region north of Moscow that orphans were at a serious disadvantage when it came time for the fateful evaluation. "It's very difficult for orphans who have no parents who can appeal the process. They are limited in opportunity at the stage of the commission evaluation, compared with kids with families. It's a human pain for us, as well as a professional one."[177]

Inappropriateness of the test

Two of the leading factors that critics blame for inaccurate diagnoses are the setting and criteria used, which they argue are inappropriate for testing children who have spent their first four years of life in confinement. Again, Dr. Vsevolod Rybchonok told Human Rights Watch:

They just look at the child and ask a couple of stupid questions and then make the diagnosis, while the child can be frozen in front of the strangers. I've seen that a few times. Coming from their little narrow world, the kids don't like it if you ask direct, bold questions...Then one of the doctors will say, "That's a mentally retarded child." Unfortunately the children don't live in this world [that we live in]. They're living outside this world.[178]

A long-time volunteer in the institutions echoed this view:

I know the people who do the psychiatric evaluation. They test the children on concepts. They test if they can walk. Now here was a child whose legs were bound up and was not allowed to walk. They go around and look at these children, who've never been outside these four walls. It's just a land of the absurd. [179]

---

[176] Ibid.

[177] Human Rights Watch interview, Dr. Mikhail M. Airumyan, March 5, 1998.

[178] Human Rights Watch interview, March 6,1998.

[179] Human Rights Watch interview, Sarah Philps, February 23, 1998.

Not only can the queries be inappropriate to the child's stultified upbringing, but the combined effect of an orphan's earliest diagnoses with the neglect in the baby house can confound even a careful examiner. One psychiatrist working in an *internat* told us, "We have an orphan who got a job in our institution. I supervise her. She's *debil*. But everything is mixed up—what's the result of congenital retardation and what is neglect? It's hard to tell after a certain point."[180]

Justice denied: the right to appeal diagnosis

Under Russian law, orphans have a right to appeal their diagnoses, particularly since "the development of intelligence is very unpredictable and at certain stages intelligence can change noticeably," we were told by an official of the Ministry of Labor and Social Development.[181] Valentina V. Terekhina went on to explain to Human Rights Watch:

I used to be a member of the commission myself and if there are (sic) any suspicions that we are not right, then the decision is made in the interest of the child...The management of all institutions have all rights to apply to the commission for a new examination of the child. And actually those children who have parents and they don't agree with the diagnosis have the right to appeal it.[182]

In practice, it is nearly impossible for a four-year-old in state care to appeal his or her diagnosis. One international charity worker described this bind to Human Rights Watch, and further expressed her concern that some diagnoses are made to discipline difficult children, "Parents have the right to insist that their kids get a reassessment. But what if the child has *no* parents. I asked this of someone from a regional children's home and she just looked at me. Obviously this hadn't occurred to her."[183] The charity worker went on:

---

[180] Human Rights Watch interview, Dr. Tatiana Moroz, Feb 12, 1998.

[181] Human Rights Watch interview, Valentina V. Terekhina, Moscow, March 6, 1998.

[182] Ibid.

[183] Human Rights Watch interview, Carole Hartigan, December 20, 1997.

The children I know who were sent to *internaty* are not all mentally handicapped. One was sent to a mental institution because the director was offended by the family. One older child was sent to a mental institution because he was smoking.[184]

While scores of specific cases of misdiagnosis are well known to the concerned staff and charity workers we interviewed, many children will never get to tell what their experience was, having been delayed and handicapped, and never taught to speak.

But another group, interviewed by Human Rights Watch, is capable of describing the terrible impact on their lives, and some even recall their encounter with the Russian Psychological-Medical-Pedagogical Commission. Now in their teens, these orphans are in a category of luckier *oligophrenics*, because they were diagnosed as only "lightly" *debil* and thereby spared the damning judgment of being ineducable. They have instead been channeled to special institutions run by the Ministry of Education, which provide minimal classroom schooling, followed by vocational training in a Pedagogical Technical Department (PTU).

As Human Rights Watch learned during a visit to a relatively well-organized PTU several hours northeast of Moscow, the discriminatory diagnosis of "*oligophrenia*" remains in the orphans' official files and stalks them into adulthood. According to a report by a leading charity in Moscow, it prevents them from applying for a driver's license.[185] Moreover, the compound stigma of abandonment and "small brain" is recorded in black and white in their personal file, which follows them from institution to institution, and can only hamper their efforts to establish themselves in society and earn a living.[186]

In a meeting with about ten articulate girls and boys and two resident *vospitateli* who were unusual in their strong advocacy for the children, Human Rights Watch noted the "Catch-22" that traps these orphans in several respects. The children said that they wished to apply to have their diagnosis lifted from their file, but they must have finished eight years of standard school in order to apply to the commission for a re-analysis. As light *oligophrenics*, however, they have only

---

[184] Ibid.

[185] Olga Alexeeva, *Who Helps Children? On the Work of Charitable Organizations* (Moscow: Charities Aid Foundation, 1994), p. 2; Human Rights Watch interview, *vospitatel'*, March 5, 1998.

[186] Human Rights Watch interviews, March 5, 1998.

had access to the equivalent of six years of standard school. According to the *vospitatel'* at the PTU, there are no teachers available to help them make up the extra two years.[187]

Even if there were a remedial school for these children, the *vospitatel'* explained that they would still need individual tutoring, "because if they haven't had the chance to catch up to the level of standard education by a certain stage, kids don't learn as well. We know two boys who were eager and willing to catch up, but it turned out to be too hard."[188]

The children, between fifteen and eighteen years of age, are now enrolled for about two years at the PTU to receive training toward trades including carpentry, sewing, and baking. They are angry that their basic rights are restricted because of the prejudicial diagnosis of *oligophrenia* in their files.

The fact that the children are so aware of their rights is extraordinary enough, and they owe it to the exceptional *vospitatel'* who instituted a program "on social pedagogy and social protection" six years ago. This again illustrates the dramatic and somewhat random variation in protection afforded orphans in Russia.

Intimidation in front of the Psychological-Medical-Pedagogical Commission

The following accounts in their own words best convey the bewilderment and injustice these adolescents feel about their fateful tests and the label of *oligophrenic*, which some told Human Rights Watch they received when they were very little, and others when they entered or transferred institutions:

> Many of us could have studied in regular school. When I was tested in first grade, I studied for two years there. But then I was sent to an *internat* (for *debily*) because I didn't do well in school. I was asked idiotic questions by the commission and I didn't want to answer. For example, "What's the weather like outside?" I said to them, "Don't you see for yourselves what the weather is like outside?" [189]

> I remember the commission asked me how to put all the cups and plates on the table. Then they asked, "What are they called?" I answered, "They're called

---

[187] Human Rights Watch interview, PTU *vospitatel'*, March 5, 1998.

[188] Human Rights Watch interview, PTU *vospitatel'*, March 5, 1998.

[189] Human Rights Watch interview, Valeria M., March 5, 1998.

dishes." A lot of things I answered. They try to ask you a lot of "trick" questions, like what's the difference between a bird and a plane?[190]

For Lyuda P., the procedure was mystifying:

I was six years old. They made me sit at a huge table. A lot of people were sitting there. I had studied first grade in a regular school. Then they came and got me and said to say "good-bye" to everybody and wave your hand. I was taken to the commission and answered two questions. I don't remember them now.[191]

The *vospitatel'* also found the procedure both intimidating and cursory. She highlighted for Human Rights Watch the extreme vulnerability of an orphan by recounting the experience of her own "healthy" son, whom she accompanied on the general pre-school evaluation administered to Russian children:

My own son was tested after kindergarten before going to school—all kids are tested. I was told they do the testing for four days. But they really conducted their test for one and a half hours. And of course parents and children are nervous. The questions are not always worded clearly. They ask questions about clothes, transportation, animals, and comparative questions. A child who could read a poem perfectly at home, may be silent in fear.[192]

Imagine, I was standing right there next to my child and he was still confused. I'm a pedagogue, myself, and I think the examiners should get involved in the world the children live in, observing and watching a kid. And then, only after that, decide. But instead, after only for an hour—they just cross out their lives![193]

---

[190] Human Rights Watch interview, Oleg A., March 5, 1998.

[191] Human Rights Watch interview, Lyuda P., March 5, 1998.

[192] Human Rights Watch interview, *vospitatel'*, March 5, 1998.

[193] Ibid.

Ruined lives: misdiagnoses by the commission

The staff of Russia's 252 baby houses and the volunteers who work with them know scores of children who have pending diagnoses as severe *oligophrenia*. They know them by face, by name, by age, condition and their real potential. There is a frantic air among some of these care givers and advocates to prevent the orphans from being transferred to psychoneurological *internaty*.

They also mourn the many they knew who could not be saved beforehand, as well as the children with severe congenital disabilities who are condemned to psychoneurological *internaty*. One exemplary case is that of the little girl with a cleft palate mentioned in the previous section of this report, who was rejected for corrective surgery. Because Alina could not talk, she was diagnosed as an *imbetsil*. Her case neatly depicts the ways in which the Russian system denies orphans with disabilities their most basic rights.

Human Rights Watch learned more about Alina in an interview with a volunteer from her orphanage who had followed her for more than a year. Alina was three years old when Theresa Jacobson met her. Her medical chart indicated the following conditions:

- Multitudinous developmental defects;
- Psychomotor delays, speech delays;
- Organic brain paralysis;
- Bilateral cleft palate and lip;
- Microcephalus;
- Premature birth.[194]

She took on the baby's case to try to get her cleft palate corrected, and possibly prevent her from going to an *internat* for the ineducable. Ms. Jacobson recalled the little girl's case with frustration and sadness:

Alina seemed to all of us quite bright. Her major problem was that she couldn't speak because of the huge crack in her palate. She basically grunted her way through life. Also, because of the huge crack in her palate, her harelip was so bad she had no upper lip. It was a huge gaping hole to her nose that turned into the hole for her mouth. When she would eat porridge, it would go up through her nose. She couldn't swallow. She was very underweight, and I think, malnourished. The saddest part, she had bright blue eyes. I'd tell her

---

[194] Notes from medical record furnished to Human Rights Watch by Theresa Jacobson, March 13,1998.

to come here and do things and she'd understand and do them. But she could only grunt.

I spent a lot of time trying to get surgery for her, and we went through several stages. First they said she had a congenital defect of the heart valve, and because of the risk that she would die under anesthesia, they couldn't do the surgery on her cleft palate. Then she was too underweight for the minimum requirement for surgery. She was only eleven kilograms at age five.

So it was just a vicious circle. Then, at one stage, I decided to get her heart condition evaluated at the Bakalev Heart Institute, and found that the valve problem had corrected itself. I had a heart surgeon who looked at her and said he'd come to do the facial surgery in case there was an emergency. We'd even been able to get a British facial surgeon interested. Then around this time I had to leave my volunteer work for personal reasons. Alina was returned to the orphanage with no explanation.[195]

According to others familiar with Alina's case, the doctor responsible for her baby house was aware of her problem. But during an interview in Moscow with Human Rights Watch, Dr. Elena Petrenko made no sign of recalling the case. To our query about potential flaws in the Psychological-Medical-Pedagogical Commission procedures, she denied there that were problems and described the process as always taking place "in a very friendly atmosphere."[196]

She added, "It depends on the level of the baby's intellectual development. Age does not play any role. For example a baby has to put together four pieces of a picture...Also, the commission tries to see if the child thinks clearly."[197]

Contrary to some views of the commission as a vehicle for one-hour, snap decisions, the doctor underscored the active participation by the staff of baby houses in making this momentous decision in the orphan's life:

---

[195] Human Rights Watch interview, Theresa Jacobson, March 8, 1998. Eventually the little girl was sent to a Moscow psychoneurological *internat* and was located in November 1998.

[196] Human Rights Watch interview, Dr. Elena Petrenko, March 2, 1998.

[197] Ibid.

They really listen to us because we've been watching the children all along. We actually decide where the child goes and actually it's a very formal procedure. We discuss with them those kids we're not sure of, but it's the interest of the baby that takes priority. I don't see any potential for problems. The same commission comes every year. They know the hospitals. I think the interest of babies is number one.[198]

Later in the interview, Human Rights Watch again asked if the doctor recalled any cases in which she did not feel satisfied about the diagnosis. She repeated her conviction that the commission gave children the benefit of the doubt, a view that sharply diverged from the observations of doctors, other institutional staff and charity workers we interviewed:

No, we stand by the diagnoses. Actually the commission works in the interest of the babies, not against them. In fact they're given even better diagnoses so they can be put in a better orphanage, even if they find out later that the child cannot manage there.[199]

When asked specifically about how the baby house handled conditions such as cleft palate, the doctor's reply again contradicted the experience of many others interviewed for this report:

Actually, those babies who should be operated on, *are* operated on... What we do actually when we get babies with any conditions, we contact the medical institute and they fix up all the problems. If the baby is really sick he is sent to the hospital.[200]

The doctor may have been convinced that Alina was an *imbetsil* because her chart contained, rightly or wrongly, conditions such as "microcephalus" and "organic brain paralysis." This of course only serves to illustrate the fact that *imbetsily* do not generally get corrective surgery.

A leading analyst of the Russian orphanage system, was however, plainly shocked by the doctor's statements and challenged their veracity. "There was gross

---

[198] Ibid.

[199] Ibid.

[200] Ibid.

misconduct in that case of the child with a cleft palate and hare lip, who never got the surgery and ended up in an insane asylum."[201]

Most likely, with her difficulty in eating and speaking, Alina's condition worsened after her transfer, and it is this terrible deterioration of wrongly diagnosed children—not to mention correctly diagnosed children with disabilities—that distresses Russian child welfare experts. One baby house director told Human Rights Watch that it was so wrenching to see the babies from his institution decline after arriving in the Ministry of Labor and Social Development *internaty*, that he avoided going to them.

> Ninety percent of what we developed with the children who we send there, is lost there. This is why we keep them here at our baby house till they're seven, eight years old, to keep developing them. But then comes the time. Even right now, we have some fine, intelligent children who have problems, but only physical ones.[202]

Dr. Airumyan's deputy director, Dr. Olga Y. Vassilieva joined our interview and quickly mentioned an eight-year-old boy named Misha.

> There's a child here who is incontinent, but smart. He could work, say, as an accountant. If he goes to the regional *internat*, in the best case he'll be in a wheel chair. Most likely, he'll be bedridden.[203]

Three years ago they said they "lost three children," whom they regretted sending to the regional *internat* of the Ministry of Labor and Social Development. The stories of these and several other Russian orphans are recounted below by people who knew them in their baby houses.

TIMKA, 6

Timka was a little boy who had a defect in the spinal column, and the related complications because of it—paralysis, incontinence, etc. He was a nervous little boy who had difficulty with speech. Then at the age of five he started to speak normally, and he sang very well. He understood everything. He used to

---

[201] Human Rights Watch interview, child welfare analyst, March 7, 1998.

[202] Human Rights Watch interview, Dr. Mikhail Airumyan, March 5, 1998.

[203] Human Rights Watch interview, March 5, 1998.

watch the American television show *Santa Barbara* on Russian television and would retell all the episodes to the staff! He had 100 percent potential for a useful life.

Then Timka went to the *internat*. After three to four months I saw him there. He was lying in bed—dressed only above his waist, lying on a rubber sheet. He recognized me and couldn't say my name. It shows there's no continuity for these children between our work here, and over there at the *internat*. That was three years ago.[204]

TASSIA, 5

Tassia was a little girl who had a spinal defect that caused the usual complications with movement and urination. But she could walk. And she would sing and take part in music here. Then she went to the *internat* three years ago, and there was a nurse who went to visit her there. Tassia asked the nurse to please take her back home here to the baby house. Now, last September (1997), the nurse went to see Tassia and saw that they only put her on the potty, and she just sits there.[205]

FEDYA, 5

Fedya was a little boy who was transferred to the *internat* in the same group with Timka and Tassia. He also suffered from a spinal defect that paralyzed him and he was incontinent. But he had potential for a useful life. He went to the *internat* three years ago.[206]

TOLYA B.

Tolya was a little boy from a baby house here in Moscow. He had a physical disability, but he could talk and reason. They diagnosed him as an *imbetsil* and whisked him away to an *internat*, where he just went downhill. That internat was one of the worst and it's since been closed.[207]

---

[204] Human Rights Watch interview, Dr. Mikail Airumyan, March 5, 1998.

[205] Human Rights Watch interview, Dr. Olga Vassilieva March 5, 1998.

[206] Ibid.

[207] Human Rights Watch interview, Sarah Philips, March 7, 1998.

NINA, 8

This little girl only has light cerebral palsy in her legs and she is so bright. But Nina has been diagnosed as *oligophrenic* and unless something is done to change it, she is headed for a psychoneurological *internat* soon.[208]

On rare occasions, someone in the charity community manages to arrange to transfer a child who has been wrongly relegated to a psychoneurological *internat,* out to an orphanage within the Ministry of Education. Another volunteer with experience working in Moscow baby houses told Human Rights Watch of one such a child who was adopted:

SERIOZH C.

Seriozh came from a baby house here in Moscow and he had only a slight physical disability. But they said he would never walk and he was diagnosed as *imbetsil* and sent to an *internat*. Then an American family managed to adopt him from that *internat* and I hear he's doing really well—and speaking fluently! They rescued him from that place.[209]

Even in the extremely rare instance when a child is "rescued" from a warehouse existence, Dr. Olga Vassilieva stresses how difficult it is to overturn the discriminatory diagnosis after all. The case she cites again illustrates how the Russian state routinely fails the children in its care. The story also highlights the need for system-wide remedies, not merely private initiatives:

There was a girl in this region who is now eighteen, who started here in our baby house. Then her mother took her, and she was put into an orphanage in another region. Finally she ended up in a psychoneurological *internat,* even though she was only *debil*. She happened to have a good staff person who helped her there. Now she studies at a cultural college, and she even had her own exhibit of paintings! But it was so hard to cancel her diagnosis. It took two people to handle her case.[210]

---

[208] Human Rights Watch interview, Sarah Philips, February 23, 1998.

[209] Human Rights Watch interview, Sarah Philips, March 7, 1998.

[210] Human Rights Watch interview, Dr. Olga Y. Vassilieva, March 5, 1998.

Conclusion

At any given time in any year thousands of abandoned children in Russian state institutions are approaching the test that will determine to what extent their basic rights to education, health, and indeed life, will be observed. Those who fail due to real or purported disabilities face a fate similar to the unfortunate children remembered above. Their *internaty*, and the inhuman treatment within their walls, are described in the chapter ahead.

VI. CHILDHOOD DOOMED:
PSYCHONEUROLOGICAL INTERNATY

They're called children with no prospects, not trainable, not treatable. A colleague called these internaty "death camps." The situation there is terrible.[211]

I could not say that I am proud of [that psychoneurological] internat, ... but in general I believe that everything that can possibly be done in the current conditions is being done . . . And for these [Down syndrome] children [who may come from alcoholic homes], life in an internat is a paradise.[212]

The desperation among those trying to prevent misdiagnosed children—indeed any children—from being shunted into the total institutions run by the Russian Ministry of Labor and Social Development is well founded.

While physical conditions in baby houses have improved significantly during the past four years, mainly with the help donated by Western charities and adoption agencies, many of the psychoneurological *internaty* for orphans classed as *imbetsily* and *idioty* have sunk into squalid obscurity.

In the course of our research we learned of at least half a dozen institutions run by the Ministry of Labor and Social Development for orphans classed as *imbetsily* and *idioty* where visitors reported alarming conditions. Our own visit to one such *internat* in February 1998 confirmed that Russian orphans with disabilities are:

- segregated in lying-down rooms where they get a minimum of maintenance and the weakest are effectively left to die;
- confined to barren and dark rooms for control and discipline;
- strait-jacketed in a cloth sack tied at the neck;
- tethered by a limb;
- given excessive sedatives;
- commingled by age and gender;
- denied their right to education.

---

[211] Human Rights Watch interview, Dr. Anatoly Severny, Moscow, February 12, 1998

[212] Natalia Tsibisova, Director of Residential Institutions, Moscow Committee for the Social Defense of the Population, in Natasha Fairweather, "Removing the Mask of Down Syndrome," *Moscow Times*, February 7, 1998.

Human Rights Watch site visit to *Internat* X

Given the time constraints during our mission to Russia, Human Rights Watch elected to visit an institution that two of our key sources had seen. They asked that we not identify it, for fear of losing access to it.

We shall call it *Internat* X, a one-story building housing some 145 orphans. It had a lying-down room for forty bedridden children from age five to seventeen, and an empty room with boarded-up windows where twenty to thirty of the most difficult children to control were penned up all day.

Internat X also had several rooms with desks and cabinets which were used as classrooms for some of the other children, but no formal education or rehabilitation were offered to these orphans.

Arriving unannounced on a freezing Sunday in February, we were accompanied by two Russian contacts who had been to the *internat* before. There we saw scenes corroborating the numerous news reports and interviews with staff and volunteers in other *internaty* who relentlessly referred to the "utter neglect of the children's human needs."[213]

We also witnessed the use of restraints and isolation. There was no evidence of education or training for the children. Privacy was nonexistent.[214] And the staff told us of the regular use of sedative drugs when children are agitated.[215] There was not a shred of dignity left in the orphans' lives.

Human Rights Watch did not find the staff of *Internat* X to be wantonly cruel; in fact we noted concern and compassion among some of the women who were on duty that day. As it was a Sunday, the director, a physician, was away. The only medically trained staff to supervise the *sanitarki* was one nurse.

---

[213] Human Rights Watch interview, Natasha Fairweather, February 20, 1998.

[214] On the matter of privacy in Russian institutions, a Russian journalist we are calling Marina Stepanova, who had visited a number of orphanages and *internaty* summarized what others had told Human Rights Watch. "There is no word for 'privacy' as you know it in Russian. The closest thing is 'your personal affairs,' but it's not what you're referring to. But you know, it's not different in the Russian schools, or kindergartens, and institutions like the army, which were supposed to discipline children. There are no locks on the doors. And in the schools, often the bathrooms have no doors. So the bosses can watch that the kids don't lock themselves in the toilet and smoke for an hour. It's different for adults, but that's how it is for children." Human Rights Watch interview, February 15, 1998.

[215] Human Rights Watch interview, Alla Sergeyeva (not her real name), *sanitarka*, February 15, 1998. We have changed all the names of staff we interviewed to protect identities.

With a staff-to-children ratio of 3:40 (versus the official standard of 1:10), the *internat* was clearly understaffed. A young *sanitarka* in the lying-down room told us that she was the only one in charge of all forty children during the overnight shift. The sheer physical demands of cleaning the bedridden children are enormous.[216]

Of greater significance is the staff's ignorance of the true medical and mental state of the children in their care. They speak bluntly and derisively of the children in their presence, while admitting at times that the children indeed understand what they say.[217]

They furthermore lack any kind of training to provide appropriate rehabilitation for them, and are largely gripped by a deterministic view that the children's physical and mental condition is unalterable.[218]

The violations of the basic rights set forth in both international and Russian law are so abundant and self-evident in *Internat* X that to enumerate them by category would diminish the interplay of prejudicial stereotypes, orphanhood and neglect. The following section, therefore, highlights the human rights abuses we documented within the context of the *internat*. (Photographs of the children, taken around the time of our visit, appear at the end of this chapter.)

The Lying-Down Room

The children lay in two rows of tightly packed little beds, running the length of a long room with bare walls. Wearing huge, faded cloth diapers, they lay directly on rubber-covered mattresses. The air was warm and thick, and the odor of human waste, mingled with disinfectant, stung the eyes.

The orphans were in the process of getting changed when we walked in and one large, bedridden boy with a bright, alert face smiled at us as he propped himself up on his strong arms and swooped the clean diaper around his waist. The staff said that they change some of the kids seven times a day. "Only a few are toilet-trained, but how could they be? They can't even sit up to sit on the potty."[219]

Human Rights Watch asked the nurse and a *sanitarka* about the children's conditions and the nurse replied, "Well they all have *oligophrenia*." When we

---

[216]   Ibid.

[217]   Human Rights Watch interview, Alla Sergeyeva, Lyuba Fokina , February 15, 1998.

[218]   Ibid.

[219]   Human Rights Watch interview, Iliana Danilova, February 15, 1998.

returned a blank stare, she repeated, "*Oligophrenia.* You know—*imbetsil* and *idiot.*" When probed for more specific conditions, she replied, "Well, some have cerebral palsy, Down syndrome, nervous system trauma. And very often we don't even know what they are here for."[220]

Motioning to two withering little girls with translucent skin and vacant eyes, the nurse went on:

> For example, we have the two little girls who can't eat. We try to feed them, and try to prepare special things for them, but they just throw up everything. They can't take milk, which we have, but they can take yogurt. But we don't get yogurt, and we only have milk. We don't know what to do with them and don't know what's wrong with them.[221]

Noticing a beaming blond, five-year-old boy walking on the callused sides of his club feet, we asked the *sanitarka* who was playing with him what his diagnosis was "*Oligophrenia.*" But when we asked specifically about his feet, she replied, "Well, it's the same... *imbetsilnost.*"[222]

Lying on a nearby bed was another boy with twisted feet, the one who had proudly changed his own diaper. He chatted and responded to one of the Russians accompanying Human Rights Watch, while a staff member explained the organization of the 145 orphans currently here. Her description reinforced our concerns about discriminatory labeling:

> We have the children divided into four groups. They're divided by their behavior. All ages are mixed together, according to their behavior. We have them divided, like we divide ourselves up, between the smart and the dumb ones. The smart ones have a room with a television to watch, and some books and a teacher. The stupid ones don't have these things because they don't understand, anyway.[223]

---

[220] Human Rights Watch interview, Alla Sergeyeva, February 15, 1998.

[221] Ibid.

[222] Human Rights Watch interview, Lyuba Fokina, February 15, 1998.

[223] Human Rights Watch interview, Iliana Danilova, February 15, 1998.

Human Rights Watch asked if any of the children could read, and all the staff quickly replied, "No, no one reads." But after a pause to reflect, one of them corrected herself:

No, wait a minute, there are two kids, a brother and sister who are fourteen years old. They were raised at home. The father went to prison and the mother—something happened to her. They can read. When the boy's old enough we're planning to send him to live in town, where there's a place with small apartments. Some of the kids can do work; they work as cleaners, and they can make paper bags.[224]

One of the other staff added that "they even get money for it, so it's interesting for them." With that, her face flushed and she added, "Some even get married!"[225]

The staff mentioned another child whom we had noticed when we were walking through the lying-down room. He had a deep voice and appeared to be well into his teens from the waist up, but his lower limbs seemed shriveled under his blanket. With a tone of affection the staff appeared to marvel at the boy's "intelligence":

He talks, understands everything. I can ask him who worked the night shift. He always knows everything that's going on. He has two grandmothers and his father, and they come for special days. He knows about it and remembers, in fact, he'll remind me when they're coming next, and it will be three months from then.[226]

Later, as we were preparing to leave, we stopped by the boy's bed and one *sanitarka* said loudly:

He has relatives who visit him, all except his mother. His mother couldn't stand to look at him. She was afraid of him, and she's still afraid to look at him

---

[224] Human Rights Watch interview, Alla Sergeyeva, February 15, 1998.

[225] Human Rights Watch interview, Iliana Danilova, February 15, 1998.

[226] Ibid.

and can't come here to see him. Can you imagine, a mother who can't look at her child?[227]

The frank, demeaning language spoken in front of the children is a nearly universal feature of Russian custodial institutions and it is spoken not only by the poorly trained *sanitarki*, but by the doctors and nurses, as well.[228] It both reflects the prejudicial stereotype against abandoned children, and reinforces its debilitating consequences.

Confinement in a dark room
Like many psychoneurological *internaty* run by the Ministry of Labor and Social Development, *Internat* X has a stark room where twenty to thirty of the "most difficult" children spend the entire day under the supervision of a *sanitarka*.[229] The only items in the fourteen-foot by twenty-foot room are a string of benches lining the perimeter, a blanket on the floor and a row of plastic potties. Planks of wood have been nailed over the windows.

A regular visitor to *Internat* X corroborated what Human Rights Watch saw in the dark room, in an interview in Moscow:

Inside there's no light, no toys, a couple of benches. They spend all day in confinement there. One time a group of ten or so kids were sitting on the blanket on the floor. It was soaked with urine and the potties were full. The smell was absolutely atrocious. It's suffocating, oppressive.

The kids are all covered with rashes, sores on hands, arms, faces and scalp. They have cuts and scars on their foreheads. Last time I was there the woman in the day room told me, "we're not hitting them anymore."[230]

---

[227] Human Rights Watch interview, Lyuba Fokina, February 15, 1998.

[228] Human Rights Watch interview, Sarah Philps, February 23, 1998; Natasha Fairweather, February 20, 1998; Marina Stepanova, February 11, 1998; Western journalist, February 17, 1998.

[229] Human Rights Watch interview, Iliana Danilova, Alla Sergeyeva, February 15, 1998.

[230] Human Rights Watch interview, Sylvia Jackson (not her real name), February 10, 1998.

As Human Rights Watch approached the dark day room, accompanied by a *sanitarka* and nurse, a dozen children rushed at us, smiling and waving their hands to greet us at the door. Their heads had been shaved and their clothes were tattered. Clamoring to come near us, a couple of them swiftly wrapped their arms around our waists and hugged us hard. Another child came close and smiled with a gesture to stroke his soft, fuzzy head. Others stroked our hands. Few said anything, although a few told us their names.

There were other children in the room, including two small ones rocking themselves on the bare floor. On the bench to the right, a tall, gaunt adolescent girl stared intently with her hands clasped and slightly twisting her torso. "She's one of the most aggressive ones who attacks the others," said the *sanitarka* on duty in the room.[231]

In the center of the room stood Galina Kirilova, who appeared to be in her fifties. "I've worked here thirty-seven years, since 1960. Sure it's difficult, but you get used to it," she told Human Rights Watch. Turning with a flourish to scan the children around her, she went on. "Look, these are the rubbish of the place. The worst."[232]

Asked for the number of boys and girls in her care, the *sanitarka* guffawed. "Hah! I don't know. I don't even notice. They're all the same!" [233]

None of the other staff accompanying Human Rights Watch on our tour of *Internat* X knew all the names of the children in the dark room that day, and no one knew all their ages. On occasion the staff members disputed the age of certain children among themselves. We asked the children their ages, and many did not know.

In replying to our query concerning the boarded-up windows, the staff told us that they put children here who misbehaved in the dark day room for punishment and applied restraints:

> They've tried to break the window and one time one of the children ran away through it and we had to chase him during the night in the village. So it's bad, but we had to hammer wooden boards up over the two windows.

---

[231] Human Rights Watch interview, Galina Kirilova, February 15, 1998.

[232] Ibid.

[233] Ibid.

When it's a cloudy day, it's dark in there. They're in there all day. And it makes them nervous. They're nervous. They have to be tied or else they would break the window and try to run away. It's very hard to control them. They're the worst group we have.[234]

The staff of *Internat* X were equally forthright about the use of sedative drugs when we asked what they did at night if the children were too active and did not want to sleep, one of the *sanitarki* immediately replied, "Oh, we give them tablets. We have *aminazine*. We give them pills to calm them down."[235]

Some of the children have "too much energy," said Iliana Danilova, the nurse. "In summer we try to take them out for some fresh air for an hour, at least those who can move. The stupid ones have so much energy and so they need exercise."[236]

Education denied

"Smart" Orphans

Our arrival in the classroom for some thirty "smart" girls came after more than an hour of interviews in other areas of *Internat* X, which allowed time for the teacher and girls to prepare for guests. The girls, ranging from about eight to seventeen years of age, sat at attention in several rows of tightly packed desks while the teacher stood in the middle.

A pleasant room with cascades of potted plants placed high above the children's reach, the classroom had as its focal point a large television mounted high on the front wall. A few cabinets displayed a limited selection of books and toys, and several pictures and drawings hung on the walls.

The teacher told Human Rights Watch that she mainly played games with the girls. When we inquired about basic education such as reading, she selected one child and instructed her to pick up the grammar-school book in English entitled

---

[234] Human Rights Watch interview, Alla Sergeyeva, February 15, 1998.

[235] Ibid.

[236] Human Rights Watch interview, February 15, 1998. One of the Russians joining Human Rights Watch on our visit to *Internat* X explained that the comment on excess energy among the "stupid" children derives from the belief that they do not use mental energy. Human Rights Watch interview, expert on *internaty*, Vyacheslav Voronin (not his real name), February 15, 1998.

"ABCs." The orphan, a mature, dark-haired young woman, struggled through a few pages and then the teacher thanked her, adding a shrug. "The others cannot read, because they cannot remember the letters," she told us. Alla Sergeyeva, the *sanitarka*, added, "They can't be taught to read."[237]

Seeking to demonstrate other skills among the group, the teacher then pointed out two sisters seated with their hands folded at their desks. She said she wanted them to sing. "There, there. These are seventeen and thirteen years old. Their father killed their mother and now they're here."[238]

After a pause of shyness, the flush-faced sister in front took the lead and began to belt out a Russian pop song, demonstrating a good voice and an entertainer's flair. Besides these brief performances, the atmosphere in the room was static. Yet it was clear that some of the children had potential for education and training and were receiving neither.

One of the older girls, for instance, approached us with a doll dressed in a turquoise gown she had sewn by hand, without patterns. The teacher and *sanitarki* praised her and encouraged her to go and get more things to show us. She returned with another doll's dress and a full-sized white robe designed like the lab coats worn by the staff. The articles were meticulously measured and stitched, with matching designs and creative details. As we were leaving she asked if we could bring some plain-colored fabric and a sewing machine the next time we came.[239]

The scene with this adolescent girl highlighted the stunted abilities and contradictions that are rife in the Russian institutions. While the teacher and *sanitarka* told Human Rights Watch that they had taught her to sew, it was up to the girl to teach herself to make the clothing. After insisting that the orphans cannot learn anything, the staff admitted that the lack of stimulation they provided the children was a partial cause of their dearth of skills: "So you see, they *can* do things. But there is really nothing to do in the place."[240]

The scene in the classroom for smart boys was similar, with the rows of desks, the cheery plants, bright walls and large wall-mounted television looming above.

Sitting at a desk just inside the door, the teacher shouted, "Okay, all of you,

---

[237] Human Rights Watch interview, Alla Sergeyeva, February 15, 1998.

[238] Human Rights Watch interview, teacher, February 15, 1998.

[239] Human Rights Watch interview, orphan, February 15, 1998.

[240] Human Rights Watch interview, teacher, *Internat X*, February 15, 1998.

shut up now and listen to what they have to say," to some thirty boys, some of whom had reached adult height; the youngest was a child of five.

There were even fewer materials for education in the boys' room; indeed the only book was a Soviet era adventure story entitled *Brigantina*, which one of the taller boys volunteered to read aloud.

The children expressed lively curiosity toward their visitors, and one boy interrupted with excited questions about the flora in the United States. Apparently the self-appointed horticulturalist for the *internat*, the boy knew a great deal about plants and trees, and pointed to some sacks of seeds which he would be planting in spring to beautify the grounds of the *internat*.

"Dumb" Orphans

Except for the fact that the windows were not boarded shut, the two day rooms for eighty "dumb" girls and boys provided the same interminable idleness as the dark room for the "most difficult" children. At the time of our visit we saw about fifteen boys and girls ranging in size, in each of their respective rooms.

The sole furnishings in each room were two benches; neither room had a single toy, table, or chair. A door led to a bathroom next to the girls' room where a *sanitarka* kept watch over a girl as she was sitting on the potty, through the open door. A crowd of girls sat in filthy, ragged clothes on the floor of the fifteen-foot-square room. On one end of a bench against the right wall, a bone-thin girl sat dangling her crossed legs and staring straight ahead. A long frayed rope anchored her by the ankle to the bench, to "prevent her from running away."[241] Her torso and arms were sheathed in a dingy cotton sack pulled over her head and drawn at the waist and neck. Without the sack, the staff said "she would break windows or something."[242]

On the opposite end of the five-foot-long bench a sixteen-year-old girl was also tethered by a rope that was knotted around her wrists. The hair on her head had begun to grow out from its last shave, and she wore a black dress and white boots. The staff told Human Rights Watch that if she were not tied, the girl would undress herself.[243]

In the barren room for some forty "dumb" boys, none of them was restrained and most of them were running around. The numbing environment here and in the

---

[241] Human Rights Watch interview, Alla Sergeyva, February 15, 1998.

[242] Ibid.

[243] Ibid.

purported classrooms for the "smart" orphans was corroborated by the experience of a regular visitor whom we interviewed in Moscow:

These kids are supposed to have modified education, but in the two classrooms there were no education materials at all, except desks and chairs. No materials. One time I went, the kids were sitting in a room, about twenty kids, watching TV. One time, the light was off and they were just sitting there. There's absolutely nothing to do.[244]

Both of the Russians who joined Human Rights Watch on the visit remarked about improvements in the *internat* since their last visits in 1997, although this was hard to imagine. Both said that the children in the lying-down room had been lying motionless and staring into space, and it was silent save for the incessant crying. As one noted:

Now there is a radio playing music in the room. The children seem to notice that there are visitors, and seem to make more eye contact. More important, there appears to be more contact between the staff and the children—they did not treat them like humans before.[245]

Unmarked graves and abuse of authority

Indeed *Internat* X has a troubled past, and some visitors hold the director accountable for it. Some twenty-four children (out of the population of 145-150) died in a single year two years ago.[246] A Western news agency reporter who visited the place with a colleague in early 1997 was stunned by the steady sobbing of the neglected children.[247] Following their visit they learned that one of the staff who

---

[244] Human Rights Watch interview, Sylvia Jackson, February 11, 1998.

[245] Human Rights Watch interview, child welfare expert and journalist, February 15, 1998. The heating system had also improved since winter 1997, when it was so frigid that the staff were wearing their coats and hats indoors.

[246] Human Rights Watch interview, Sylvia Jackson, February 11, 1998.

[247] Human Rights Watch interview, Western journalist, January 22, 1998.

had talked with them was fired, and then that food they had brought did not reach the children.[248]

In June 1998, four months after we saw *Internat* X, Human Rights Watch received a report from a regular visitor there that one of the emaciated children—a nine year old girl—had died. The visitor, Sylvia Jackson, thought that the girl had not been getting enough food, and used to go there to wash her. She watched her deteriorate, and saw the girl shortly after she died in the *internat*.

The orphanage misinformed the visitor of the burial time, and when she arrived, it had already taken place, she told Human Rights Watch. At the site, she saw a lot of unmarked graves, and she learned that the other children from the orphanage were made to dig the grave for the dead child.

According to Ms. Jackson, the director of *Internat* X told her that she does not report deaths to the authorities in order to keep the $300 allocated to the deceased child per month earmarked for her institution.[249]

Discovery of *Internat* Y

In February 1998, during Human Rights Watch's mission to Russia, yet another psychoneurological *internat* run by the Ministry of Labor and Social Development in a region north of Moscow was exposed by a cameraman from the British network Independent Television News (ITN). The footage was ghastly, and it corroborated our findings from *Internat* X.

From the driveway, *Internat* Y is a two-story, beige brick building. From 224 to 230 children, aged five to eighteen years, are housed here, and all are diagnosed as *imbetsily* or *idioty*. The cameraman threads through the dimly lit corridor on the first floor, and then stops and turns to a closed door. As it opens a gale of children's shrieks and giggles bursts from inside, and a group of adolescents with shaved heads emerge like zombies, blinded by the glare. At the sight of the cameraman some of them begin to clap their hands and their screeches turn to grunts and growls. The *sanitarka*, tells them, "Stop it. Enough. We have a guest here."

The children appear unwashed, with bruises and scratches on their skin and scalp. Their clothes are torn and filthy, and the camera focuses on a pair of tattered

---

[248] Ibid. This could not be confirmed with the director who was not on duty the day of Human Rights Watch's visit. We did not contact her.

[249] Human Rights Watch interview, Sylvia Jackson, June 10, 1998, October 22, 1998. Exchange rate as of March 1998.

slippers. The cameraman was told that the children were wearing their only clothes.[250]

Within minutes about ten children gather in the corridor, including a spastic girl with contorted legs who has crawled out of the room. According to the Russian cameraman, "It was hot like a sauna and the smell was horrible."[251]

While most of the children smile and point at the camera, a tall, solidly built girl named Marina M. stands against the wall, staring sullenly with down-turned mouth. The staff say that she is thirteen years old and "a Down." Her nose runs and she is biting her puffed, red lips. Her cotton sweatshirt is askew, and falls off her left shoulder. To the right, a girl gazes with her mouth agape.

Upstairs, the cameraman enters a lying-down room much like those in *Internat* X, as well as baby houses across Russia, and finds rows of children half the size for their age, with spindly legs, lying on small beds. Some are sitting up and rocking themselves. The *internat's* one staff doctor, who has been summoned from home by the director on this Saturday, strolls among the rows of bedridden orphans, none of whom has a stuffed animal or toy.

As the doctor approaches the frail children to demonstrate the severity of their disabilities, she abruptly hoists them up by the shoulders and pokes at their heart and other organs. One child has loose stomach skin which the doctor points out to the cameraman by pulling at it while she talks to him. There is no appearance of any relationship between the staff and children, and no spontaneous effort to comfort the children as the doctor performs the brief demonstrations.

One child she approaches is lying motionless, face down. At eight years old, Tanya is the size of a child less than half her age. She suffers from a heart condition and has very red hands, and groans as the doctor pulls her up to face the camera. Her tongue lies limp in her open mouth, and she is barely conscious. She will die before she reaches adulthood, says the doctor, in front of the children.

Sitting folded over in front of Tanya is a little girl with bright eyes, who rocks and bounces, trying to play with the camera man.

After viewing the ITN tape in Moscow, Human Rights Watch interviewed the Russian cameraman for information about any education or activities provided to the ambulatory children who did not appear for much time on his tape. "They showed me some classrooms, and showed me some games they play," he said.

---

[250] Human Rights Watch interview, Russian cameraman, March 4, 1998.

[251] Ibid.

"Some got education. But there are so many children with different mental conditions. With the difficult children, it's rough for them."[252]

The cameraman saw no activities going on in any of these rooms, albeit, it was a Saturday when he visited. When he inquired about the children's names and conditions, the staff replied, "I don't know." As poor as the conditions were, however, the cameraman told Human Rights Watch that the *internat* was the only place in town where officials found money in the empty public coffers to pay the staff.[253]

The director, who had been reluctant to allow the cameraman into the *internat* in the first place, did not tell the him the annual mortality rate among the 224 children. Rather he said that the "prospects" for half of the orphans were "okay," but for the other half, "the prospects were "not okay."[254]

Those who do reach the age of eighteen will move to a "mental hospital for adults," the staff said to him. Wincing, the camera man told Human Rights Watch that he had been on assignment to several such state institutions, including one for mentally retarded adults. He said, "There—it will be even worse."[255]

Within a week of ITN's visit to *Internat* Y, Human Rights Watch interviewed two Russian welfare workers who had visited that same *internat* several times. Confirming the description of gross neglect that was obvious from the video footage, they added their own concerns about the deterioration of children's condition upon entry, and the commingling of older children with little ones. The scene they described was chaotic:

WORKER No.1:

When I went, there was a woman who cut long bread in half and just handed it to the children and they just grabbed pieces off of it. Some were on beds without a pillow, or cotton sheets—just on bare rubber sheets. Others were crawling on the floor, rising up to grab the bread. They were half naked, wearing only shirts. These were the "invalids," the ones who couldn't really walk. Because the ones who could walk went into the *stalovaya* (dining hall)

---

[252] Human Rights Watch interview, Russian cameraman, March 4, 1998.

[253] Ibid.

[254] Ibid.

[255] Ibid.

to eat and feed themselves. These "invalids" were fed in their place, and there were old children with young children, boys and girls all in the same room.[256]

Another periodic visitor to *Internat* Y was particularly jolted by the debilitating effect that the institution had had on several children she had known before they were committed there:

WORKER No. 2:
The first time I went there I cried all the way back from the place. When you get there you see only those kids who are "invalids." And because the baby houses are under the Ministry of Health, and the *internaty* are under the Ministry of Labor, there's a really big difference. At the baby house where the children came from they really got treatment. But at the *internaty*, all they do is feed them. It's horrible there.

There's a dreadful smell, you really need a respirator. They're all naked from the waist down and they wet the bed. You can imagine the smell. There are rubber sheets under them. Or they put them on the potty on the floor. There are older kids who have no continence and don't feel when they're wetting themselves. What I saw there was such a nightmare.

I saw kids just sitting on pots, some were on beds, some were crawling. Some of the deeply disabled ones were sitting on potties and some were fed with bottles.[257]

In view of the debilitating neglect depicted in the footage shot by ITN on February 28, 1998, it is difficult to imagine that it was much worse when Worker No.2 made her first trip there. "The first time I went in September 1995, it was really bad there. Last time it was better, they'd finished a renovation and it was better."[258]

---

[256] Human Rights Watch interview, March 5, 1998.

[257] Human Rights Watch interview, Worker No. 2, March 5, 1998.

[258] Ibid. Human Rights Watch received a report in October 1998 that conditions in Internat Y had improved further, and that officials in that region had initiated an experimental program of an ombudsman for children. We commend such efforts, but

Human Rights Watch commends action taken by the Russian authorities to improve the physical environment for some of the children under its care. But we conclude from interviews with a range of doctors, institution staff, volunteers and journalists who have visited all of the *internaty* in Moscow and various outlying regions, that the state fails to allocate appropriate resources to the critical developmental needs of these children.

One doctor who has directed a large baby house for more than twenty-five years and is familiar with *Internat* Y and other institutions in Russia told Human Rights Watch, "*Internat* Y is bad, but there's one like it in every region of Russia. And not only one."[259]

Additional reports from visitors to other *internaty* heighten the need to put an end to commingling of different age groups. One charity volunteer described to Human Rights Watch how older orphans of the psychoneurological *internat* change and clean the bedridden ones:

In the *internaty*, a lot of the main caretakers are the older inmates. If they're put to work feeding and taking care of the kids, there's potential for abuse. Everything I say here, I have seen ten times. In some you'll get a fifteen-to-sixteen-year-old perfectly normal child, wrongly diagnosed, looking after these children who are "becoming" *imbetsily* themselves.[260]

A Western journalist who traveled to a number of *internaty* for feature articles on the state of *internaty* echoed this observation to Human Rights Watch as well:

You must remember that the people who are changing the babies and clothes are often the older "*debily*," who are not qualified. I saw a big guy pick up a child by his hands and feet to transfer him to the next bed to change.[261]

---

remain deeply concerned about the pervasive features of the custodial system already mentioned in this report which violate the fundamental rights of disabled children to live in their families and develop to their full potential.

[259] Human Rights Watch interview, Dr. Mikhail Airumyan, March 5, 1998.

[260] Human Rights Watch interview, Sarah Philps, February 23, 1998.

[261] Human Rights Watch interview, Sam Hutchinson, February 17, 1998.

Internat Z

During our mission to Russia, a third *internat* for orphans with disabilities was featured in a lengthy article in the *Moscow Times* on February 7, 1998, about children with Down syndrome. Human Rights Watch interviewed the journalist, who asked that we not identify the institution, despite the fact that her research indicated that it was "one of the smaller and better ones in Moscow."[262]

Clean, fitted with new curtains and a new coat of paint on the walls, *Internat* Z is home to 150 children. Although the staff are overworked, they know the names of all the children.

It is especially noteworthy that *Internat* Z does provide education to the children who are classed as *imbetsily* and *debily*.[263] The journalist found that most of these older children had learned to read and write, and one of them had just started working as full-paid member of the staff there. The child had somehow inherited an apartment as well, and was going to live outside. The younger children with lighter disabilities were taking music lessons, and at the time of her visit, they were making Christmas cutouts. [264]

Yet even in this "good" *internat*, the journalist told Human Rights Watch, there was no education at all provided for the children with the severest classification as *idioty*. And she described the lying down room to Human Rights Watch as "just horrific":

There were three tiny children. They looked about eighteen months old. Completely emaciated, wasted legs. One was in a straitjacket; the other two were dying—completely lifeless. Then there were four or three older children lying in beds with cerebral palsy as far as I could tell.

There were four children in a playpen with no toys. One was screaming, screaming, screaming. And two other were prostrate, face down and hunched over, like in fetal position.[265]

---

[262] Human Rights Watch interview, Natasha Fairweather, February 12, 1998.

[263] Ibid.

[264] Ibid.

[265] Ibid.

General observations on abuses of orphans classed as *imbetsily* and *idioty*

Malign neglect of medical needs

As in Russia's baby houses, children in the *internaty* of the Ministry of Labor and Social Development are often passed over for needed medical or surgical treatment. Dr. Anatoly Severny, a child psychiatrist and leading critic of the cycle of discrimination against abandoned and disabled children, described the problem in an interview with Human Rights Watch:

> In the *internaty* they really don't treat the children as if they're people. These children are viewed as hopeless. Recently a colleague of mine who is a psychiatrist in an *internat* transferred a child to an infectious disease hospital. The hospital refused to place that child in intensive care, because supposedly there is a directive not to spend money on expensive medicine for children with a mental disability. The child had cerebral palsy and had a lung infection. In Russia there's always been a system of "unwritten rules": supervisors give oral instructions and nothing is written.[266]

Human Rights Watch interviewed Dr. Severny's colleague, who provided further details on the eight-year-old boy who was denied medical care:

> When we tried to explain they were violating the child's rights, and that he should be in intensive care, they said, "We just do what we can do." And they refused. It's true that he has severe pathology. The boy had pneumonia, respiratory infection, cerebral palsy, and he has a problem swallowing food so that it goes down his windpipe. He's very skinny because he cannot be fed, and he looks more like five years old. But he is responsive, he reacts. We called every day to check on the child, and he's still alive![267]

Again, as Chapter IV of this report documented the malfeasance and neglect concerning medical referrals from baby houses, this case illustrates the disadvantages of abandoned and disabled children in *internaty* who are truly without parents:

---

[266] Human Rights Watch interview, Dr. Anatoly Severny, February 12, 1998.

[267] Human Rights Watch interview, Dr. Tatiana Moroz, psychiatrist, February 12, 1998.

The surgeons refuse to operate on the heart because the operations are expensive. If this child lives in a family, the parent insists on surgery and sometimes gets it. Sometimes they obtain money somewhere, but those in *internaty* never get such operations. Children with disabilities like this will not be cared for even when they're in the maternity hospital. Really, these children are not examined properly. We can't get special medical care for them.[268]

A similar case in *Internat Z* was featured in the *Moscow Times* article on February 7, 1998. In the following excerpt, the chief psychiatrist at *Internat Z* expresses the prejudice that denies orphans like Tanya Chekhovskaya a life-saving heart operation:

Tanya smiles as Lydia Petrovna, the chief psychiatrist at the *internat*, or home for disabled children where she lives, declares to a visitor that the girl suffers from acute mental retardation; "the worst kind of oligophrenic (small brain); an *idiot*."

Tanya smiles as the doctor explains that Down Syndrome children go through phases of being "evil, sullen, and withdrawn," as well as times when they are happy to dust furniture if lavishly praised.

Tanya even smiles as the doctor describes how the Moscow cardiological center deemed her "unsuitable" for a heart operation on which her long-term survival depends because the center does not waste resources on disabled children.

As Petrovna continues describing how children with Down syndrome are incapable of playing with toys, let alone learning to speak, Tanya slides out of her chair and begins to explore the room, chattering happily to herself as she moves. She discovers a piece of patterned paper in the trash can. "Ineducable Tanya" repeats, after she hears them spoken, the names of each of the colors."[269]

---

[268] Ibid.

[269] Natasha Fairweather, "Removing the Mask of Down Syndrome," *Moscow Times*, February 7, 1998.

Excessive use of strong drugs

The reports of sedatives being used in *Internat* X were substantiated by a Moscow psychiatrist interviewed by Human Rights Watch. She explained how, in the previous *internat* where she worked, every evening a nurse gave the children a psychotropic drug—tizercine, relanium or aminazine—all without a doctor's prescription. "There's a slang term for that—*ukol beznorm*—which means 'injections without doctors' orders.' "[270]

Dr. Anatoly Severny told Human Rights Watch that children he has seen in institutions have also told him about the administration of "*ukol beznorm.*"[271] Asked about the drugs that are commonly used, Dr. Severny told us:

> The regular ones are: *aminazine*—a neuroleptic—*haloperidol*, and *neuleptil*, which especially retards strongly, and is given for restless behavior. Other drugs are *ceduxen, relanim, nazepam, rudotel*. These drugs can actually retard the child further. You can quite surely say that this is a common practice. For *internaty*, that's for sure.[272]

Conclusion

Russian Orphans classed as *imbetsily* and *idioty* are subjected to a lifetime of malign neglect, deprived in some cases of their most basic right to life. The malfeasance on the part of the Russian authorities, notably the Ministry of Labor and Social Development, is all the more deplorable in light of the remarkable recoveries achieved by a group of orphans who were permitted to enter the care of several ordinary volunteers from Russian society.[273] The dramatic results of this effort are presented in Chapter VIII of this report.

But first, the unique genre of corporal punishment and gratuitous violence encouraged in orphanages for school-aged children is documented in Chapter VII.

---

[270] Human Rights Watch interview, Dr. Tatiana Moroz, February 12, 1998.

[271] Human Rights Watch interview, Dr. Anatoly Severny, February 12, 1998.

[272] Ibid.

[273] This project was organized by the newly formed, independent Russian group, the Down Syndrome Association.

VII. THE DYETSKII DOM:
TRUNCATED LIVES AND GRATUITOUS CRUELTY

The director or a teacher does not always punish the children directly. They can get the older kids to punish the other kids. One of our teachers would just say, "Okay, now you two fight each other! They could do this for punishment, maybe, but also for amusement.[274]

Or for pure sadism. Sadism.[275]

Introduction

Like most of the baby houses in Russia, some of the orphanages run by the Education Ministry for school-aged children have been the beneficiaries of charitable donations since 1991 and have seen significant improvements in furnishings, clothing and supplies. These improvements were corroborated during Human Rights Watch's mission to Russia, through extensive research and interviews with six Russian children's advocates, four orphanage teachers, and thirty-one Russian orphans, who represented at least seventeen *dyetskiye doma* of the Ministry of Education. We also interviewed a Western journalist who had visited five *dyetskiye doma* six baby houses and three *internaty*.

The orphans and their teachers we interviewed resided in institutions in Moscow, St. Petersburg, and a third town some miles north of the capital. In Moscow, we arranged our interviews through local children's rights advocates who had collected the orphans' initial testimonies of abuse at the hands of several orphanage staff. We interviewed four teenaged children and two *vospitateli* from Orphanage A, and a girl from Orphanage M.

In St. Petersburg, a different independent children's rights advocate informed us of particularly abusive orphanages in that city and its environs. Based on that information, Human Rights Watch made an unannounced visit to a group of orphans aged fifteen to seventeen who had "graduated" from a variety of local *dyetskiye doma* in the area and were taking vocational training until the age of eighteen. They resided in a large state-run dormitory—Dormitory X—which we

---

[274] Human Rights Watch interview, Yegor P., St. Petersburg, February 27, 1998. (The names of all orphans cited in this chapter have been changed to protect their identities.)

[275] Human Rights Watch interview, Yuri T., St. Petersburg, February 27, 1998.

visited three times. In the course of those visits, Human Rights Watch conducted interviews with fifteen boys in a group setting, and seven individually.

The third group of teenaged orphans Human Rights Watch interviewed were referred to us through children's rights advocates in Moscow who had received reports of their grievances from a sympathetic child welfare worker in their region north of Moscow. Also aged fifteen to seventeen and taking vocational training, the orphans in that region had been diagnosed as *debil* or "lightly *oligoprhenic*," in the state orphanage system and raised in institutions run by the Ministry of Education for children with mild disabilities. We interviewed about ten of them in a group setting, along with two *vospitateli* who were unusually active in informing these children of their rights under Russian law and attempting to appeal their stigmatizing diagnosis of *oligophrenia*.

Human Rights Watch concluded that the standard orphanages run by the Russian Education Ministry were relatively clean, with only two to three beds per room, and provided adequate food. The children had access to a local public school and sometimes even had extracurricular activities in the *dyetskii dom*.[276]

Yet from our investigation, a dark tableau of abuse, dereliction of responsibility, and gratuitous cruelty also emerged. Orphanages for school-aged children breed their own genre of brutalizing punishment. It is distinct from the discipline found in the baby houses or the *internaty*, but well known in the Russian bastions of gang-rule: the military and the GULAG prisons.

First, Human Rights Watch received reports that adult staff members of Russian orphanages had abused children by:

- slapping or striking them
- shoving their heads in the toilet
- squeezing a hand in a vise
- squeezing testicles while interrogating them
- stripping their clothes off in front of peers
- locking them in a freezing, unheated room for days
- engaging them in sexual relations
- sending them to a psychiatric institute to punish them for misdeeds such as attempting to run away.[277]

---

[276] Human Rights Watch interviews, Moscow, February 20, 1998; St. Petersburg, February 27, 1998.

[277] Human Rights Watch interview, orphans, Moscow, February 20, 1998, March 2, 1998; orphans, St. Petersburg, February 27, 28, March 1, 1998.

Secondly, Human Rights Watch heard reports that older or stronger orphans, goaded by the adult staff had maliciously abused younger or weaker ones by such measures as:

• beating them on the neck, forehead and cheeks
• throwing them out the window in a wooden chest
• wiring a metal bed to electricity and shocking a child forced to lie on it
• forcing a child to beg or steal for them.[278]

The variations on acts of corporal and psychological punishment fell into two broad patterns. In the first instance, adult staff members, with the informal consent of the orphanage director, strike and humiliate children. Then, in an elaborate version of this direct abuse, the adults engage other orphans with them to punish a child "collectively."

For children who hardly have a positive alternative social role model from the world beyond the institution, the orphanage staff set an unconscionable example of degrading discipline. In doing so, the adults helped reinforce a survival-of-the-fittest hierarchy among the orphans, which they fostered in a second pattern to control and punish children by proxy.

This proxy pattern was particularly insidious because the favored children, delegated to "govern" like minor feudal lords, developed a repertoire of vicious and injurious punishments which the older, stronger orphans inflicted upon the younger or weaker ones. In Russian, this is known by its familiar colloquial term *"dyedovshchina,"* or hazing, which is taken from military slang; it was not surprising to Human Rights Watch when orphans in St. Petersburg spontaneously used *dyedovshchina* to describe the gratuitous violence in orphanage life.

It is worth remembering that this practice of hazing as a means of internal control is understood by Russians as malicious and even deadly; it is not to be confused with the typical roughhousing among fraternity brothers at universities in the United States. A brief catalogue of frequently used punishments appears later in this chapter.

As the testimonies herein depict, orphanages for school-aged children in Russia violate the essential tenets of international human rights law, which prohibit cruel,

---

[278] Human Rights Watch interviews, orphans, St. Petersburg, February 27, 29, 1998.

inhuman and degrading treatment, and guarantee the right to live in dignity.[279] Moreover, while it offers children a nominal public school education, the state orphanage system fails to prepare them for the responsibilities of creating homes and families, and finding a decent place in society.[280]

While numerous experts interviewed by Human Rights Watch stressed their alarm at the lack of appropriate social training to prepare institutionalized children for life as adults on their own, [281] the evidence assembled here shows that state orphanage system does acquaint children with the pecking order of the streets. Indeed one orphan told Human Rights Watch that he planned to be a *"vor v zakonye"* (Russian *mafiya* boss) some day, while he was flanked by two meeker looking orphans whose admiration was apparent.[282]

Several boys in the St. Petersburg dormitory we visited told Human Rights Watch matter of factly that they made their pocket money by picking pockets in the market.[283] One of them said plainly, "We all learn to steal," as he showed us some rooms with considerable furnishings that he and his friends had stolen from shops while distracting salespeople.[284]

One of the reports that we found most disturbing from the orphans we interviewed in Moscow and St. Petersburg was the psychological abuse with which the adults infused their discipline. "Humiliation" was the word the children we interviewed repeated like an intrusive memory—from the denigrating curses that staff members use, to public shaming in the presence of their teenaged peers.

---

[279] International Covenant on Civil and Political Rights, GA Res. 2200 A (XXI) Dec. 16, 1966, March 23, 1976, Articles 4(2) and 7; U.N. Convention on the Rights of the Child, GA res. 44/25, annex, 44 U.N. GAOR Supp. (No. 49), Article 37(a); Declaration on the Protection of All Persons from Being Subjected to Torture and Other Cruel, Inhuman or Degrading Treatment or Punishment, GA res. 3452 (XXX), Dec. 9, 1975.

[280] Human Rights Watch interview, Dr. Anatoly Severny, February 12, 1998; *vospitatel'*, Moscow, February 20, 1998; *vospitatel'* in region north of Moscow, March 5, 1998, among others.

[281] Human Rights Watch interview, Dr. Anatoly Severny, February 12, 1998; Dr. Tatiana Moroz, February 12, 1998; Boris Altshuler, February 16, 1998.

[282] Human Rights Watch interview, orphan, St. Petersburg, February 27, 1998.

[283] Human Rights Watch interview, orphans, St. Petersburg, February 27, 1998.

[284] Human Rights Watch interview, Yegor P., St. Petersburg, February 27, 1998.

Further, children who had grown up in one St. Petersburg *dyetskii dom* reported to Human Rights Watch that their director had encouraged orphans to ridicule certain children as homosexual, thereby reinforcing an intolerance that runs deep in Russian society.

Although knowledgeable people we interviewed knew of *dyetskiye doma* where physical and psychological abuse were not routine, the findings in this report call attention to discernible patterns detailed to us by people living and working in some institutions. Moreover, their testimonies, which included cases of sexual abuse and institutional corruption, signaled the need for a thorough, independent investigation across the Russian Federation.

Russian children's rights activists and an attorney we interviewed shared the concern of international child welfare experts that far more abuse takes place in institutions run by the Ministry of Education and Ministry of Labor and Social Development than ever gets reported. One expert told Human Rights Watch that the several reports we received about official action taken against abusive orphanage staff were "definitely the exception," and that:

> I have no doubt that abuse is going on in places far from Moscow that we will never hear about. There is no standard means for children in institutions to make a confidential complaint about abuse by staff. [285]

A leading Russian children's rights expert based in Moscow also told Human Rights Watch that the only way for many orphans in the more remote regions of Russia to expose abuse in their *dyetskii dom* is to run away from it and report it. She continued:

> Most of the *dyetskiye doma* are fully closed institutions, and almost no one gets access to them. No NGOs, no private citizens, only government control. Even children living in homes do not complain to officials when they are abused by their parents because they feel ashamed about it and they are scared and do not know what they can do. The orphans live in isolation. They do not know their own human rights and rights in general. They get a very bad education and no one gives them information about the structure of society. [286]

---

[285] Human Rights Watch interview, international child welfare expert, Moscow, October 15, 1998.

[286] Human Rights Watch interview, Lyubov Kushnir, October 15, 1998.

Furthermore, a Russian lawyer who is experienced in juvenile law told Human Rights Watch that even some children's advocates felt a disincentive to talk about abuses in the *dyetskyei doma*, because they need to maintain a working relationship with the orphanage directors in order to obtain information for legal cases they prepare on behalf of the children. Some advocates fear that they would lose the directors' cooperation if they were to expose abuses.[287]

In sum, one of the great impediments that children's advocates face in attempting to glean a picture of Russian state institutions is the lack of access and the *de facto* reliance on the few children who escape and seek out some independent nongovernmental group or even the Russian media, to report the abuse in their orphanages. The interviews conducted for this report indicated that children in orphanages tolerated a certain level of neglect and abuse. The cases that reached the stage of official investigation in Moscow and St. Petersburg involved particularly egregious offenses or repetitious cruelty that prompted children or sympathetic staff members to seek out known human rights advocates or outlets in the mass media.[288]

Adult perpetrators of crimes against children in their care must be prosecuted under Russian law, which provides criminal penalties for those who endanger the welfare of a minor. And the system encouraging minors to inflict abuse upon each other must be dismantled.

Corporal punishment by orphanage director and staff

In order to speak candidly with school-aged orphans in Moscow, Human Rights Watch arranged to meet a group of four teenagers in the apartment of a former member of their orphanage staff who had supported the children's complaints about abuses in their *dyetskii dom*. We shall call it Orphanage A. Our meeting was organized through the leading children's rights group in Moscow, Rights of the Child, which had learned of frequent corporal punishment by staff members. In our individual interview with Masha K., sixteen, she told us that as in baby houses and *internaty*, abandoned children in *dyetskiye doma* who had no parents were more likely to be mistreated:

> That teacher in my orphanage was a very cruel woman. She used to work in a *kolonia* [prison] for kids and really loved to beat up children. That was her

---

[287] Human Rights Watch interview, Moscow attorney, February 1998.

[288] Human Rights Watch interview, Boris Altshuler, February 16, 1998; children from Moscow Orphanage *A*; Lyubov Kushnir, February 23, 1998.

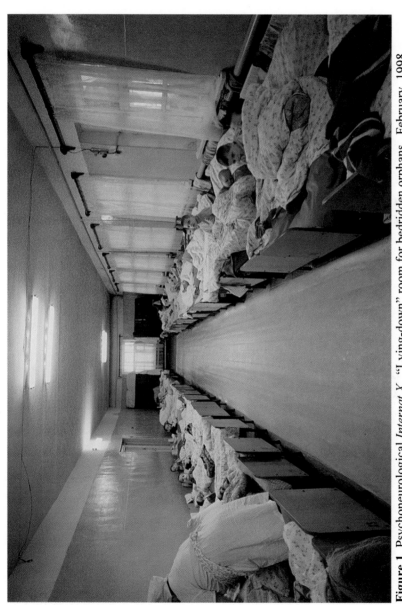

Figure 1 Psychoneurological *Internat X*. "Lying-down" room for bedridden orphans. February 1998.
© Kate Brooks

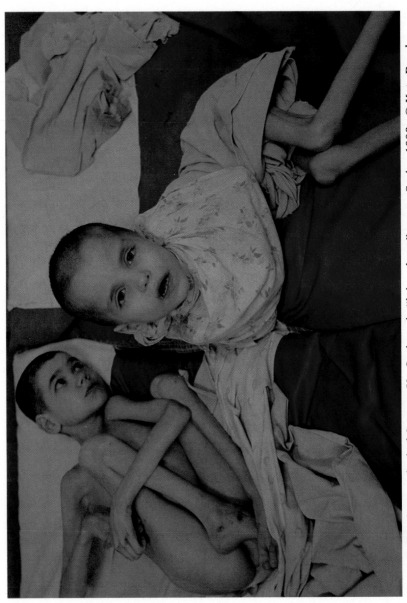

Figure 2 Psychoneurological *Internat* X. Orphans in "lying-down" room. Spring 1998. © Kate Brooks

Figure 3 Psychoneurological *Internat* X. Orphans pass the day in the barren, dark room with boarded-up windows. February 1998. © Kate Hunt.

Figure 4 Psychoneurological *Internat* X. Orphans in barren, dark room emerge to receive candies from sanitarka. February 1998. © Kate Brooks

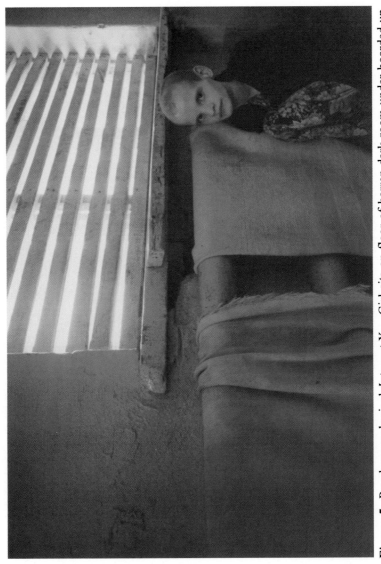

Figure 5 Psychoneurological *Internat* X. Girl sits on floor of barren dark room under boarded-up window. February 1998. © Kate Brooks

Figure 6 *Psychoneurological Internat* X. Boy sits on bench in barren dark room. February 1998. © Kate Brooks

Figure 7 Psychoneurological *Internat* X. Orphan boys sit in corner of barren day room for "dumb" boys. February 1998. © Kate Brooks

Figure 8 Psychoneurological *Internat* X. Orphan girl tied to seat of bench in day room for "dumb" girls. Summer 1998. © Kate Brooks

Figure 9 Psychoneurological *Internat* X. Orphans usually confined to the dark room, see outside world through the bars of this annexed room. Summer 1998. © Kate Brooks

Figure 10 Psychoneurological *Internat* X. Orphan boy, sixteen, with arms tied to back of a wooden bench. Summer 1998. © Kate Brooks

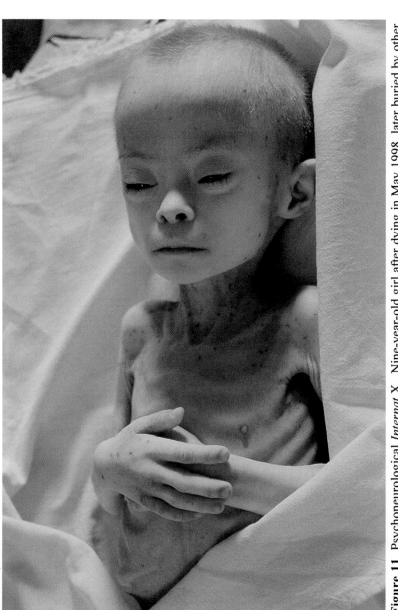

Figure 11 Psychoneurological *Internat* X. Nine-year-old girl after dying in May 1998, later buried by other orphans in unmarked grave. © Kate Brooks.

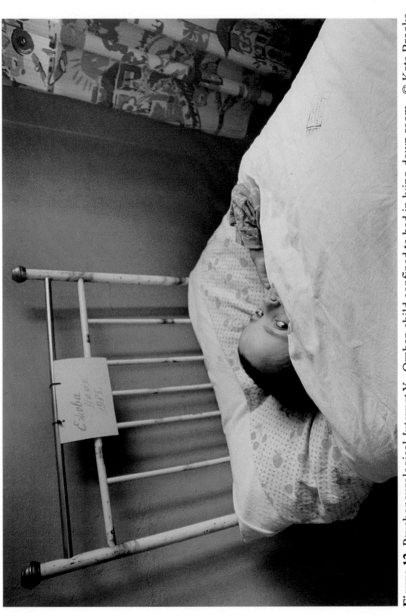

Figure 12 Psychoneurological *Internat* Y. Orphan child confined to bed in lying-down room. © Kate Brooks

Figure 13 Psychoneurological *Internat* Y. Orphan child confined to bed in lying-down room.
© Kate Brooks

Figure 14 Psychoneurological *Internat* Z. Orphan child tied up in sheet. December 1997. © Natasha Fairweather

method with me. She'd catch me by my hair. There was another girl in my class whom the teacher would grab by the hair and bang her head against the wall. That girl also had no parents. There were very poor children there, and we had refugee kids, too. The director was very energetic as a director, but as a person—terrible.[289]

Human Rights Watch conducted a separate interview with Kirina G. from the same orphanage. Small boned and slender, Kirina G. told us that she had been abandoned at birth, and spent the first three years of her life in a baby house before being transferred to Orphanage A where she has lived ever since. Kirina G. also described how the staff of her present orphanage treated children without parents more harshly, knowing that there was no one who would complain:

"When I was little, Svetlana Petrovna put my head in the toilet and beat me on the behind, hips, and arms. At first she would hit me on my hand—that was while I was small, until I was nine years old. After that she could take a slipper and slap us on the lips. Of course, a kid couldn't do anything or say anything. We were so afraid of her.

"They could put you in the bedroom and make you stay there. They also kept food from you to punish you, too. Right now it's the staff that's the worst thing about life here—especially Svetlana Petrovna. She's been here six or seven years. There are about six or seven staff who are about the same."[290]

In another individual interview with a girl from Moscow Orphanage A, Irina V., we were told what she witnessed in their orphanage:

I saw what happened to Kirina G. She was very afraid of the group *vospitatel'* and would lie to her about her grades. Svetlana Petrovna said, "If you lie to me again, I'll put *fekali* [excrement] in your mouth." She lied the next time and Svetlana Petrovna beat her all over. Her lip was bleeding.

Svetlana Petrovna also once put Valentin T.'s head in the toilet. It was summer 1994 when we were on vacation and we went to the summer camp.

---

[289] Human Rights Watch interview, Masha K., sixteen, February 20, 1998.

[290] Human Rights Watch interview, Kirina G., February 20, 1998.

Valentin T. left and went into the neighborhood near us and Svetlana Petrovna took him to the outhouse and—as he said—she put his head in the toilet.

She also did this with Julia B. That was last November (1997). One evening Julia B. came back a little drunk and decided to go to the teacher and tell her what she thought of her. The teacher took her to the shower and physically put her head in the toilet.[291]

Dmitri P., fifteen, lived with his family until the age of thirteen, and has since lived in Moscow Orphanage A as well. He told Human Rights Watch:

I see kids punished almost every day. Slapped. Kids could be humiliated verbally with words that are too bad to say. I personally haven't been punished physically by the teacher, but I have been punished verbally.[292]

Like nearly all Russian children, Dmitri P. became too embarrassed in front of foreign visitors to pronounce the "bad words" used to humiliate them, including the young children. One of the others from his orphanage agreed to write the following list for Human Rights Watch: *pizdiuk* (cunt), *pridurok* (jerk, said very angrily), *suka* (vulgar term for bitch), and *kozyol* (literally, "goat;" but in the prison world, it is the worst possible insult to Russians, connoting "passive homosexual").

In St. Petersburg's Dormitory X which we visited, children we interviewed told of excessive physical punishment as well. One child from Orphanage C described to Human Rights Watch how the director and a teacher in his orphanage severely punished a boy named Mitya K. for the alleged theft of humanitarian aid received by the orphanage:

The director and the teacher locked Mitya K. in the hardware storage room of our orphanage, and then put his hand in a vise and turned it. He experienced a lot of pain, and they had to send him to the hospital by emergency ambulance.[293]

---

[291] Human Rights Watch interview, Irina V., February 20, 1998.

[292] Human Rights Watch interview, Dmitri P., Moscow, February 20, 1998.

[293] Human Rights Watch interview, Piotr C., seventeen, St. Petersburg, February 27, 1998.

Another boy from Orphanage C told Human Rights Watch that, "The director grabbed me by the balls and squeezed while he was asking me questions."[294]

Isolation in a frigid room

Anya D., sixteen, from Moscow, had been put in Orphanage M by her parents, and later got them to take her home after complaining of the physical abuse taking place there. But in 1996, in the midst of the real estate boom in Moscow, her mother sold her four-room apartment and moved to a rural area in the surrounding region. "My mother's an alcoholic, and she claims she put 40 million rubles (about $8,000 at the time) in a bank account for me and my brother, but it's not true. I'm from Moscow, and I didn't want to live out there, so I came here."[295]

Human Rights Watch interviewed Anya D. at a small, privately run refuge for runaways in Moscow, where she described Orphanage M where she had lived from the time she was eight to eleven years old. She told us how the staff punished orphans who tried to run away:

> There was a punishment there: they would put kids for two to three days in a freezing cold room with no food and lock the door. It was on the third floor at the end of the building. They would lock the door from the outside. There was no heating there.

> They warned us, if you escape, we'll put you in the "*komnata*" [the room]. There was a boy who was eleven years old, who ran away for a day. He was caught outside and brought back and put in the cold room. The *vospitatel'* put him in the room. I saw them going there. Two men dragged the boy. He was resisting, and crying, of course.

> He was in there for two days, only wearing his indoor clothes and slippers on his feet. When he came out, he was freezing. I can even say that he couldn't think clearly. He was crying. When his parents came, he told them everything, and they applied to the court. I don't know what happened after that.[296]

---

[294] Human Rights Watch interview, orphan, St. Petersburg, March 1, 1998.

[295] Human Rights Watch interview, Anya D., March 2, 1998.

[296] Human Rights Watch interview, Anya D., Moscow, March 2, 1998.

Other children in Orphanage M were similarly confined to the unheated isolation room during the Moscow winters, as Anya D. recalled:

One girl went in because she was rude to the *vospitatel'*. We were watching TV, and the girl said something and had an argument with the *vospitatel'*. The *vospitatel'* said, "If you're going to argue with me, you'll go into the room."

So they started to fight with each other and the girl swore at the *vospitatel'*. Then the *vospitatel'* grabbed her and pulled her to the room, and left her in there for five days. It was winter. She was really pale.[297]

In another instance, teachers struck students for answering questions incorrectly, according to Anya D.:

If you give a wrong answer in class, they can hit you with a stick. I was eleven and got hit fifteen or twenty times. This wasn't when I misbehaved, but when I gave a wrong answer to my lessons. It went on the whole time I was there. We had five teachers and two were nice, three were bad.[298]

Corporal punishment sharpened by public shaming

Kiril V.'s Story

In February 1997, a young Moscow teenager we shall call Kiril V. accused staff members of Orphanage A of stealing yogurt that was intended for the orphans, and then grabbed a couple of yogurt containers and ran off to another part of the building.[299]

In an interview with another orphan, whose testimony was corroborated in a separate interview with a teacher from the orphanage, Human Rights Watch was told that Kiril V. was punished for stealing the yogurts by three members of the staff—the psychologist, the teacher of household tasks, and the deputy director of the orphanage. Together they threw him out a window on the first floor of the

---

[297] Ibid.

[298] Ibid.

[299] Human Rights Watch interview, Masha K., February 20, 1998.

orphanage.[300] Another teacher on the staff witnessed it, and sought help from the Moscow advocacy group, Rights of the Child, in filing a complaint.[301]

Kiril V.'s story continues, because he complained to the director about being thrown out the window by the staff. His subsequent punishment exemplifies the peculiar practice of publicly shaming children by stripping them or exposing them in some way to their peers, as orphans in both Moscow and St. Petersburg told us.

Public shaming was a recurring motif in our interviews conducted with some thirty-one children housed by the Russian Ministry of Education. In the following testimony, a fifteen-year-old orphan in Moscow named Masha K. told Human Rights Watch how she witnessed Kiril V.'s public mortification in Orphanage A:

> I was having a German class with a group of five kids when Kiril V. came into the room. It was a big room—and maybe the teacher who is in charge of him had learned that he had complained to the director about being thrown out the window. She walked in after him and said, "You don't have any right to complain about goods. You're wearing German stuff (donations). You don't like it? I'm the one who gets it for you."

> Kiril's very small, and she grabbed him and she took off all his clothes—his briefs, too. Because *all* the clothes were donated by the German group. He was naked. And she threw the stuff out. He cried because he was very ashamed and so upset and confused. After that she called all the kids together to a meeting to make an announcement. You know it's a tradition for us to call her "Mom"—even though we don't mean it for affection—and she told Kiril, "From now on you can't call me Mom. You don't deserve to."[302]

Such public humiliation appears to have been a signature punishment in this Moscow orphanage for years. Irina V., sixteen, recalls another incident involving the same staff member:

---

[300] Human Rights Watch interview, Irina V., Moscow, February 20, 1998.

[301] Human Rights Watch interviews, orphanage teacher, Moscow, February 20, 1998; Rights of the Child, February 17, 1998.

[302] Human Rights Watch interview, Masha K., February 20, 1998. Kiril V. was also sent to a psychiatric hospital as punishment when other children went to a summer camp, as reported below.

It was at the summer camp about four years ago when Kirina G. tried to smoke. To punish her, Svetlana Petrovna dragged her in her panties *only*, to the boy's shower to humiliate her.[303]

"Collective Punishment"

Human Rights Watch heard reports of even more elaborate rituals of wanton cruelty in our meetings and interviews with about fifteen teenaged orphan boys taking vocational training at a Pedagogical Technical Directorate (PTU) in St. Petersburg. The boys had "graduated" from seven Ministry of Education *dyetskiye doma* in and around St. Petersburg, and described a barrage of violence at the hands of their orphanage directors and staff throughout their childhood.

Children who had spent time in Orphanage C recounted to us how a teacher used the punishment of stripping to convey a stern warning to the others:

> The teacher would punish children by bringing everyone into the classroom, and then making the ones who did something wrong get undressed and stand in front of the open window when it was very cold. Several children would be stripped and have to stand like that while the others had to watch the child in front of the window as a threat.[304]

Piotr C., who had lived in Orphanage C, told Human Rights Watch about a teacher in that orphanage who would grab a girl or boy and force him or her to crawl on all fours in front of everyone. Then she would make the others join in on it:

> For punishment, a teacher named Alexandra Kalugina would strip off a child's clothes until he was completely nude, and make him get down on all fours. Then the rest of the children had to kick the child and sit on him like a horse—to humiliate him. The kids could push and kick and pull hair and ride him like an animal. She was an active sadist.[305]

Piotr C. told us that this same staff member later ordered children to punish another child, which resulted in that child's injury. That incident was reported and

---

[303] Human Rights Watch interview, Moscow, February 20, 1998.

[304] Human Rights Watch interview, St. Petersburg, February 27, 1998.

[305] Human Rights Watch interview, Piotr C., February 27, 1998.

she left the orphanage.[306] Based on the reports received from these children and those interviewed in Moscow, many abuses go unreported, but some extreme incidents, especially causing injury to a child, have been punished.[307]

Nikita M., also from St. Petersburg, complained to Human Rights Watch about the constant ridicule he suffered from his orphanage director at Orphanage B, who, according to others from the same institution, told the children that Nikita was gay. The boy himself did not go into details, except to say:

> I was crying a lot of the time, because the director was shaming me. It was very tough for me, because he was trying to humiliate me and isolate me from other children.[308]

Murky areas of misconduct founded on humiliation of this kind were impossible for Human Rights Watch to corroborate case by case. However, we were alarmed by the level of detail and consistency in the testimonies taken from children in different cities, interviewed individually, and by their apparent role as a prelude to overt physical punishment.

For instance, in further interviews with other children who had lived in Orphanage B one child described to us the progression from verbal abuse to physical violence against Nikita M., seventeen, whom the director alleged to be homosexual:

> The director suspected Nikita of being *"malchik-devochka"* [passive homosexual] and this was why the director hated him. He was very aggressive to him and accused him in front of the other kids of being homosexual. One time the director told me that he saw Nikita with another boy playing "house," and Nikita was playing the passive role. The way the director told me, Nikita was asking the other kid to play the game and wanted the boy to play the father and Nikita would play the mother.

---

[306] Ibid.

[307] Ibid.

[308] Human Rights Watch interview, Nikita M., St. Petersburg, February 27, 1998. This orphanage director was one of two we heard of in St. Petersburg whose particularly abusive treatment prompted complaints and criminal investigations. One of them was convicted and sentenced to a one year prison sentence, but problems persisted with his orphanage, as described by an independent children's rights advocate later in this chapter.

Now, then there was some humanitarian aid we received and it was stolen in the orphanage. So the director decided to check the classrooms, in case it was the kids who stole it. While he was checking the rooms, he found Nikita and Sergei C. in a classroom and at that moment, Nikita was naked and masturbating. Sergei C. was dressed. The director told Nikita to put his clothes on and follow him to the study. Then the director told me to come in with them to be a witness.

So the director started to ask Nikita about this situation where he was naked with the other boy and Nikita started to cry. Then Nikita insulted the director who hit Nikita on the neck. Nikita cried some more and the director told both of us to leave.[309]

According to Pavel N., after the incident in the study, Nikita filed a complaint against the director. To this, the director of the orphanage called a meeting of the orphans aged twelve to fourteen years, to validate his actions against Nikita and to enlist the orphans to punish Nikita for him:

The director told to us that every time he punished Nikita it was *"za delo"* [for a real reason]. Nikita was there and he was crying. Then the director told us, "I can't punish Nikita, but you should do what you think you should" and left the room. When he left, the kids—the *lyubimchiki* ["favorites"]—pushed Nikita into a corner and hit him on the arms and the legs. Nikita shouted loudly enough that the director could have heard him from the hallway, but he did nothing. Finally one of the teachers heard the noise and came and stopped the violence.[310]

Punishment-by-proxy and vicious hazing

The progression from verbal debasement to beatings instigated by adults provided a graphic illustration of the practice of punishment by proxy which was repeatedly described to Human Rights Watch. In the process, the orphans learned a code of cruelty which the older children used against the younger and weaker ones. At times, the children told us, the staff pitted them against each other for

---

[309] Human Rights Watch interview, Pavel N., St. Petersburg, February 28, 1998.

[310] Human Rights Watch interview, Pavel N., St. Petersburg, March 1, 1998.

their own entertainment.[311]   In any case, the orphanage staff must bear direct responsibility for allowing the abusive treatment to flourish.

Many of the punishments meted out by St. Petersburg children themselves had ironic nicknames, as Human Rights Watch was told by orphans interviewed in Dormitory X. Among the most egregious was a torture applied to a sixteen-year-old boy named Grigory Z., who told us how the older boys in his orphanage had given him the "electric chair":

> They did a torture called "electric chair" on me. I was laid on a metal bed, naked. Then someone takes wires that are connected to 220 volt electricity and touches the metal bed. The power runs through it and the kid lying on the bed shakes.

> Also, the older orphans used to play something called "*Russkii Fashist*" when I was small. They came to our dormitory where we were sleeping and told us to use our pillow like a shield and run around the room while they beat on us. They'd also tell kids, "You have to fight with your friend. And if you don't fight him really hard, or it doesn't look real enough, then we'll beat you up."[312]

Another extremely dangerous practice which was reported to Human Rights Watch by children raised in St. Petersburg orphanages was the appalling act of forcing a smaller child into the small wooden chest [*tumbochka*] that they each have for their clothes and throwing him out a window. [313]

One of the orphans interviewed in St. Petersburg described yet another gratuitous punishment that involved standing for hours in a half-crouch:

> The older ones also punished the smaller kids like this: they'd make the small ones stand at attention, or with their legs bent and their hands stretched out in front. Then they'd put one or two pillows on our hands. We'd have to stand there for one to two hours. How can anyone take this without falling down? And when a small kid fell down or dropped the pillow, someone would hit him

---

[311] Human Rights Watch interview, Yegor P., St. Petersburg, February 27, 1998.

[312] Human Rights Watch interview, Grigory Z., St. Petersburg, February 27, 1998.

[313] Human Rights Watch interview, Pavel N., St. Petersburg, February 27, 29, 1998.

on his head and forehead. After that, they would start all over again until the child sometimes fainted.[314]

Hanging a fellow orphan from an open window was another form of intimidation among orphans interviewed by Human Rights Watch in St. Petersburg. Misha T., seventeen, said he was a victim:

The older kids held me and Anatoly Z. upside down out the window of the fourth floor, just to scare us. In our orphanage we called this kind of intimidation "in the wind." [315]

As training sessions for sadistic bullying, these gratuitous punishments can also become a conduit to crime, as Fyodor T., fifteen, told us:

The oldest kid in our orphanage was Anton M.—he's in prison now for theft. He beat me very often for refusing to steal some equipment from the hardware storage room of the school. He also beat me very cruelly when I wouldn't steal a walkie-talkie from a policeman. He demanded from me that I bring him money, and made me beg for money on the street and bring it to him. When I didn't do that, Anton M. beat me very cruelly.[316]

As in the Russian military, this form of violent hazing can lead to accidental death, as one orphan in St. Petersburg recounted to us with a degree of regret:

One boy named Piotr A. even was killed accidentally in my orphanage, Orphanage F, when some older kids made him steal eggs from the refrigerator. But the refrigerator was old and it had only three legs, so it fell over on top of him. The other boy who was with him was very scared and ran off, and didn't tell anyone about it all day. When they finally found Piotr A., he was dead.[317]

---

[314] Human Rights Watch interview, orphan, St. Petersburg, February 27, 1998.

[315] Human Rights Watch interview, Misha T., St. Petersburg, March 3, 1998.

[316] Human Rights Watch interview, Fyodor T., March 3, 1998.

[317] Human Rights Watch interview, Yegor P., February 27, 1998.

Code of Cruelty

The following are a selection of malicious punishments with their nicknames, used by older orphans on younger ones. They are described by the boys Human Rights Watch interviewed in St. Petersburg during February and March 1998:

"Makaronina" ("little macaroni"): They make you rock your head to the left and right, and while you do that, someone strikes each side of your neck.

"Fashka" (no real translation): You have to fill your cheek with air and someone hits you on the cheek. It's very painful because your teeth cut the inside of your cheek.

"Locya" ("deer"): You have to stand with your palms crossed, facing out, on your forehead. And someone beats you with his fist. Your knuckles hit your forehead. It's very painful.

"Oduvanchik" ("dandelion"): In this one, the older kids beat with their fists on top of head of younger ones.

"Velociped" ("bicycle"; well known in the army): When someone's in bed, you take balls of cotton and put them between their toes. Then you set fire to the cotton and the person kicks his legs as if he's peddling a bicycle.

Psychiatric hospital as punishment

One of the most abhorrent hallmarks of the Soviet Union was the psychiatric profession's collaboration in the punishment of political dissidents.[318] Today, based on an alarming number of reports from orphans and institution staff, Human Rights Watch has found that children in the care of the Ministry of Education who misbehave can be sent to closed psychiatric hospitals for "treatment" and discipline.

---

[318] Helsinki Watch, *Psychiatric Abuse in the Soviet Union* (New York: Human Rights Watch, 1990).

The children even used the sardonic diminutive "*psykhushka*" for such hospitals, a holdover from Soviet times.[319]

During one of our visits to the dormitory of orphans who had lived in a variety of St. Petersburg *dyetskiye doma*, we asked them what the staff of their orphanages did when children ran away. Several of them instantly replied, "They're sent to the *psykhushka*! They think you're abnormal for running away so they send you there."[320]

One of the boys, Piotr C., told Human Rights Watch:

When I was in Orphanage C, the administrator sent me many times to the *psykhushka* for punishment. I tried to run away to the region where I had lived before.[321]

In Moscow, the teenaged children from Orphanage A whom we interviewed echoed what we were told in St. Petersburg about children who tried to run away, or even about children who broke something. According to Dimitri P., fifteen, the staff of Orphanage A would "yell at you and send you to a psychiatric hospital."[322]

"I was told about many kids from other groups in my orphanage, They call the hospital and an emergency car comes. I've seen the ambulance come for a kid three times with my own eyes. And then I'd hear about it when the child comes back from the hospital."[323]

A *vospitatel'* from that same orphanage in Moscow also told us how he had tried to intervene to prevent a child from being sent:

I twice had to accompany them in the emergency vehicle to psychiatric hospital Number 6 on Donskoi Proezd. And once, around October or

---

[319] Human Rights Watch interviews, Moscow, February 20, 1998; St. Petersburg, February 27, 1998.

[320] Human Rights Watch interview, Piotr C., Yegor P., Valery P., Yuri T.. St. Petersburg, February 27, 1998.

[321] Human Rights Watch interview, St. Petersburg, February 27, 1998.

[322] Human Rights Watch interview, Dmitri P., Moscow, February 20, 1998.

[323] Ibid.

November 1997, a car came to get a child and we managed to protect him from being taken.[324]

According to orphans and children's rights advocates who monitor the Education Ministry's institutions, the children return from their internment in the *"psykhushka"* in a terrible state. Dmitri P., fifteen, from Orphanage A in Moscow, described it as follows:

They really feel withdrawn, isolated. Because they've been there for two or three months. Some come back to normal. But they get drugs—round pills—to calm down. I don't remember the name of the drugs now. The kids, after they come back from the hospital they've had drugs, and they're very confused.

They can spend three months there. In summer kids would go to camp and our friend Kiril V. would spend all the time at the hospital. They lied to him that he was going to a sanitorium and so he packed his swim suit and everything for a vacation. Then he found out he was going to the hospital.[325]

Human Rights Watch condemns the use of psychiatric lockups and powerful drugs to discipline children whose behavior is deemed "abnormal" by institution staff. But it is also impossible to know to what degree the children sent to psychiatric hospitals do have a need for legitimate psychiatric care. Dr. Anatoly Severny, one of the leading Russian advocates for the protection of institutionalized children, told Human Rights Watch that one cannot conclude that all children are systematically committed to psychiatric hospitals simply for punishment:

Breaking the rules of behavior can be seen by an orphanage director as a psychological or psychiatric problem. But what can they do? They're not provided with enough medical staff and educational staff, and the personnel are not taught either biology or pedagogy. So, children are sent to the psychiatric clinic to calm down. As a doctor, I can't say it's a "system" to treat healthy children that way. You would need wide-scale research so we would know how and where and what they do. But nobody does this research. We're

---

[324] Human Rights Watch interview, orphanage staff member, Moscow, February 20, 1998.

[325] Human Rights Watch interview, Dmitri P., Moscow, February 20, 1998.

very scared to say "generally." But the children are certainly singled out if their behavior is not "normal."[326]

The use of psychiatric hospitals to discipline children who misbehave was corroborated by a Western charity working in Russia whose staff visited the orphanages in St. Petersburg during autumn 1997. In an interview with Human Rights Watch, an official of the charity recounted the words of one orphanage director which summarized these harmful practices. The charity worker reported to Human Rights Watch:

> This is what the director told me: "One child was sent to the psychiatric hospital last fall (1997). The girl ran away, so obviously she was psychologically disturbed. We sent her away last fall and she hasn't come back so I guess she really does have problems. Another one had a behavior problem. He didn't do his homework. He hasn't come back."[327]

Based on considerable experience working in Russia, the charity official told Human Rights Watch, "They really do fill [the orphans] up with drugs."[328]

Corruption, abuse of authority, and alleged crime

During our mission to Russia in February-March 1998, Human Rights Watch received numerous reports from human rights activists and children from orphanages in Moscow and St. Petersburg alleging abuse of authority and financial corruption among the directors and staff of *dyetskiye doma*.

Of all the cases, Human Rights Watch was most alarmed by reports we received about Dormitory X in St. Petersburg. According to orphans interviewed in that high-rise dormitory, the children who had reached the age of eighteen and not yet obtained lodging from the state, were permitted to move from the "orphan" floor of the dorm to live temporarily on another floor. One of the orphans we interviewed summarized the conditions on that floor as follows:

> It's horrible there. They call it the "*otstoinik*," which means the reservoir where the rancid water stays. The kids live like homeless people, and they

---

[326] Human Rights Watch interview, Dr. Anatoly Severny, February 20, 1998.

[327] Human Rights Watch interview, Western charity official, February 24, 1998.

[328] Ibid.

spent the allowance we get when we leave the system on "sexodromes" [huge beds].[329]

At the time of our unannounced visit to Dormitory X in February 1998, the building itself was a crumbling, concrete wreck with a rattling elevator and empty light sockets. But the floor delegated for the "graduates" was particularly squalid.[330]

The orphans interviewed by Human Rights Watch reported that the director of Dormitory X permitted older adult males from outside to live in vacant rooms in the building. The children had observed that some of these people were the directors' friends and had reportedly made advances to the girls living in the "*otstoinik*." The orphans we interviewed, who were friends of the girls in the "*otstoinik*," told Human Rights Watch that the girls were in a "complex" position to turn down the men's advances, because of their connection with the director.[331]

Yuri T., a seventeen-year-old orphan, told us:

When the police come to look for something criminal, the director takes them only to the floors where we [the current orphans] live, and makes a signal to the criminal guys on the lower floors so they escape through the windows there.[332]

Many of the incidents of misconduct by orphanage staff which were reported to Human Rights Watch were not as injurious as the potential corruption of minors in Dormitory X in St. Petersburg. But they did represent an appalling abrogation of responsibility to the children in their care. Often orphans told Human Rights Watch in interviews that the director and orphanage staff were siphoning off humanitarian donations of food and clothing intended for the orphans. Valery P.'s story of Orphanage G. in St. Petersburg was representative:

---

[329] Human Rights Watch interview, Yuri T., St. Petersburg, February 27, 1998.

[330] Time and circumstances did not permit us to conduct confidential interviews with the teenaged girls we encountered on our unannounced tour of the *otstoinik*.

[331] Human Rights Watch interview, Yuri T., St. Petersburg, February 27, 1998.

[332] Human Rights Watch interview, Yuri T., St. Petersburg, February 27, 1998.

The administration of our orphanage constantly took the humanitarian donations for themselves and sold them. Especially chocolate and other food. They stole it, and they used big trucks for transferring the large quantity of things. All the children saw this. All of us got the worst things from the administration—like shoes and clothes that looked so poor that we just couldn't wear them outside.[333]

Grievances and impunity

One of the people interviewed by Human Rights Watch in St. Petersburg was Alexander Rodin, a former member of the city council and independent children's advocate who has exposed the abuses in orphanages and juvenile detention centers for more than eight years.

While Rodin considered the criminal action against the directors of Orphanages B and C in St. Petersburg to be important victories, he pointed out to us the mixed benefits for the children:

The director of orphanage C was an ex-Soviet military officer, and he was sentenced to a one-year term. But now the new director of this orphanage is a friend of the former director, and the St. Petersburg officials have changed the orphanage's status to an institution for juvenile delinquents.[334]

Rodin went on to stress the importance of an orphanage director's power, not only to commit abuses, but also to cover them up:

The problem with all the institutions is that the director hires all the personnel. That means that doctors and nurses are required to write papers according to what the director wants. So if something is done by the director, they can't report it because they will be fired. Also if a kid has to go to a local medical center for an injury, he brings the records back and the director keeps them all. He can destroy them, hiding any chance of implicating the staff.[335]

---

[333] Human Rights Watch interview, Valery P., St. Petersburg, February 27, 1998.

[334] Human Rights Watch interview, March 6, 1998.

[335] Human Rights Watch interview, February 26, 1998.

In interviews with thirty-one orphans and experts in Russia, Human Rights Watch found that the fear of retribution was only one deterrent to exposing abuses within the institutions. For instance, ignorance of grievance procedures also stand in the way of many children we interviewed, as does the doubt that much will come of their complaints anyway:

> We really don't know about the channels and mechanisms for changing things. If we knew what mechanism there was we would use it. We tried to protect the small kids at our place when the staff took their fruit away. We wrote a letter and sent one copy to the director and one to the municipal department. Well, of course, the municipal department told us, "You didn't catch anyone doing it. So you saw someone doing this, but you didn't catch anyone."[336]

> Once we called for a TV crew to come, and they interviewed us and we answered their questions. The teachers were busy when they arrived, so the crew went with us and interviewed kids personally. It helped a little, but not so much. Some high officials saw it on TV and asked a high official named Zernova what was going on. So because those top officials yelled at her, she came to the orphanage and talked to the staff, and it helped a little. Before, they would really yell and humiliate us, and not even think about who was around. Now they say things to us only after they look around to see who's there. They're more *careful* with yelling and humiliation.[337]

The financial interest in orphanages
Financial interests were also a recurrent theme in the critiques Human Rights Watch received of Russian state orphanages. The government blames its lack of resources for its inability to train and pay for qualified staff, while critics, including some institution staff, claim that it is more a matter of misappropriation of the current budget.

One doctor summarized what Human Rights Watch heard from numerous knowledgeable people working in institutions:

---

[336] Human Rights Watch interview, Masha K., Moscow Orphanage A, February 20, 1998.

[337] Ibid.

It's a very expensive system. But the child only gets 25 percent of all the funds that are allocated. Seventy-five percent goes to keeping the system going. For instance, a Ministry of Labor official recently told a roundtable gathering in January (1998) that they budget 2,500 rubles ($400) per child per month in the orphanage.

But we know from colleagues who work in *internaty* that they spend only from 500 to 600 rubles ($100) a month specifically on the care of each child. So when I went to the Ministry of Labor to confirm how much was spent on children, they refused to say. But I heard myself at the roundtable [conference] that they budget 2,500 rubles.[338]

A psychiatrist working in an *internat* corroborated Dr. Severny's calculations with the following report:

We are supposed to spend on each child 17 rubles (three U.S. dollars) a day for food and 1.7 rubles for medicine.[339]

The psychiatrist also told Human Rights Watch that the actual number of staff they are budgeted for on her service is kept "top secret," and only the administrator knows the figure.[340]

The potential for financial mismanagement concerning the state pension accounts for orphans is another matter that concerns children's rights advocates, as Dr. Anatoly Severny summarized for us:

Starting from the age of sixteen years, the children in the psychoneurological *internaty* get a pension from the state because they're considered officially as invalids. This is supposed to be used for their care in the *internat*. But where does the pension go? There's a legal problem. By law the court can rule a person not capable of taking care of himself. Officially, they don't have legal rights to manage their own affairs like a pension.

---

[338] Human Rights Watch interview, Dr. Anatoly Severny, February 12, 1998. Exchange rate as of February 1998.

[339] Human Rights Watch report, Dr. Tatiana Moroz, February 16, 1998.

[340] Ibid.

So, on one hand the state gives the pension. But we don't see where that money goes. That's one reason the ministries want to maintain the system as it is. The ministries receive a huge amount of money.[341]

Conclusion

Human Rights Watch condemns the use of violent punishment—physical or psychological, whether administered by officials or children acting at their behest—of children in institutions operated by the Ministry of Education. Moreover, rather than condoning or turning a blind eye to the savage hazing among school-aged orphans within some institutions, the Russian authorities are obliged to protect the children it has accepted in its custody. They must halt all forms of cruel, inhuman, and degrading treatment immediately, investigate existing reports of corruption and other wrongdoing, and further conduct unannounced investigations in distant regions where few children's rights activists are available to advocate on behalf of abused orphans.

In the following section of this report, Part VIII, we present some recent progress as well as systemic impediments relevant to the future protection of orphans' rights in Russia.

---

[341] Ibid.

VIII. PROGRESS AND IMPEDIMENTS
IN ENSURING ORPHANS' RIGHTS

Skeletons come back to life

A striking indictment of the discrimination, neglect and degrading punishment in Russian state orphanages, can be seen in a series of photographs of a few dozen orphans with disabilities, taken from 1994 to 1997.[342]

Several years ago these children were found in psychoneurological *internaty*, lying with gnarled, limp legs, effectively left to die. Within six months they had flesh on their bones and were out of their beds, smiling, walking and playing.

These were the effects of what began as a volunteer program organized by a group of Russians with no specialized training in the rehabilitation of children with disabilities. Rather they provided basic daily care—feeding, holding, talking, bathing, massaging, and getting needed health services. As the program grew, the group gathered support from western donors and received three in-service training courses from visiting experts from three European countries. They also earned the agreement of government ministries to work with more than 100 disabled orphans in a Moscow psychoneurological *internat*. The results, captured in the photographs at the end of this chapter, are startling.

First there is nine year old Irina, once languishing like a famine victim in a Moscow psychoneurological *internat*, later standing and playing with other children. There is also the emaciated frame of Nina, a little girl tottering on her spindly legs with the help of a steady hand, hardly recognizable a year later. The same can be said of frail little Andrei, once a gruesome sight with his ulcer-covered face, sitting folded up in a large pen for the children; or for Petrushka or Pavel.

The horrors of Russia's "total institutions" came to light in 1994 through the action of Sergei Koloskov, the father of a girl born with Down syndrome, who resisted pressure to abandon his baby and decided to raise her in her family. Shortly afterwards, he founded the Russian Down Syndrome Association for families in similar circumstances, and sought information and assistance from Western donor and disability experts as well as the Russian state association for disabled people.

---

[342] The photographs, appearing at the end of this chapter, are from the collection of Sergei Koloskov, president of the Down Syndrome Association (DSA), and are part of a joint project between the DSA and the European-based nongovernmental organization International Catholic Children's Bureau.

In 1994, responding to reports of acutely ill orphans in the squalid state institutions in Moscow, Koloskov began to explore the state institutions in Moscow, and came upon a hollow-eyed nine-year-old orphan named Irina in psychoneurological *internat* Number 11. Born with Down syndrome, she had been restrained from the neck down in a cloth sack, and apparently left to die.

Koloskov filmed Irina's deathly figure and his footage aired on Russian television, awakening the audience to a hidden world of neglect known to very few. The haunting images provoked a fiery debate in Russia, and prompted national and international news media to probe the archipelago of locked institutions across Russia. Their exposés revealed considerable variation in the level of care from place to place, but also documented the horrific neglect and punishment. They also spurred Russian volunteers to work with the newly formed Down Syndrome Association, and inspired international volunteers in Moscow such as the International Women's Club, to expand their work in the desperate *internaty* and baby houses.[343]

Over time, Koloskov felt that his public critique of the state institutions bore few results, and took a more practical approach to seeking ways to work in cooperation with the authorities.[344] This led to a formal agreement with government officials to expand the innovative care begun with Irina to include thirty orphans with similar disabilities. He also got the agreement and financial support of the authorities to translate and publish the respected educational series for disabled children called "Small Steps."

A remarkable intervention

The most startling transformation in a group of children has been documented in the work with Irina who was tended to full-time by two volunteers while she received medical treatment in a Moscow hospital in 1995. From that one case, Koloskov gradually recruited several dozen workers through the Russian Orthodox Church to care for as many as 100 orphans in a ward of a large Moscow psychoneurological internat. Although many of the children have serious hereditary conditions such as Down syndrome that may limit their potential over

---

[343] Human Rights Watch interview, volunteer, December 20, 1998. Over the years, new charities, notably Action for Russia's Children (ARC) and Downside Up, have provided services to a range of institutions.

[344] Human RightsWatch interview, Sergei Koloskov, November 13, 1998.

the long term, they have been spared a lifetime deteriorating in lying-down rooms.[345]

During our mission to Russia, Human Rights Watch visited the Moscow *internat* where the children in these photographs have come back to life, and saw them at play on tricycles and slides. It was nothing short of incredible; and it was powerful proof of how the systematic neglect in Russian institutions denies children their basic rights.

It is also an alarming sign that an untold number of children are indeed wrongly consigned to bed through misdiagnosis and neglect. It is unclear how many more children with twisted, useless legs could be walking and developing to the maximum of their individual potential.

Showing the pictures at *Internat* X

During our visit to *Internat* X, Human Rights Watch explored the real potential of the orphans there in our initial interview with the staff. We took along a large selection of "before and after" photographs from the Down Syndrome Associations pilot project to show the staff. We were interested in seeking their reaction to the contrast in the children's conditions after the intervention of attentive caretakers, albeit caretakers with no professional expertise in disabilities.

Human Rights Watch found that the older staff *sanitarki* appeared disbelieving and disinterested, while a couple of younger *sanitarki* and one nurse studied the pictures carefully.[346] They noted the children who were emaciated and seemingly deformed in the state *internat*, and later appeared chubby and playful as they crouched on those previously "deformed" legs.[347]

"This one's like ours," said one *sanitarka* pointing to one of the skeletal images. "We have one like this here."[348]

Among the photographs of the orphans were several snapshots taken of Russian adults with Down syndrome, who were playing recorders in a group. An

---

[345] Human Rights Watch interview, Moscow psychiatrist, Dr. Tatiana Moroz, February 12, 1998.

[346] Human Rights Watch interview, Iliana Danilova, Alla Sergeyeva, Lyuba Fokina, February 15, 1998.

[347] Human Rights Watch interview, Alla Sergeyeva, February 15, 1998.

[348] Ibid.

older *sanitarka* shook her head and remarked, "They play music, they speak!—these with Down! None of ours can speak."[349]

While studying the photographs, and comparing those children with some of the orphans in their care, one of the staff members of *Internat* X told Human Rights Watch that she thought perhaps ten of their 145 children had potential for a life outside the *internat*.[350]

But the general reaction of the staff at *Internat* X to the photographs indicated that they had accepted their orphans' fate as given, indeed permanent. The idea of encouraging the bedridden children to use their legs and start to crawl was roundly dismissed when one of our Russian contacts mentioned a "great floor mat" that was being used with these transformed orphans. Even though it was clear that the nurse and *sanitarki* were not in a position to make policy changes in the *internat*, we asked if they might be able to use such a floor mat in *Internat X*. Their response was unanimous, as put by one of their number, who said, "Oh no, there's no room for them to crawl, if they started to."[351]

Other progress

Since 1996, when another flurry of media reports revealed the persistent neglect and maltreatment of children in Russian institutions, several of the worst *internaty* have been shut down, and others, such as *Internat* Y, have undergone some physical improvements in their physical surroundings. And recent reports from the Down Syndrome Association suggest that some progress is being made with the Ministry of Social Labor and Ministry of Education in considering better care and education for children with disabilities.[352]

Human Rights Watch also learned of at least two orphanages for school-aged children in St. Petersburg, where the directors were either under criminal investigation or serving a year for charges of abuse brought by advocates of the orphans. In Moscow, too, children's rights activists had succeeded in opening a

---

[349] Human Rights Watch interview, *internat sanitarka*, February 15, 1998.

[350] Human Rights Watch interview, Iliana Danilova, February 15, 1998.

[351] Human Rights Watch interview, Iliana Danilova, Alla Sergeyeva, February 15, 1998.

[352] Human Rights Watch interview, Sergei Koloskov, October 23,1998.

government investigation into abuse by directors in one orphanage and a residential shelter for children in the suburb of Lubertsy.[353]

Children's rights advocates interviewed by Human Rights Watch in Moscow corroborated the difficulties Alexander Rodin described in trying to remove abusive orphanage directors and staff. One such case involved a residential shelter called "Good Friend," in the Moscow suburb of Lubertsy, where a representative of Rights of the Child investigated reports of deplorable conditions and corporal punishment.[354]

Arriving unannounced on February 18, 1997, Lyubov Kushnir found the children freezing and hungry, as she told Human Rights Watch:

> It was not heated at all, and so cold inside that I couldn't take off my heavy coat. Maybe it was three degrees celsius. I saw bedrooms with no beds at all. All the beds were taken to the gym floor. They were tiny, like kindergarten size, and they were lined up, one next to another in a row. Boys and girls were mixed. I saw two beds with the ends cut off to extend the length for older children. There were no warm blankets—only thin ones. There were about five or six children lying there for the quiet hour, just huddled there, looking pale and scared. They looked about eight or nine years old.
>
> The senior medical nurse told me that she had no medicines and had to go and beg for them. The cook said she had nothing to feed them for dinner, only tea and dried bread.[355]

Kushnir told Human Rights Watch that despite the apparent poverty of the center, 1.5 billion rubles (about $300,000) had been allocated four years ago for a major renovation of the building.[356]

---

[353] Human Rights Watch interview, Lyuba Kushnir, February 23, 1998.

[354] Human Rights Watch interview, February 16, 1998. Although a residential shelter is a more temporary facility for the burgeoning population of street children, "Good Friend" operates under the supervision of the Ministry of Education and should therefore be subject to the same scrutiny accorded other custodial institutions. Russian children's advocates regard this case as a good example of corruption.

[355] Human Rights Watch interview, February 23, 1998.

[356] Ibid. Exchange rate as of February 1998.

Eventually, the Russian procuracy (prosecutor) commenced an investigation and according to Kushnir, the director was charged in September 1997 with exploitation, humiliation, cruelty to children, and financial wrongdoing.[357]

But by February 1998, Kushnir was informed by friends of the director that the case had been closed in January. At that time, children's rights advocates told Human Rights Watch that due to the director's relations with the Ministry of Education's Moscow Committee, the local branch of the Education Ministry in Lubertsy feared that they could lose their jobs if they did not accept the decision.[358] Kushnir also reported that the director's supporters tried to intimidate her by threatening to bring some kind of action against her nongovernmental organization Rights of the Child. [359]

Through her organization, Kushnir nevertheless appealed to the procuracy and the case was re-opened. In the end, the children's advocates prevailed, and the director was fired.[360]

Further progress was reported by the Moscow-based NGO Rights of the Child, which together with several independent child development specialists and psychiatrists, has engaged the Russian government to consider their proposal for an independent citizens' oversight committee to monitor children's rights in the institutions.

But as the above account illustrates, progress is slow, tainted with official intimidation, and advocates for children's rights told us that they still face several systemic obstacles.

Russian government reaction to critics

In general, the Russian authorities have reacted to the critiques of their orphanages by blocking access to the institutions; punishing or threatening to fire workers if they speak about abuses; and, in some instances, promoting those who are responsible for the wrongdoing.

Senior officials of the three ministries charged with maintaining the orphanages have consistently rejected requests from human rights groups and child

---

[357] Ibid.

[358] Ibid.

[359] Human Rights Watch interview, Lyuba Kushnir, September 30, 1998.

[360] Ibid.

welfare experts to visit the particularly inhumane psychoneurological *internaty* run by the Ministry of Labor and Social Development.[361]

Nor do they easily share information that should be in the public domain, according to Dr. Anatoly Severny:

> When I went to the Ministry of Social Welfare and asked for data on *internaty*, they refused me and said I needed special permission from the deputy minister. I sent an official request to the Deputy Minister, and there's been no reply for three weeks. [362]

Dr. Severny further described to Human Rights Watch how high-level officials discriminate against children deemed to be "untrainable," in blocking proposals to shift orphans to institutions for more appropriate care:

> One year ago we started to try to get the mentally disabled children transferred from the Ministry of Labor to the Ministry of Health, so they would get better treatment. But the Ministry of Health does not want these children. We called press conferences. We went to the Duma (lower house of Parliament). But everybody said these children are not trainable; they don't need to be treated. What's the use of transferring them to the Ministry of Health?[363]

High risk for Russian orphans

Among the greatest perils facing orphans in Russia is their entry into society at large. Their lack of preparation for life on their own was a frequent concern of experts and orphanage staff interviewed by Human Rights Watch. UNICEF, too, calls the children who leave state care the "most vulnerable group of children.[364]

One staff teacher of Moscow Orphanage A—herself raised in a *dyetskii dom*—poignantly summarized what Human Rights Watch heard again and again:

---

[361] Human Rights Watch interview, Boris Altshuler, February 16, 1998; Dr. Anatoly Severny, February 12, 1998.

[362] Human Rights Watch interview, February 12, 1998.

[363] Ibid.

[364] UNICEF, *Children at Risk*, p. 89.

The most dreadful thing about the whole system of education and training is that the orphans are well equipped in electronic things, decent furniture, and a little spending money. But they're not prepared for future life. They don't know how to *make* money, even how to make *tea*! Look at the official statistics.[365]

The statistics are grim indeed. According to the Russian Procuracy General, some 15,000 children leave state *dyetskiye doma* every year. Within several years, 5,000 will be unemployed; 6,000 will be homeless; 3,000 will have criminal records; and 1,500 will commit suicide.[366]

When orphans leave the state institutions at eighteen years of age, they receive a lump sum—about seven million rubles in St. Petersburg—which is barely enough to buy the furniture for a single room.[367] We also heard reports from the staff of Education Ministry orphanages who claimed that these children were also victims of financial corruption:

In principle, each child should have a private bank account. But in practice, really few of them get one. Also they're supposed to have an apartment where they are officially registered if they have a family member or guardian but who knows what they do with the apartment.

For example, the apartment where a boy named Maxim A. was registered had been occupied for several years by a state organization which used it for storage. That's not the only case. Also some are taken by Moscow and sold off.[368]

The same teacher from Orphanage A in Moscow cited another case he knew of a girl whose family was allegedly misusing the apartment that was legally hers:

---

[365] Human Rights Watch interview, teacher, Orphanage A, February 20, 1998.

[366] Cited in UNICEF, *Children at Risk*, p. 89.

[367] Human Rights Watch interview, Yuri T., St. Petersburg, February 27, 1998.

[368] Human Rights Watch interview, teacher, Orphanage A, February 20, 1998. The misallocation of apartments intended for orphans leaving state custodial institutions was corroborated by an attorney specializing in juvenile law in a Human Rights Watch interview, October 14, 1998.

Take the case of Vika Z. Her aunt rents out the apartment and all the money she gets for it she doesn't give to Vika. It's Vika's money, and it should go to her bank account for when she gets out of the orphanage. [369]

But the problems for the orphans start earlier, in the socialization they receive in the institution, and the second-class treatment they report that they receive in the public schools they attend. According to another teacher from Moscow Orphanage A, himself a product of a *dyetskii dom*, the children do not receive the same attention and encouragement from the public school teachers as children from families:

> They go to regular public schools, but they're not welcomed there. In the regular school the teachers don't know the mentality of this place or the atmosphere of the place where they grow up. Also, the other kids try to exclude them. For example, instead of studying the whole nine classes for a diploma, the orphans often study only up through the sixth year. Only one of the girls in our group finished the standard nine years. [370]

Conclusion

Legion are the difficulties facing abandoned children in Russian state institutions. For those who are not doomed to a life in a locked asylum, the full effects of their discrimination still awaits them when they leave the sheltered and stunting world of the orphanage.

While certain progress has been made, we are aware of the views we heard again and again, from Russians and international experts deeply involved in the care of abandoned children, summarized below by this experienced volunteer:

> It's attitude, plus no feeling at all of responsibility by anyone who looks after them. I know this sounds extreme, but I've seen it again and again. It's also ignorance. The most horrific thing, you can meet officials of the Ministry of Health, or the Ministry of Social Welfare, who've actually seen how children can be treated and taught to walk, and learn. Officials who've been to other countries.

---

[369] Ibid.

[370] Human Rights Watch interview with teacher, Orphanage A, Moscow, February 20, 1998.

One of these is the head of the psycho-neurological *internaty* for Moscow. But under her care, children are in straitjackets, little skeletons like in Romania. The first time I was at one of the *internaty* there was a child in cloth bag and another in a straitjacket. And she [the official] railed on about how the boy has to be tied up or else he'll swallow his fist.

"So we are not talking about money at all. We are talking about no conscience, no soul. And if she is not responsible for these children, then who is?"

IX. CONCLUSION

The evidence gathered and presented in this report shows that Russian policies toward abandoned children impose an invidious discrimination due to their status as orphans or "social orphans." This effectively relegates them to an underclass, in clear violation of the fundamental principles of international human rights treaties to which the Russian Federation is obligated.

The stigma of abandonment or disability, when deepened by an official diagnosis of mental retardation, subjects Russian children to prejudicial stereotypes of ineducability and inherited deviance. These, in turn, spawn a cycle of institutional neglect and further debilitation, resulting in the denial of such fundamental rights as education and health care; the right not to be cruelly punished and degraded; the right to vote; and in some cases, the right to life.

This violation of human rights is a product of state action, be it by official policy, or by disregard for Russian and international legal standards. In either case, the consequence is the violation of orphans' civil and political rights; to remedy it, the Russian authorities must first ensure that a child's rights are respected without discrimination of any kind.

There are clear, practical measures to address the discrimination due to status as orphans—or disabled orphans—that would cost the Russian Federation relatively little. These include:

- prohibiting medical personnel from frightening parents into abandoning infants with birth defects;

- actively promoting state support for alternatives to institutionalization, such as state aid to parents or relatives rearing disabled or abandoned children; foster families; and local and international adoption;

- undertaking a serious public education effort to raise awareness on the rights and potential of abandoned children and children with disabilities;

- prohibiting the official diagnosis of *retardation or oligophrenia* in infants until they are old enough to be evaluated adequately;

- abolishing any barriers to civil rights posed by the diagnosis of *debil* (light *oligophrenic*), and removing from identification papers and passports indicators that the bearer was an orphan or institutionalized child;

- issuing strict orders to the three ministries involved in custodial care to halt corporal and cruel and humiliating punishment, as well as the use of dehumanizing language in front of orphans, and ensuring that perpetrators of such violations will be investigated and disciplined.

In addition, the Russian government should immediately authorize the establishment of an independent oversight committee of experts in child development, who would be mandated to visit institutions without prior notice, and empowered to impose sanctions when they documented malfeasance and neglect.

The moment is overdue for the Russian authorities to respect their many commitments to the protection of children, including the ratification of the U.N. Convention on the Rights of the Child, and the passage of important civil and criminal laws pertinent to minors.

Human Rights Watch recognizes the economic difficulties facing the Russian government as it navigates the turbulent waters of post-communist transition. But Russia is not a land entirely razed by war, nor is it ravaged by drought and natural disaster.

To the contrary, a visit to Moscow and some other cities dramatically demonstrates a sector enjoying considerable prosperity, a tax base that has so far succeeded in eluding government collectors. The international community should insist that Russia meet its obligations to its most vulnerable citizens as vigorously as it insists on compliance with international arms control treaties.

In the coming months, thousands of Russian children risk being abandoned and homeless at a pace quickened by the recent collapse of the Russian financial system. The solution is not to build new institutions for abandoned children. In the long run, the Russian Federation must plan to close down those institutions gradually, and provide practical support to struggling families.

Until that can be accomplished, the authorities, urged by the international community and the advocacy groups from their own citizenry, must take every measure to abolish the cruelty and neglect that stunt the lives of orphans in their care.

APPENDICES

APPENDIX A. INTERNATIONAL LAW

U.N. Convention on the Rights of the Child

Convention on the Rights of the Child, G.A. res. 44/25, annex, 44 U.N. GAOR Supp. (No. 49) at 167, U.N. Doc. A/44/49 (1989).

PREAMBLE

The States Parties to the present Convention,

Considering that, in accordance with the principles proclaimed in the Charter of the United Nations, recognition of the inherent dignity and of the equal and inalienable rights of all members of the human family is the foundation of freedom, justice and peace in the world,

Bearing in mind that the peoples of the United Nations have, in the Charter, reaffirmed their faith in fundamental human rights and in the dignity and worth of the human person, and have determined to promote social progress and better standards of life in larger freedom,

Recognizing that the United Nations has, in the Universal Declaration of Human Rights and in the International Covenants on Human Rights, proclaimed and agreed that everyone is entitled to all the rights and freedoms set forth therein, without distinction of any kind, such as race, colour, sex, language, religion, political or other opinion, national or social origin, property, birth or other status,

Recalling that, in the Universal Declaration of Human Rights, the United Nations has proclaimed that childhood is entitled to special care and assistance,

Convinced that the family, as the fundamental group of society and the natural environment for the growth and well-being of all its members and particularly children, should be afforded the necessary protection and assistance so that it can fully assume its responsibilities within the community,

Recognizing that the child, for the full and harmonious development of his or her personality, should grow up in a family environment, in an atmosphere of happiness, love and understanding,

Considering that the child should be fully prepared to live an individual life in society, and brought up in the spirit of the ideals proclaimed in the Charter of the United Nations, and in particular in the spirit of peace, dignity, tolerance, freedom, equality and solidarity,

Bearing in mind that the need to extend particular care to the child has been stated in the Geneva Declaration of the Rights of the Child of 1924 and in the Declaration of the Rights of the Child adopted by the General Assembly on 20 November 1959 and recognized in the Universal Declaration of Human Rights, in the International Covenant on Civil and Political Rights (in particular in articles 23 and 24), in the International Covenant on Economic, Social and Cultural Rights (in particular in article 10) and in the statutes and relevant instruments of specialized agencies and international organizations concerned with the welfare of children, '

Bearing in mind that, as indicated in the Declaration of the Rights of the Child, "the child, by reason of his physical and mental immaturity, needs special safeguards and care, including appropriate legal protection, before as well as after birth",

Recalling the provisions of the Declaration on Social and Legal Principles relating to the Protection and Welfare of Children, with Special Reference to Foster Placement and Adoption Nationally and Internationally; the United Nations Standard Minimum Rules for the Administration of Juvenile Justice (The Beijing Rules) ; and the Declaration on the Protection of Women and Children in Emergency and Armed Conflict,

Recognizing that, in all countries in the world, there are children living in exceptionally difficult conditions, and that such children need special consideration,

Taking due account of the importance of the traditions and cultural values of each people for the protection and harmonious development of the child,

Recognizing the importance of international co-operation for improving the living conditions of children in every country, in particular in the developing countries,

Have agreed as follows:

PART I

Article 1

For the purposes of the present Convention, a child means every human being below the age of eighteen years unless under the law applicable to the child, majority is attained earlier.

Article 2

1. States Parties shall respect and ensure the rights set forth in the present Convention to each child within their jurisdiction without discrimination of any kind, irrespective of the child's or his or her parent's or legal guardian's race, colour, sex, language, religion, political or other opinion, national, ethnic or social origin, property, disability, birth or other status.

2. States Parties shall take all appropriate measures to ensure that the child is protected against all forms of discrimination or punishment on the basis of the status, activities, expressed opinions, or beliefs of the child's parents, legal guardians, or family members.

Article 3

1. In all actions concerning children, whether undertaken by public or private social welfare institutions, courts of law, administrative authorities or legislative bodies, the best interests of the child shall be a primary consideration.

2. States Parties undertake to ensure the child such protection and care as is necessary for his or her well-being, taking into account the rights and duties of his or her parents, legal guardians, or other individuals legally responsible for him or her, and, to this end, shall take all appropriate legislative and administrative measures.

3. States Parties shall ensure that the institutions, services and facilities responsible for the care or protection of children shall conform with the standards established by competent authorities, particularly in the areas of safety, health, in the number and suitability of their staff, as well as competent supervision.

Article 4

States Parties shall undertake all appropriate legislative, administrative, and other measures for the implementation of the rights recognized in the present Convention. With regard to economic, social and cultural rights, States Parties shall undertake such measures to the maximum extent of their available resources and, where needed, within the framework of international co-operation.

Article 5
States Parties shall respect the responsibilities, rights and duties of parents or, where applicable, the members of the extended family or community as provided for by local custom, legal guardians or other persons legally responsible for the child, to provide, in a manner consistent with the evolving capacities of the child, appropriate direction and guidance in the exercise by the child of the rights recognized in the present Convention.

Article 6
1. States Parties recognize that every child has the inherent right to life.

2. States Parties shall ensure to the maximum extent possible the survival and development of the child.

Article 7
1. The child shall be registered immediately after birth and shall have the right from birth to a name, the right to acquire a nationality and. as far as possible, the right to know and be cared for by his or her parents.

2. States Parties shall ensure the implementation of these rights in accordance with their national law and their obligations under the relevant international instruments in this field, in particular where the child would otherwise be stateless.

Article 8
1. States Parties undertake to respect the right of the child to preserve his or her identity, including nationality, name and family relations as recognized by law without unlawful interference.

2. Where a child is illegally deprived of some or all of the elements of his or her identity, States Parties shall provide appropriate assistance and protection, with a view to re-establishing speedily his or her identity.

Article 9
1. States Parties shall ensure that a child shall not be separated from his or her parents against their will, except when competent authorities subject to judicial

review determine, in accordance with applicable law and procedures, that such separation is necessary for the best interests of the child. Such determination may be necessary in a particular case such as one involving abuse or neglect of the child by the parents, or one where the parents are living separately and a decision must be made as to the child's place of residence.

2. In any proceedings pursuant to paragraph 1 of the present article, all interested parties shall be given an opportunity to participate in the proceedings and make their views known.

3. States Parties shall respect the right of the child who is separated from one or both parents to maintain personal relations and direct contact with both parents on a regular basis, except if it is contrary to the child's best interests.

4. Where such separation results from any action initiated by a State Party, such as the detention, imprisonment, exile, deportation or death (including death arising from any cause while the person is in the custody of the State) of one or both parents or of the child, that State Party shall, upon request, provide the parents, the child or, if appropriate, another member of the family with the essential information concerning the whereabouts of the absent member(s) of the family unless the provision of the information would be detrimental to the well-being of the child. States Parties shall further ensure that the submission of such a request shall of itself entail no adverse consequences for the person(s) concerned.

Article 10

1. In accordance with the obligation of States Parties under article 9, paragraph 1, applications by a child or his or her parents to enter or leave a State Party for the purpose of family reunification shall be dealt with by States Parties in a positive, humane and expeditious manner. States Parties shall further ensure that the submission of such a request shall entail no adverse consequences for the applicants and for the members of their family.

2. A child whose parents reside in different States shall have the right to maintain on a regular basis, save in exceptional circumstances personal relations and direct contacts with both parents. Towards that end and in accordance with the obligation of States Parties under article 9, paragraph 1, States Parties shall respect the right of the child and his or her parents to leave any country, including their own, and to enter their own country. The right to leave any country shall be subject only to such restrictions as are prescribed by law and which are necessary to protect the

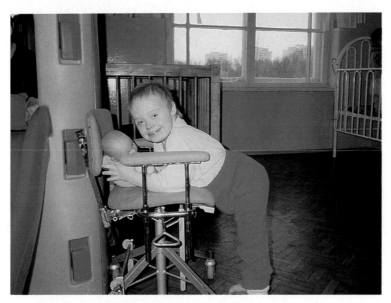

Petrushka (not her real name) in 1996 (above, upper left) and 1997 (below).

Pavel (not his real name) in 1997.

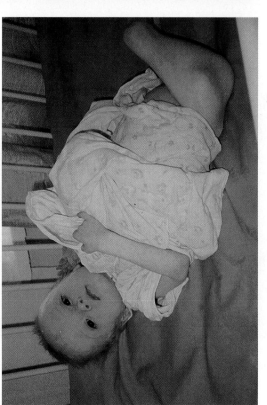

Pavel (not his real name) in 1996.

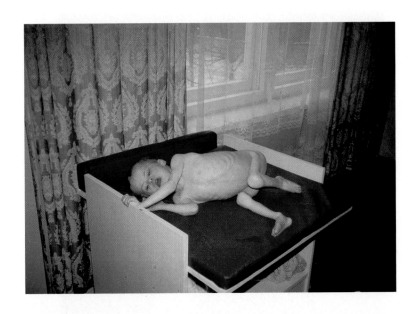

Marina (not her real name) in 1996 (above) and 1997 (below).

Andrei (not his real name) in 1997.

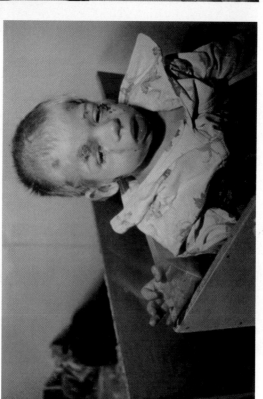

Andrei (not his real name) in 1996.

Irina (not her real name) in 1994 (above) and 1995 (below).

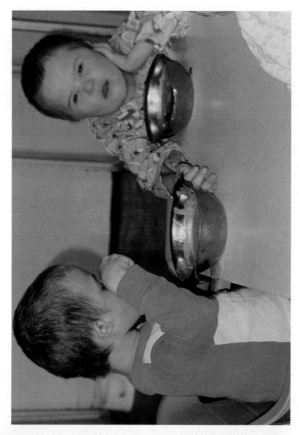

Nina (not her real name) in 1997.

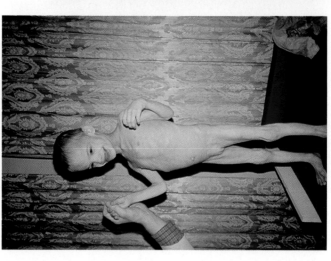

Nina (not her real name) in 1996.

national security, public order (ordre public), public health or morals or the rights and freedoms of others and are consistent with the other rights recognized in the present Convention.

Article 11

1. States Parties shall take measures to combat the illicit transfer and non-return of children abroad.

2. To this end, States Parties shall promote the conclusion of bilateral or multilateral agreements or accession to existing agreements.

Article 12

1. States Parties shall assure to the child who is capable of forming his or her own views the right to express those views freely in all matters affecting the child, the views of the child being given due weight in accordance with the age and maturity of the child.

2. For this purpose, the child shall in particular be provided the opportunity to be heard in any judicial and administrative proceedings affecting the child, either directly, or through a representative or an appropriate body, in a manner consistent with the procedural rules of national law.

Article 13

1. The child shall have the right to freedom of expression; this right shall include freedom to seek, receive and impart information and ideas of all kinds, regardless of frontiers, either orally, in writing or in print, in the form of art, or through any other media of the child's choice.

2. The exercise of this right may be subject to certain restrictions, but these shall only be such as are provided by law and are necessary:
(a) For respect of the rights or reputations of others; or
(b) For the protection of national security or of public order (ordre public), or of public health or morals.

Article 14

1. States Parties shall respect the right of the child to freedom of thought, conscience and religion.

2. States Parties shall respect the rights and duties of the parents and, when applicable, legal guardians, to provide direction to the child in the exercise of his or her right in a manner consistent with the evolving capacities of the child.

3. Freedom to manifest one's religion or beliefs may be subject only to such limitations as are prescribed by law and are necessary to protect public safety, order, health or morals, or the fundamental rights and freedoms of others.

Article 15

1. States Parties recognize the rights of the child to freedom of association and to freedom of peaceful assembly.

2. No restrictions may be placed on the exercise of these rights other than those imposed in conformity with the law and which are necessary in a democratic society in the interests of national security or public safety, public order (ordre public), the protection of public health or morals or the protection of the rights and freedoms of others.

Article 16

1. No child shall be subjected to arbitrary or unlawful interference with his or her privacy, family, home or correspondence, nor to unlawful attacks on his or her honour and reputation.

2. The child has the right to the protection of the law against such interference or attacks.

Article 17

States Parties recognize the important function performed by the mass media and shall ensure that the child has access to information and material from a diversity of national and international sources, especially those aimed at the promotion of his or her social, spiritual and moral well-being and physical and mental health. To this end, States Parties shall:
(a) Encourage the mass media to disseminate information and material of social and cultural benefit to the child and in accordance with the spirit of article 29;
(b) Encourage international co-operation in the production, exchange and dissemination of such information and material from a diversity of cultural, national and international sources;
(c) Encourage the production and dissemination of children's books;

(d) Encourage the mass media to have particular regard to the linguistic needs of the child who belongs to a minority group or who is indigenous;

(e) Encourage the development of appropriate guidelines for the protection of the child from information and material injurious to his or her well-being, bearing in mind the provisions of articles 13 and 18.

Article 18

1. States Parties shall use their best efforts to ensure recognition of the principle that both parents have common responsibilities for the upbringing and development of the child. Parents or, as the case may be, legal guardians, have the primary responsibility for the upbringing and development of the child. The best interests of the child will be their basic concern.

2. For the purpose of guaranteeing and promoting the rights set forth in the present Convention, States Parties shall render appropriate assistance to parents and legal guardians in the performance of their child-rearing responsibilities and shall ensure the development of institutions, facilities and services for the care of children.

3. States Parties shall take all appropriate measures to ensure that children of working parents have the right to benefit from child-care services and facilities for which they are eligible.

Article 19

1. States Parties shall take all appropriate legislative, administrative, social and educational measures to protect the child from all forms of physical or mental violence, injury or abuse, neglect or negligent treatment, maltreatment or exploitation, including sexual abuse, while in the care of parent(s), legal guardian(s) or any other person who has the care of the child.

2. Such protective measures should, as appropriate, include effective procedures for the establishment of social programmes to provide necessary support for the child and for those who have the care of the child, as well as for other forms of prevention and for identification, reporting, referral, investigation, treatment and follow-up of instances of child maltreatment described heretofore, and, as appropriate, for judicial involvement.

Article 20

1. A child temporarily or permanently deprived of his or her family environment, or in whose own best interests cannot be allowed to remain in that environment, shall be entitled to special protection and assistance provided by the State.

2. States Parties shall in accordance with their national laws ensure alternative care for such a child.

3. Such care could include, inter alia, foster placement, kafalah of Islamic law, adoption or if necessary placement in suitable institutions for the care of children. When considering solutions, due regard shall be paid to the desirability of continuity in a child's upbringing and to the child's ethnic, religious, cultural and linguistic background.

Article 21

States Parties that recognize and/or permit the system of adoption shall ensure that the best interests of the child shall be the paramount consideration and they shall:
(a) Ensure that the adoption of a child is authorized only by competent authorities who determine, in accordance with applicable law and procedures and on the basis of all pertinent and reliable information, that the adoption is permissible in view of the child's status concerning parents, relatives and legal guardians and that, if required, the persons concerned have given their informed consent to the adoption on the basis of such counseling as may be necessary;
(b) Recognize that inter-country adoption may be considered as an alternative means of child's care, if the child cannot be placed in a foster or an adoptive family or cannot in any suitable manner be cared for in the child's country of origin;
(c) Ensure that the child concerned by inter-country adoption enjoys safeguards and standards equivalent to those existing in the case of national adoption;
(d) Take all appropriate measures to ensure that, in inter-country adoption, the placement does not result in improper financial gain for those involved in it;
(e) Promote, where appropriate, the objectives of the present article by concluding bilateral or multilateral arrangements or agreements, and endeavour, within this framework, to ensure that the placement of the child in another country is carried out by competent authorities or organs.

Article 22

1. States Parties shall take appropriate measures to ensure that a child who is seeking refugee status or who is considered a refugee in accordance with applicable international or domestic law and procedures shall, whether unaccompanied or

accompanied by his or her parents or by any other person, receive appropriate protection and humanitarian assistance in the enjoyment of applicable rights set forth in the present Convention and in other international human rights or humanitarian instruments to which the said States are Parties.

2. For this purpose, States Parties shall provide, as they consider appropriate, co-operation in any efforts by the United Nations and other competent intergovernmental organizations or non-governmental organizations co-operating with the United Nations to protect and assist such a child and to trace the parents or other members of the family of any refugee child in order to obtain information necessary for reunification with his or her family. In cases where no parents or other members of the family can be found, the child shall be accorded the same protection as any other child permanently or temporarily deprived of his or her family environment for any reason , as set forth in the present Convention.

Article 23

1. States Parties recognize that a mentally or physically disabled child should enjoy a full and decent life, in conditions which ensure dignity, promote self-reliance and facilitate the child's active participation in the community.

2. States Parties recognize the right of the disabled child to special care and shall encourage and ensure the extension, subject to available resources, to the eligible child and those responsible for his or her care, of assistance for which application is made and which is appropriate to the child's condition and to the circumstances of the parents or others caring for the child.

3. Recognizing the special needs of a disabled child, assistance extended in accordance with paragraph 2 of the present article shall be provided free of charge, whenever possible, taking into account the financial resources of the parents or others caring for the child, and shall be designed to ensure that the disabled child has effective access to and receives education, training, health care services, rehabilitation services, preparation for employment and recreation opportunities in a manner conducive to the child's achieving the fullest possible social integration and individual development, including his or her cultural and spiritual development

4. States Parties shall promote, in the spirit of international cooperation, the exchange of appropriate information in the field of preventive health care and of medical, psychological and functional treatment of disabled children, including dissemination of and access to information concerning methods of rehabilitation,

education and vocational services, with the aim of enabling States Parties to improve their capabilities and skills and to widen their experience in these areas. In this regard, particular account shall be taken of the needs of developing countries.

Article 24

1. States Parties recognize the right of the child to the enjoyment of the highest attainable standard of health and to facilities for the treatment of illness and rehabilitation of health. States Parties shall strive to ensure that no child is deprived of his or her right of access to such health care services.

2. States Parties shall pursue full implementation of this right and, in particular, shall take appropriate measures:
(a) To diminish infant and child mortality;
(b) To ensure the provision of necessary medical assistance and health care to all children with emphasis on the development of primary health care;
(c) To combat disease and malnutrition, including within the framework of primary health care, through, inter alia, the application of readily available technology and through the provision of adequate nutritious foods and clean drinking-water, taking into consideration the dangers and risks of environmental pollution;
(d) To ensure appropriate pre-natal and post-natal health care for mothers;
(e) To ensure that all segments of society, in particular parents and children, are informed, have access to education and are supported in the use of basic knowledge of child health and nutrition, the advantages of breastfeeding, hygiene and environmental sanitation and the prevention of accidents;
(f) To develop preventive health care, guidance for parents and family planning education and services.

3. States Parties shall take all effective and appropriate measures with a view to abolishing traditional practices prejudicial to the health of children.

4. States Parties undertake to promote and encourage international co-operation with a view to achieving progressively the full realization of the right recognized in the present article. In this regard, particular account shall be taken of the needs of developing countries.

Article 25

States Parties recognize the right of a child who has been placed by the competent authorities for the purposes of care, protection or treatment of his or her physical or mental health, to a periodic review of the treatment provided to the child and all other circumstances relevant to his or her placement.

Article 26

1. States Parties shall recognize for every child the right to benefit from social security, including social insurance, and shall take the necessary measures to achieve the full realization of this right in accordance with their national law.

2. The benefits should, where appropriate, be granted, taking into account the resources and the circumstances of the child and persons having responsibility for the maintenance of the child, as well as any other consideration relevant to an application for benefits made by or on behalf of the child.

Article 27

1. States Parties recognize the right of every child to a standard of living adequate for the child's physical, mental, spiritual, moral and social development.

2. The parent(s) or others responsible for the child have the primary responsibility to secure, within their abilities and financial capacities, the conditions of living necessary for the child's development.

3. States Parties, in accordance with national conditions and within their means, shall take appropriate measures to assist parents and others responsible for the child to implement this right and shall in case of need provide material assistance and support programmes, particularly with regard to nutrition, clothing and housing.

4. States Parties shall take all appropriate measures to secure the recovery of maintenance for the child from the parents or other persons having financial responsibility for the child, both within the State Party and from abroad. In particular, where the person having financial responsibility for the child lives in a State different from that of the child, States Parties shall promote the accession to international agreements or the conclusion of such agreements, as well as the making of other appropriate arrangements.

Article 28

1. States Parties recognize the right of the child to education, and with a view to achieving this right progressively and on the basis of equal opportunity, they shall, in particular:
(a) Make primary education compulsory and available free to all;

(b) Encourage the development of different forms of secondary education, including general and vocational education, make them available and accessible to every child, and take appropriate measures such as the introduction of free education and offering financial assistance in case of need;
(c) Make higher education accessible to all on the basis of capacity by every appropriate means;
(d) Make educational and vocational information and guidance available and accessible to all children;
(e) Take measures to encourage regular attendance at schools and the reduction of drop-out rates.

2. States Parties shall take all appropriate measures to ensure that school discipline is administered in a manner consistent with the child's human dignity and in conformity with the present Convention.

3. States Parties shall promote and encourage international cooperation in matters relating to education, in particular with a view to contributing to the elimination of ignorance and illiteracy throughout the world and facilitating access to scientific and technical knowledge and modern teaching methods. In this regard, particular account shall be taken of the needs of developing countries.

Article 29
1. States Parties agree that the education of the child shall be directed to:
(a) The development of the child's personality, talents and mental and physical abilities to their fullest potential;
(b) The development of respect for human rights and fundamental freedoms, and for the principles enshrined in the Charter of the United Nations;
(c) The development of respect for the child's parents, his or her own cultural identity, language and values, for the national values of the country in which the child is living, the country from which he or she may originate, and for civilizations different from his or her own;
(d) The preparation of the child for responsible life in a free society, in the spirit of understanding, peace, tolerance, equality of sexes, and friendship among all peoples, ethnic, national and religious groups and persons of indigenous origin;
(e) The development of respect for the natural environment.

2. No part of the present article or article 28 shall be construed so as to interfere with the liberty of individuals and bodies to establish and direct educational institutions, subject always to the observance of the principle set forth in paragraph

1 of the present article and to the requirements that the education given in such institutions shall conform to such minimum standards as may be laid down by the State.

Article 30

In those States in which ethnic, religious or linguistic minorities or persons of indigenous origin exist, a child belonging to such a minority or who is indigenous shall not be denied the right, in community with other members of his or her group, to enjoy his or her own culture, to profess and practice his or her own religion, or to use his or her own language.

Article 31

1. States Parties recognize the right of the child to rest and leisure, to engage in play and recreational activities appropriate to the age of the child and to participate freely in cultural life and the arts.

2. States Parties shall respect and promote the right of the child to participate fully in cultural and artistic life and shall encourage the provision of appropriate and equal opportunities for cultural, artistic, recreational and leisure activity.

Article 32

1. States Parties recognize the right of the child to be protected from economic exploitation and from performing any work that is likely to be hazardous or to interfere with the child's education, or to be harmful to the child's health or physical, mental, spiritual, moral or social development.

2. States Parties shall take legislative, administrative, social and educational measures to ensure the implementation of the present article. To this end, and having regard to the relevant provisions of other international instruments, States Parties shall in particular:
(a) Provide for a minimum age or minimum ages for admission to employment;
(b) Provide for appropriate regulation of the hours and conditions of employment;
(c) Provide for appropriate penalties or other sanctions to ensure the effective enforcement of the present article.

Article 33

States Parties shall take all appropriate measures, including legislative, administrative, social and educational measures, to protect children from the illicit use of narcotic drugs and psychotropic substances as defined in the relevant international treaties, and to prevent the use of children in the illicit production and trafficking of such substances.

Article 34

States Parties undertake to protect the child from all forms of sexual exploitation and sexual abuse. For these purposes, States Parties shall in particular take all appropriate national, bilateral and multilateral measures to prevent:
(a) The inducement or coercion of a child to engage in any unlawful sexual activity;
(b) The exploitative use of children in prostitution or other unlawful sexual practices;
(c) The exploitative use of children in pornographic performances and materials.

Article 35

States Parties shall take all appropriate national, bilateral and multilateral measures to prevent the abduction of, the sale of or traffic in children for any purpose or in any form.

Article 36

States Parties shall protect the child against all other forms of exploitation prejudicial to any aspects of the child's welfare.

Article 37

States Parties shall ensure that:
(a) No child shall be subjected to torture or other cruel, inhuman or degrading treatment or punishment. Neither capital punishment nor life imprisonment without possibility of release shall be imposed for offenses committed by persons below eighteen years of age;
(b) No child shall be deprived of his or her liberty unlawfully or arbitrarily. The arrest, detention or imprisonment of a child shall be in conformity with the law and shall be used only as a measure of last resort and for the shortest appropriate period of time;
(c) Every child deprived of liberty shall be treated with
humanity and respect for the inherent dignity of the human person, and in a manner which takes into account the needs of persons of his or her age. In particular, every child deprived of liberty shall be separated from adults unless it is considered in the child's best interest not to do so and shall have the right to maintain contact with his or her family through correspondence and visits, save in exceptional circumstances;

(d) Every child deprived of his or her liberty shall have the right to prompt access to legal and other appropriate assistance, as well as the right to challenge the legality of the deprivation of his or her liberty before a court or other competent, independent and impartial authority, and to a prompt decision on any such action.

Article 38

1. States Parties undertake to respect and to ensure respect for rules of international humanitarian law applicable to them in armed conflicts which are relevant to the child.

2. States Parties shall take all feasible measures to ensure that persons who have not attained the age of fifteen years do not take a direct part in hostilities.

3. States Parties shall refrain from recruiting any person who has not attained the age of fifteen years into their armed forces. In recruiting among those persons who have attained the age of fifteen years but who have not attained the age of eighteen years, States Parties shall endeavor to give priority to those who are oldest.

4. In accordance with their obligations under international humanitarian law to protect the civilian population in armed conflicts, States Parties shall take all feasible measures to ensure protection and care of children who are affected by an armed conflict.

Article 39

States Parties shall take all appropriate measures to promote physical and psychological recovery and social reintegration of a child victim of: any form of neglect, exploitation, or abuse; torture or any other form of cruel, inhuman or degrading treatment or punishment; or armed conflicts. Such recovery and reintegration shall take place in an environment which fosters the health, self-respect and dignity of the child.

Article 40

1. States Parties recognize the right of every child alleged as, accused of, or recognized as having infringed the penal law to be treated in a manner consistent with the promotion of the child's sense of dignity and worth, which reinforces the child's respect for the human rights and fundamental freedoms of others and which takes into account the child's age and the desirability of promoting the child's reintegration and the child's assuming a constructive role in society.

2. To this end, and having regard to the relevant provisions of international instruments, States Parties shall, in particular, ensure that:

(a) No child shall be alleged as, be accused of, or recognized as having infringed the penal law by reason of acts or omissions that were not prohibited by national or international law at the time they were committed;

(b) Every child alleged as or accused of having infringed the penal law has at least the following guarantees:

(i) To be presumed innocent until proven guilty according to law;

(ii) To be informed promptly and directly of the charges against him or her, and, if appropriate, through his or her parents or legal guardians, and to have legal or other appropriate assistance in the preparation and presentation of his or her defense;

(iii) To have the matter determined without delay by a competent, independent and impartial authority or judicial body in a fair hearing according to law, in the presence of legal or other appropriate assistance and, unless it is considered not to be in the best interest of the child, in particular, taking into account his or her age or situation, his or her parents or legal guardians;

(iv) Not to be compelled to give testimony or to confess guilt; to examine or have examined adverse witnesses and to obtain the participation and examination of witnesses on his or her behalf under conditions of equality;

(v) If considered to have infringed the penal law, to have this decision and any measures imposed in consequence thereof reviewed by a higher competent, independent and impartial authority or judicial body according to law;

(vi) To have the free assistance of an interpreter if the child cannot understand or speak the language used;

(vii) To have his or her privacy fully respected at all stages of the proceedings.

3. States Parties shall seek to promote the establishment of laws, procedures, authorities and institutions specifically applicable to children alleged as, accused of, or recognized as having infringed the penal law, and, in particular:

(a) The establishment of a minimum age below which children shall be presumed not to have the capacity to infringe the penal law;

(b) Whenever appropriate and desirable, measures for dealing with such children without resorting to judicial proceedings, providing that human rights and legal safeguards are fully respected.

4. A variety of dispositions, such as care, guidance and supervision orders; counseling; probation; foster care; education and vocational training programmes and other alternatives to institutional care shall be available to ensure that children

are dealt with in a manner appropriate to their well-being and proportionate both to their circumstances and the offense.

Article 41

Nothing in the present Convention shall affect any provisions which are more conducive to the realization of the rights of the child and which may be contained in:

(a) The law of a State party; or

(b) International law in force for that State.

PART II

Article 42

States Parties undertake to make the principles and provisions of the Convention widely known, by appropriate and active means, to adults and children alike.

Article 43

1. For the purpose of examining the progress made by States Parties in achieving the realization of the obligations undertaken in the present Convention, there shall be established a Committee on the Rights of the Child, which shall carry out the functions hereinafter provided.

2. The Committee shall consist of ten experts of high moral standing and recognized competence in the field covered by this Convention. The members of the Committee shall be elected by States Parties from among their nationals and shall serve in their personal capacity, consideration being given to equitable geographical distribution, as well as to the principal legal systems.

3. The members of the Committee shall be elected by secret ballot from a list of persons nominated by States Parties. Each State Party may nominate one person from among its own nationals.

4. The initial election to the Committee shall be held no later than six months after the date of the entry into force of the present Convention and thereafter every second year. At least four months before the date of each election, the Secretary-General of the United Nations shall address a letter to States Parties inviting them to submit their nominations within two months. The Secretary-General shall subsequently prepare a list in alphabetical order of all

persons thus nominated, indicating States Parties which have nominated them, and shall submit it to the States Parties to the present Convention.

5. The elections shall be held at meetings of States Parties convened by the Secretary-General at United Nations Headquarters. At those meetings, for which two thirds of States Parties shall constitute a quorum, the persons elected to the Committee shall be those who obtain the largest number of votes and an absolute majority of the votes of the representatives of States Parties present and voting.

6. The members of the Committee shall be elected for a term of four years. They shall be eligible for re-election if renominated. The term of five of the members elected at the first election shall expire at the end of two years; immediately after the first election, the names of these five members shall be chosen by lot by the Chairman of the meeting.

7. If a member of the Committee dies or resigns or declares that for any other cause he or she can no longer perform the duties of the Committee, the State Party which nominated the member shall appoint another expert from among its nationals to serve for the remainder of the term, subject to the approval of the Committee.

8. The Committee shall establish its own rules of procedure.

9. The Committee shall elect its officers for a period of two years.

10. The meetings of the Committee shall normally be held at United Nations Headquarters or at any other convenient place as determined by the Committee. The Committee shall normally meet annually. The duration of the meetings of the Committee shall be determined, and reviewed, if necessary, by a meeting of the States Parties to the present Convention, subject to the approval of the General Assembly.

11. The Secretary-General of the United Nations shall provide the necessary staff and facilities for the effective performance of the functions of the Committee under the present Convention.

12. With the approval of the General Assembly, the members of the Committee established under the present Convention shall receive emoluments from United Nations resources on such terms and conditions as the Assembly may decide.

Article 44

1. States Parties undertake to submit to the Committee, through the Secretary-General of the United Nations, reports on the measures they have adopted which give effect to the rights recognized herein and on the progress made on the enjoyment of those rights:

(a) Within two years of the entry into force of the Convention for the State Party concerned;

(b) Thereafter every five years.

2. Reports made under the present article shall indicate factors and difficulties, if any, affecting the degree of fulfilment of the obligations under the present Convention. Reports shall also contain sufficient information to provide the Committee with a comprehensive understanding of the implementation of the Convention in the country concerned.

3. A State Party which has submitted a comprehensive initial report to the Committee need not, in its subsequent reports submitted in accordance with paragraph 1 (b) of the present article, repeat basic information previously provided.

4. The Committee may request from States Parties further information relevant to the implementation of the Convention.

5. The Committee shall submit to the General Assembly, through the Economic and Social Council, every two years, reports on its activities.

6. States Parties shall make their reports widely available to the public in their own countries.

Article 45

In order to foster the effective implementation of the Convention and to encourage international co-operation in the field covered by the Convention:

(a) The specialized agencies, the United Nations Children's Fund, and other United Nations organs shall be entitled to be represented at the consideration of the implementation of such provisions of the present Convention as fall within the scope of their mandate. The Committee may invite the specialized agencies, the United Nations Children's Fund and other competent bodies as it may consider appropriate to provide expert advice on the implementation of the Convention in areas falling within the scope of their respective mandates. The Committee may invite the specialized agencies, the United Nations Children's Fund, and other

United Nations organs to submit reports on the implementation of the Convention in areas falling within the scope of their activities;

(b) The Committee shall transmit, as it may consider appropriate, to the specialized agencies, the United Nations Children's Fund and other competent bodies, any reports from States Parties that contain a request, or indicate a need, for technical advice or assistance, along with the Committee's observations and suggestions, if any, on these requests or indications;

(c) The Committee may recommend to the General Assembly to request the Secretary-General to undertake on its behalf studies on specific issues relating to the rights of the child;

(d) The Committee may make suggestions and general recommendations based on information received pursuant to articles 44 and 45 of the present Convention. Such suggestions and general recommendations shall be transmitted to any State Party concerned and reported to the General Assembly, together with comments, if any, from States Parties.

PART III

Article 46
The present Convention shall be open for signature by all States.

Article 47
The present Convention is subject to ratification. Instruments of ratification shall be deposited with the Secretary-General of the United Nations.

Article 48
The present Convention shall remain open for accession by any State. The instruments of accession shall be deposited with the Secretary-General of the United Nations.

Article 49
1. The present Convention shall enter into force on the thirtieth day following the date of deposit with the Secretary-General of the United Nations of the twentieth instrument of ratification or accession.

2. For each State ratifying or acceding to the Convention after the deposit of the twentieth instrument of ratification or accession, the Convention shall enter into force on the thirtieth day after the deposit by such State of its instrument of ratification or accession.

Article 50

1. Any State Party may propose an amendment and file it with the Secretary-General of the United Nations. The Secretary-General shall thereupon communicate the proposed amendment to States Parties, with a request that they indicate whether they favor a conference of States Parties for the purpose of considering and voting upon the proposals. In the event that, within four months from the date of such communication, at least one third of the States Parties favor such a conference, the Secretary-General shall convene the conference under the auspices of the United Nations. Any amendment adopted by a majority of States Parties present and voting at the conference shall be submitted to the General Assembly for approval.

2. An amendment adopted in accordance with paragraph 1 of the present article shall enter into force when it has been approved by the General Assembly of the United Nations and accepted by a two-thirds majority of States Parties.

3. When an amendment enters into force, it shall be binding on those States Parties which have accepted it, other States Parties still being bound by the provisions of the present Convention and any earlier amendments which they have accepted.

Article 51

1. The Secretary-General of the United Nations shall receive and circulate to all States the text of reservations made by States at the time of ratification or accession.

2. A reservation incompatible with the object and purpose of the present Convention shall not be permitted.

3. Reservations may be withdrawn at any time by notification to that effect addressed to the Secretary-General of the United Nations, who shall then inform all States. Such notification shall take effect on the date on which it is received by the Secretary-General

Article 52

A State Party may denounce the present Convention by written notification to the Secretary-General of the United Nations. Denunciation becomes effective one year after the date of receipt of the notification by the Secretary-General.

Article 53

The Secretary-General of the United Nations is designated as the depositary of the present Convention.

Article 54

The original of the present Convention, of which the Arabic, Chinese, English, French, Russian and Spanish texts are equally authentic, shall be deposited with the Secretary-General of the United Nations.

IN WITNESS THEREOF the undersigned plenipotentiaries, being duly authorized thereto by their respective governments, have signed the present Convention.

Excerpts from the International Covenant on Economic, Social and Cultural Rights

International Covenant on Economic, Social and Cultural Rights, G.A. res. 2200A (XXI), 21 U.N.GAOR Supp. (No. 16) at 49, U.N. Doc. A/6316 (1966), 993 U.N.T.S. 3, entered into force Jan. 3, 1976.

Adopted and opened for signature, ratification and accession by General Assembly resolution 2200 A (XXI) on 16 December 1966

PREAMBLE

"Considering that, in accordance with the principles proclaimed in the Charter of the United Nations, recognition of the inherent dignity and of the equal and inalienable rights of all members of the human family is the foundation of freedom, justice and peace in the world,

Recognizing that these rights derive from the inherent dignity of the human person,

Recognizing that, in accordance with the Universal Dec of Human Rights, the ideal of free human beings enjoying freedom from fear and want can only be achieved if conditions are created whereby everyone may enjoy his economic, social and cultural rights, as well as his civil and political rights...

PART II

Article 2
2. The States Parties to the present Covenant undertake to guarantee that the rights enunciated in the present Covenant will be exercised without discrimination of any kind as to race colour, sex, language, religion, political or other opinion, national or social origin, property, birth or other status. ***

Article 4
The States Parties to the present Covenant recognize that, in the enjoyment of those rights provided by the state in conformity with the present Covenant, the State may subject such rights only to such limitations as are determined by law only in so far as this may be compatible with the nature of these rights and solely for the purpose of promoting the general welfare in a democratic society.

169

PART III

Article 6

1. The States Parties to the present Covenant recognize the right to work, which includes the right of everyone to the opportunity to gain his living by work which he freely chooses or accepts, and will take appropriate steps to safeguard this right.

2. The steps to be taken by a State Party to the present Covenant to achieve the full realization of this right shall include technical and vocational guidance and training programmes, policies and techniques to achieve steady economic, social and cultural development and full and productive employment under conditions safeguarding fundamental political and economic freedoms to the individual.

Article 7

The States Parties to the present Covenant recognize the right of everyone to the enjoyment of just and favourable conditions of work which ensure, in particular:
(a) Remuneration which provides all workers, as a minimum, with:
(I) Fair wages and equal remuneration for work of equal value without distinction of any kind, in particular women being guaranteed conditions of work not inferior to those enjoyed by men, with equal pay for equal work.
(ii) A decent living for themselves and their families in accordance with the provisions of the present Covenant;...

Article 11

1. The States Parries to the present Covenant recognize the right of everyone to an adequate standard of living for himself and his family, including adequate food, clothing and housing, and to the continuous improvement of living conditions. ...

Article 12

1. The States Parties to the present Covenant recognize the right of everyone to the enjoyment of the highest attainable standard of physical and mental health.

2. The steps to be taken by the States Parties to the present Covenant to achieve the full realization of this right shall include those necessary for:
(a) The provision for the reduction of the stillbirth-rate and of infant mortality and for the healthy development of the child:
(d) The creation of conditions which would assure to all medical service and medical attention in the event of sickness.

Article 13

1. The States Parties to the present Covenant recognize the right of everyone to education. They agree that education shall be directed to the full development of the human personality and the sense of its dignity, and shall strengthen the respect for human rights and fundamental freedoms. They further agree that education shall enable all persona to participate effectively in a free society, promote understanding , tolerance and friendship among all nations and all racial, ethnic or religious groups, and further the activities of the United Nations for the maintenance of peace.

2. The States Parties to the present Covenant recognize that, with a view to achieving the full realization of this right:
(a) primary education shall be compulsory and available free to all;
(b) Secondary education in its different forms, including technical and vocational secondary education, shall be made generally available and accessible to all by every appropriate means, and in particular by the progressive introduction of free education'
(c) Higher education shall be made equally accessible to all, on the basis of capacity, by every appropriate means, and in particular by the progressive introduction of free education;
(d) Fundamental education shall be encouraged or intensified as far as possible for those person who have not received or completed the whole period of their primary education;
(e) The development of a system of schools at all levels shall be actively pursued, and adequate fellowship system shall be established, and the material conditions of teaching staff shall be continuously improved.

Article 15

1. The States Parties to the present Covenant recognize the right of everyone:
(a) To take part in cultural life;
(b) To enjoy the benefits of scientific progress and its applications   ****

Excerpts from the International Covenant on Civil and Political Rights

International Covenant on Civil and Political Rights, G.A. res. 2200A (XXI), 21 U.N. GAOR Supp. (No. 16) at 52, U.N. Doc. A/6316 (1966), 999 U.N.T.S. 171, entered into force Mar. 23, 1976.

PART II

Article 2

3. Each State party to the present Covenant undertakes:

(a) To ensure that any person whose rights or freedoms as herein recognized are violated shall have an effective remedy, notwithstanding that the violation has been committed by personal acting in an official capacity;

(b) To ensure that any person claiming such a remedy shall have his right thereto determined by competent judicial, administrative or legislative authorities, or by any other competent authority provided for by the legal system of the State, and to develop the possibilities of judicial remedy.

PART III

Article 6

1. Every human being has the inherent right to life. This right shall be protected by law. No one shall be arbitrarily deprived of his life.

Article 7

No one shall be subjected to torture or to cruel, inhuman or degrading treatment or punishment. In particular, no one shall be subjected without his free consent to medical or scientific experimentation.

Article 8

(3a) No one shall be required to perform forced or compulsory labour;

(3c) For the purpose of this paragraph the term "forced or compulsory labour shall not include:

(I) any work or service, not referred to in subparagraph b, normally required of a person who is under detention in consequence of a lawful order of a court, of a person during conditional release from such detention;

Article 9

1. Everyone has the right to liberty and security of person. No one shall be subjected to arbitrary arrest or detention. No one shall be deprived of his liberty

except on such grounds and in accordance with such procedure as are established by law.

Article 10

1. All persons deprived of their liberty shall be treated with humanity and with respect for the inherent dignity of the human person.

Article 17

1. No one shall be subjected to arbitrary or unlawful interference with his privacy, family, home or correspondence, not to unlawful attacks on his honour and reputation.

Article 18

1. Everyone shall have the right to freedom of thought, conscience and religion

Article 19

2. Everyone shall have the right to freedom of expression; this right shall include freedom to seek, receive and impart information and ideas of all kinds, regardless of frontiers, either orally, in writing or in print, in the form of art, or through any other media of his choice.

Article 23

1. The family is the natural and fundamental group unit of society and is entitled to protection by society and the State.

Article 24

1. Every child shall have, without any discrimination as to race, colour, sex, language, religion, national or social origin, property or birth, the right to such measure of protection as are required by his status as a minor, on the part of his family, society and the State.

Article 26

All persons are equal before the law and are entitled without any discrimination to the equal protection of the law. In this respect, the law shall prohibit any discrimination and guarantee to all persons equal and effective protection against discrimination on any ground such as race, colour, sex, language, religion, political or other opinion , national or social origin, property, birth or other status.

PART IV

Article 28
1. There shall be established a Human Rights Committee ...

United Nations Rules for the Protection of Juveniles Deprived of their Liberty

United Nations Rules for the Protection of Juveniles Deprived of their Liberty G.A. res. 45/113, annex, 45 U.N. GAOR Supp. (No. 49A) at 205, U.N. Doc. A/45/49 (1990) ("U.N. Rules").

I. FUNDAMENTAL PERSPECTIVES

1. The juvenile justice system should uphold the rights and safety and promote the physical and mental well-being of juveniles. Imprisonment should be used as a last resort.

2. Juveniles should only be deprived of their liberty in accordance with the principles and procedures set forth in these Rules and in the United Nations Standard Minimum Rules for the Administration of Juvenile Justice (The Beijing Rules). Deprivation of the liberty of a juvenile should be a disposition of last resort and for the minimum necessary period and should be limited to exceptional cases. The length of the sanction should be determined by the judicial authority, without precluding the possibility of his or her early release.

3. The Rules are intended to establish minimum standards accepted by the United Nations for the protection of juveniles deprived of their liberty in all forms, consistent with human rights and fundamental freedoms, and with a view to counteracting the detrimental effects of all types of detention and to fostering integration in society.

4. The Rules should be applied impartially, without discrimination of any kind as to race, color, sex, age, language, religion, nationality, political or other opinion, cultural beliefs or practices, property, birth or family status, ethnic or social origin, and disability. The religious and cultural beliefs, practices and moral concepts of the juvenile should be respected.

5. The Rules are designed to serve as convenient standards of reference and to provide encouragement and guidance to professionals involved in the management of the juvenile justice system.

6. The Rules should be made readily available to juvenile justice personnel in their national languages. Juveniles who are not fluent in the language spoken by the personnel of the detention facility should have the right to the services of an

interpreter free of charge whenever necessary, in particular during medical examinations and disciplinary proceedings.

7. Where appropriate, States should incorporate the Rules into their legislation or amend it accordingly and provide effective remedies for their breach, including compensation when injuries are inflicted on juveniles. States should also monitor the application of the Rules.

8. The competent authorities should constantly seek to increase the awareness of the public that the care of detained juveniles and preparation for their return to society is a social service of great importance, and to this end active steps should be taken to foster open contacts between the juveniles and the local community.

9. Nothing in the Rules should be interpreted as precluding the application of the relevant United Nations and human rights instruments and standards, recognized by the international community, that are more conducive to ensuring the rights, care and protection of juveniles, children and all young persons.

10. In the event that the practical application of particular Rules contained in sections II to V, inclusive, presents any conflict with the Rules contained in the present section, compliance with the latter shall be regarded as the predominant requirement.

II. SCOPE AND APPLICATION OF THE RULES

11. For the purposes of the Rules, the following definitions should apply:
(a) A juvenile is every person under the age of 18. The age limit below which it should not be permitted to deprive a child of his or her liberty should be determined by law;
(b) The deprivation of liberty means any form of detention or imprisonment or the placement of a person in a public or private custodial setting, from which this person is not permitted to leave at will, by order of any judicial, administrative or other public authority.

12. The deprivation of liberty should be effected in conditions and circumstances which ensure respect for the human rights of juveniles. Juveniles detained in facilities should be guaranteed the benefit of meaningful activities and programmes which would serve to promote and sustain their health and self-respect, to foster

their sense of responsibility and encourage those attitudes and skills that will assist them in developing their potential as members of society.

13. Juveniles deprived of their liberty shall not for any reason related to their status be denied the civil, economic, political, social or cultural rights to which they are entitled under national or international law, and which are compatible with the deprivation of liberty.

14. The protection of the individual rights of juveniles with special regard to the legality of the execution of the detention measures shall be ensured by the competent authority, while the objectives of social integration should be secured by regular inspections and other means of control carried out, according to international standards, national laws and regulations, by a duly constituted body authorized to visit the juveniles and not belonging to the detention facility.

15. The Rules apply to all types and forms of detention facilities in which juveniles are deprived of their liberty. Sections I, II, IV and V of the Rules apply to all detention facilities and institutional settings in which juveniles are detained, and section III applies specifically to juveniles under arrest or awaiting trial.

16. The Rules shall be implemented in the context of the economic, social and cultural conditions prevailing in each Member State.

III. JUVENILES UNDER ARREST OR AWAITING TRIAL

17. Juveniles who are detained under arrest or awaiting trial ("untried") are presumed innocent and shall be treated as such. Detention before trial shall be avoided to the extent possible and limited to exceptional circumstances. Therefore, all efforts shall be made to apply alternative measures. When preventive detention is nevertheless used, juvenile courts and investigative bodies shall give the highest priority to the most expeditious processing of such cases to ensure the shortest possible duration of detention. Untried detainees should be separated from convicted juveniles.

18. The conditions under which an untried juvenile is detained should be consistent with the rules set out below, with additional specific provisions as are necessary and appropriate, given the requirements of the presumption of innocence, the duration of the detention and the legal status and circumstances of the juvenile. These provisions would include, but not necessarily be restricted to, the following:

(a) Juveniles should have the right of legal counsel and be enabled to apply for free legal aid, where such aid is available, and to communicate regularly with their legal advisers. Privacy and confidentiality shall be ensured for such communications;
(b) Juveniles should be provided, where possible, with opportunities to pursue work, with remuneration, and continue education or training, but should not be required to do so. Work, education or training should not cause the continuation of the detention;
(c) Juveniles should receive and retain materials for their leisure and recreation as are compatible with the interests of the administration of justice.

IV. THE MANAGEMENT OF JUVENILE FACILITIES

A. Records
19. All reports, including legal records, medical records and records of disciplinary proceedings, and all other documents relating to the form, content and details of treatment, should be placed in a confidential individual file, which should be kept up to date, accessible only to authorized persons and classified in such a way as to be easily understood. Where possible, every juvenile should have the right to contest any fact or opinion contained in his or her file so as to permit rectification of inaccurate, unfounded or unfair statements. In order to exercise this right, there should be procedures that allow an appropriate third party to have access to and to consult the file on request. Upon release, the records of juveniles shall be sealed, and, at an appropriate time, expunged.

20. No juvenile should be received in any detention facility without a valid commitment order of a judicial, administrative or other public authority. The details of this order should be immediately entered in the register. No juvenile should be detained in any facility where there is no such register.

B. Admission, registration, movement and transfer
21. In every place where juveniles are detained, a complete and secure record of the following information should be kept concerning each juvenile received:
(a) Information on the identity of the juvenile;

(b) The fact of and reasons for commitment and the authority therefor;
(c) The day and hour of admission, transfer and release;
(d) Details of the notifications to parents and guardians on every admission, transfer or release of the juvenile in their care at the time of commitment;

(e) Details of known physical and mental health problems, including drug and alcohol abuse.

22. The information on admission, place, transfer and release should be provided without delay to the parents and guardians or closest relative of the juvenile concerned.

23. As soon as possible after reception, full reports and relevant information on the personal situation and circumstances of each juvenile should be drawn up and submitted to the administration.

24. On admission, all juveniles shall be given a copy of the rules governing the detention facility and a written description of their rights and obligations in a language they can understand, together with the address of the authorities competent to receive complaints, as well as the address of public or private agencies and organizations which provide legal assistance. For those juveniles who are illiterate or who cannot understand the language in the written form, the information should be conveyed in a manner enabling full comprehension.

25. All juveniles should be helped to understand the regulations governing the internal organization of the facility, the goals and methodology of the care provided, the disciplinary requirements and procedures, other authorized methods of seeking information and of making complaints and all such other matters as are necessary to enable them to understand fully their rights and obligations during detention.

26. The transport of juveniles should be carried out at the expense of the administration in conveyances with adequate ventilation and light, in conditions that should in no way subject them to hardship or indignity. Juveniles should not be transferred from one facility to another arbitrarily.

C. Classification and placement

27. As soon as possible after the moment of admission, each juvenile should be interviewed, and a psychological and social report identifying any factors relevant to the specific type and level of care and programme required by the juvenile should be prepared. This report, together with the report prepared by a medical officer who has examined the juvenile upon admission, should be forwarded to the director for purposes of determining the most appropriate placement for the juvenile within the facility and the specific type and level of care and programme

required and to be pursued. When special rehabilitative treatment is required, and the length of stay in the facility permits, trained personnel of the facility should prepare a written, individualized treatment plan specifying treatment objectives and time-frame and the means, stages and delays with which the objectives should be approached.

28. The detention of juveniles should only take place under conditions that take full account of their particular needs, status and special requirements according to their age, personality, sex and type of offense, as well as mental and physical health, and which ensure their protection from harmful influences and risk situations. The principal criterion for the separation of different categories of juveniles deprived of their liberty should be the provision of the type of care best suited to the particular needs of the individuals concerned and the protection of their physical, mental and moral integrity and well-being.

29. In all detention facilities juveniles should be separated from adults, unless they are members of the same family. Under controlled conditions, juveniles may be brought together with carefully selected adults as part of a special programme that has been shown to be beneficial for the juveniles concerned.

30. Open detention facilities for juveniles should be established. Open detention facilities are those with no or minimal security measures. The population in such detention facilities should be as small as possible. The number of juveniles detained in closed facilities should be small enough to enable individualized treatment. Detention facilities for juveniles should be decentralized and of such size as to facilitate access and contact between the juveniles and their families. Small-scale detention facilities should be established and integrated into the social, economic and cultural environment of the community.

D. Physical environment and accommodation
31. Juveniles deprived of their liberty have the right to facilities and services that meet all the requirements of health and human dignity.

32. The design of detention facilities for juveniles and the physical environment should be in keeping with the rehabilitative aim of residential treatment, with due regard to the need of the juvenile for privacy, sensory stimuli, opportunities for association with peers and participation in sports, physical exercise and leisure-time activities. The design and structure of juvenile detention facilities should be such as to minimize the risk of fire and to ensure safe evacuation from the premises.

There should be an effective alarm system in case of fire, as well as formal and drilled procedures to ensure the safety of the juveniles. Detention facilities should not be located in areas where there are known health or other hazards or risks.

33. Sleeping accommodation should normally consist of small group dormitories or individual bedrooms, while bearing in mind local standards. During sleeping hours there should be regular, unobtrusive supervision of all sleeping areas, including individual rooms and group dormitories, in order to ensure the protection of each juvenile. Every juvenile should, in accordance with local or national standards, be provided with separate and sufficient bedding, which should be clean when issued, kept in good order and changed often enough to ensure cleanliness.

34. Sanitary installations should be so located and of a sufficient standard to enable every juvenile to comply, as required, with their physical needs in privacy and in a clean and decent manner.

35. The possession of personal effects is a basic element of the right to privacy and essential to the psychological well-being of the juvenile. The right of every juvenile to possess personal effects and to have adequate storage facilities for them should be fully recognized and respected. Personal effects that the juvenile does not choose to retain or that are confiscated should be placed in safe custody. An inventory thereof should be signed by the juvenile. Steps should be taken to keep them in good condition. All such articles and money should be returned to the juvenile on release, except in so far as he or she has been authorized to spend money or send such property out of the facility. If a juvenile receives or is found in possession of any medicine, the medical officer should decide what use should be made of it.

36. To the extent possible juveniles should have the right to use their own clothing. Detention facilities should ensure that each juvenile has personal clothing suitable for the climate and adequate to ensure good health, and which should in no manner be degrading or humiliating. Juveniles removed from or leaving a facility for any purpose should be allowed to wear their own clothing.

37. Every detention facility shall ensure that every juvenile receives food that is suitably prepared and presented at normal meal times and of a quality and quantity to satisfy the standards of dietetics, hygiene and health and, as far as possible, religious and cultural requirements. Clean drinking water should be available to every juvenile at any time.

E. Education, vocational training and work

38. Every juvenile of compulsory school age has the right to education suited to his or her needs and abilities and designed to prepare him or her for return to society. Such education should be provided outside the detention facility in community schools wherever possible and, in any case, by qualified teachers through programmes integrated with the education system of the country so that, after release, juveniles may continue their education without difficulty. Special attention should be given by the administration of the detention facilities to the education of juveniles of foreign origin or with particular cultural or ethnic needs. Juveniles who are illiterate or have cognitive or learning difficulties should have the right to special education.

39. Juveniles above compulsory school age who wish to continue their education should be permitted and encouraged to do so, and every effort should be made to provide them with access to appropriate educational programmes.

40. Diplomas or educational certificates awarded to juveniles while in detention should not indicate in any way that the juvenile has been institutionalized.

41. Every detention facility should provide access to a library that is adequately stocked with both instructional and recreational books and periodicals suitable for the juveniles, who should be encouraged and enabled to make full use of it.

42. Every juvenile should have the right to receive vocational training in occupations likely to prepare him or her for future employment.

43. With due regard to proper vocational selection and to the requirements of institutional administration, juveniles should be able to choose the type of work they wish to perform.

44. All protective national and international standards applicable to child labor and young workers should apply to juveniles deprived of their liberty.

45. Wherever possible, juveniles should be provided with the opportunity to perform remunerated labor, if possible within the local community, as a complement to the vocational training provided in order to enhance the possibility of finding suitable employment when they return to their communities. The type of work should be such as to provide appropriate training that will be of benefit to the juveniles following release. The organization and methods of work offered in

detention facilities should resemble as closely as possible those of similar work in the community, so as to prepare juveniles for the conditions of normal occupational life.

46. Every juvenile who performs work should have the right to an equitable remuneration. The interests of the juveniles and of their vocational training should not be subordinated to the purpose of making a profit for the detention facility or a third party. Part of the earnings of a juvenile should normally be set aside to constitute a savings fund to be handed over to the juvenile on release. The juvenile should have the right to use the remainder of those earnings to purchase articles for his or her own use or to indemnify the victim injured by his or her offense or to send it to his or her family or other persons outside the detention facility.

F. Recreation

47. Every juvenile should have the right to a suitable amount of time for daily free exercise, in the open air whenever weather permits, during which time appropriate recreational and physical training should normally be provided. Adequate space, installations and equipment should be provided for these activities. Every juvenile should have additional time for daily leisure activities, part of which should be devoted, if the juvenile so wishes, to arts and crafts skill development. The detention facility should ensure that each juvenile is physically able to participate in the available programmes of physical education. Remedial physical education and therapy should be offered, under medical supervision, to juveniles needing it.

G. Religion

48. Every juvenile should be allowed to satisfy the needs of his or her religious and spiritual life, in particular by attending the services or meetings provided in the detention facility or by conducting his or her own services and having possession of the necessary books or items of religious observance and instruction of his or her denomination. If a detention facility contains a sufficient number of juveniles of a given religion, one or more qualified representatives of that religion should be appointed or approved and allowed to hold regular services and to pay pastoral visits in private to juveniles at their request. Every juvenile should have the right to receive visits from a qualified representative of any religion of his or her choice, as well as the right not to participate in religious services and freely to decline religious education, counseling or indoctrination.

H. Medical care

49. Every juvenile shall receive adequate medical care, both preventive and remedial, including dental, ophthalmological and mental health care, as well as pharmaceutical products and special diets as medically indicated. All such medical care should, where possible, be provided to detained juveniles through the appropriate health facilities and services of the community in which the detention facility is located, in order to prevent stigmatization of the juvenile and promote self-respect and integration into the community.

50. Every juvenile has a right to be examined by a physician immediately upon admission to a detention facility, for the purpose of recording any evidence of prior ill-treatment and identifying any physical or mental condition requiring medical attention.

51. The medical services provided to juveniles should seek to detect and should treat any physical or mental illness, substance abuse or other condition that may hinder the integration of the juvenile into society. Every detention facility for juveniles should have immediate access to adequate medical facilities and equipment appropriate to the number and requirements of its residents and staff trained in preventive health care and the handling of medical emergencies. Every juvenile who is ill, who complains of illness or who demonstrates symptoms of physical or mental difficulties, should be examined promptly by a medical officer.

52. Any medical officer who has reason to believe that the physical or mental health of a juvenile has been or will be injuriously affected by continued detention, a hunger strike or any condition of detention should report this fact immediately to the director of the detention facility in question and to the independent authority responsible for safeguarding the well-being of the juvenile.

53. A juvenile who is suffering from mental illness should be treated in a specialized institution under independent medical management. Steps should be taken, by arrangement with appropriate agencies, to ensure any necessary continuation of mental health care after release.

54. Juvenile detention facilities should adopt specialized drug abuse prevention and rehabilitation programmes administered by qualified personnel. These programmes should be adapted to the age, sex and other requirements of the juveniles concerned, and detoxification facilities and services staffed by trained personnel should be available to drug- or alcohol-dependent juveniles.

55. Medicines should be administered only for necessary treatment on medical grounds and, when possible, after having obtained the informed consent of the juvenile concerned. In particular, they must not be administered with a view to eliciting information or a confession, as a punishment or as a means of restraint. Juveniles shall never be testers in the experimental use of drugs and treatment. The administration of any drug should always be authorized and carried out by qualified medical personnel.

I. Notification of illness, injury and death
56. The family or guardian of a juvenile and any other person designated by the juvenile have the right to be informed of the state of health of the juvenile on request and in the event of any important changes in the health of the juvenile. The director of the detention facility should notify immediately the family or guardian of the juvenile concerned, or other designated person, in case of death, illness requiring transfer of the juvenile to an outside medical facility, or a condition requiring clinical care within the detention facility for more than 48 hours. Notification should also be given to the consular authorities of the State of which a foreign juvenile is a citizen.

57. Upon the death of a juvenile during the period of deprivation of liberty, the nearest relative should have the right to inspect the death certificate, see the body and determine the method of disposal of the body. Upon the death of a juvenile in detention, there should be an independent inquiry into the causes of death, the report of which should be made accessible to the nearest relative. This inquiry should also be made when the death of a juvenile occurs within six months from the date of his or her release from the detention facility and there is reason to believe that the death is related to the period of detention.

58. A juvenile should be informed at the earliest possible time of the death, serious illness or injury of any immediate family member and should be provided with the opportunity to attend the funeral of the deceased or go to the bedside of a critically ill relative.

J. Contacts with the wider community
59. Every means should be provided to ensure that juveniles have adequate communication with the outside world, which is an integral part of the right to fair and humane treatment and is essential to the preparation of juveniles for their return to society. Juveniles should be allowed to communicate with their families, friends and other persons or representatives of reputable outside organizations, to

leave detention facilities for a visit to their home and family and to receive special permission to leave the detention facility for educational, vocational or other important reasons. Should the juvenile be serving a sentence, the time spent outside a detention facility should be counted as part of the period of sentence.

60. Every juvenile should have the right to receive regular and frequent visits, in principle once a week and not less than once a month, in circumstances that respect the need of the juvenile for privacy, contact and unrestricted communication with the family and the defense counsel.

61. Every juvenile should have the right to communicate in writing or by telephone at least twice a week with the person of his or her choice, unless legally restricted, and should be assisted as necessary in order effectively to enjoy this right. Every juvenile should have the right to receive correspondence.

62. Juveniles should have the opportunity to keep themselves informed regularly of the news by reading newspapers, periodicals and other publications, through access to radio and television programmes and motion pictures, and through the visits of the representatives of any lawful club or organization in which the juvenile is interested.

K. Limitations of physical restraint and the use of force
63. Recourse to instruments of restraint and to force for any purpose should be prohibited, except as set forth in rule 64 below.

64. Instruments of restraint and force can only be used in exceptional cases, where all other control methods have been exhausted and failed, and only as explicitly authorized and specified by law and regulation. They should not cause humiliation or degradation, and should be used restrictively and only for the shortest possible period of time. By order of the director of the administration, such instruments might be resorted to in order to prevent the juvenile from inflicting self-injury, injuries to others or serious destruction of property. In such instances, the director should at once consult medical and other relevant personnel and report to the higher administrative authority.

65. The carrying and use of weapons by personnel should be prohibited in any facility where juveniles are detained.

L. Disciplinary procedures

66. Any disciplinary measures and procedures should maintain the interest of safety and an ordered community life and should be consistent with the upholding of the inherent dignity of the juvenile and the fundamental objective of institutional care, namely, instilling a sense of justice, self-respect and respect for the basic rights of every person.

67. All disciplinary measures constituting cruel, inhuman or degrading treatment shall be strictly prohibited, including corporal punishment, placement in a dark cell, closed or solitary confinement or any other punishment that may compromise the physical or mental health of the juvenile concerned. The reduction of diet and the restriction or denial of contact with family members should be prohibited for any purpose. Labor should always be viewed as an educational tool and a means of promoting the self-respect of the juvenile in preparing him or her for return to the community and should not be imposed as a disciplinary sanction. No juvenile should be sanctioned more than once for the same disciplinary infraction. Collective sanctions should be prohibited.

68. Legislation or regulations adopted by the competent administrative authority should establish norms concerning the following, taking full account of the fundamental characteristics, needs and rights of juveniles:
(a) Conduct constituting a disciplinary offense;
(b) Type and duration of disciplinary sanctions that may be inflicted;
(c) The authority competent to impose such sanctions;
(d) The authority competent to consider appeals.

69. A report of misconduct should be presented promptly to the competent authority, which should decide on it without undue delay. The competent authority should conduct a thorough examination of the case.

70. No juvenile should be disciplinarily sanctioned except in strict accordance with the terms of the law and regulations in force. No juvenile should be sanctioned unless he or she has been informed of the alleged infraction in a manner appropriate to the full understanding of the juvenile, and given a proper opportunity of presenting his or her defense, including the right of appeal to a competent impartial authority. Complete records should be kept of all disciplinary proceedings.

71. No juveniles should be responsible for disciplinary functions except in the supervision of specified social, educational or sports activities or in self-government programmes.

M. Inspection and complaints

72. Qualified inspectors or an equivalent duly constituted authority not belonging to the administration of the facility should be empowered to conduct inspections on a regular basis and to undertake unannounced inspections on their own initiative, and should enjoy full guarantees of independence in the exercise of this function. Inspectors should have unrestricted access to all persons employed by or working in any facility where juveniles are or may be deprived of their liberty, to all juveniles and to all records of such facilities.

73. Qualified medical officers attached to the inspecting authority or the public health service should participate in the inspections, evaluating compliance with the rules concerning the physical environment, hygiene, accommodation, food, exercise and medical services, as well as any other aspect or conditions of institutional life that affect the physical and mental health of juveniles. Every juvenile should have the right to talk in confidence to any inspecting officer.

74. After completing the inspection, the inspector should be required to submit a report on the findings. The report should include an evaluation of the compliance of the detention facilities with the present rules and relevant provisions of national law, and recommendations regarding any steps considered necessary to ensure compliance with them. Any facts discovered by an inspector that appear to indicate that a violation of legal provisions concerning the rights of juveniles or the operation of a juvenile detention facility has occurred should be communicated to the competent authorities for investigation and prosecution.

75. Every juvenile should have the opportunity of making requests or complaints to the director of the detention facility and to his or her authorized representative.

76. Every juvenile should have the right to make a request or complaint, without censorship as to substance, to the central administration, the judicial authority or other proper authorities through approved channels, and to be informed of the response without delay.

77. Efforts should be made to establish an independent office (ombudsman) to receive and investigate complaints made by juveniles deprived of their liberty and to assist in the achievement of equitable settlements.

78. Every juvenile should have the right to request assistance from family members, legal counselors, humanitarian groups or others where possible, in order to make a complaint. Illiterate juveniles should be provided with assistance should they need to use the services of public or private agencies and organizations which provide legal counsel or which are competent to receive complaints.

N. Return to the community

79. All juveniles should benefit from arrangements designed to assist them in returning to society, family life, education or employment after release. Procedures, including early release, and special courses should be devised to this end.

80. Competent authorities should provide or ensure services to assist juveniles in re-establishing themselves in society and to lessen prejudice against such juveniles. These services should ensure', to the extent possible, that the juvenile is provided with suitable residence, employment, clothing, and sufficient means to maintain himself or herself upon release in order to facilitate successful reintegration. The representatives of agencies providing such services should be consulted and should have access to juveniles while detained, with a view to assisting them in their return to the community.

V. PERSONNEL

81. Personnel should be qualified and include a sufficient number of specialists such as educators, vocational instructors, counselors, social workers, psychiatrists and psychologists. These and other specialist staff should normally be employed on a permanent basis. This should not preclude part-time or volunteer workers when the level of support and training they can provide is appropriate and beneficial. Detention facilities should make use of all remedial, educational, moral, spiritual, and other resources and forms of assistance that are appropriate and available in the community, according to the individual needs and problems of detained juveniles.

82. The administration should provide for the careful selection and recruitment of every grade and type of personnel, since the proper management of detention

facilities depends on their integrity, humanity, ability and professional capacity to deal with juveniles, as well as personal suitability for the work.

83. To secure the foregoing ends, personnel should be appointed as professional officers with adequate remuneration to attract and retain suitable women and men. The personnel of juvenile detention facilities should be continually encouraged to fulfil their duties and obligations in a humane, committed, professional, fair and efficient manner, to conduct themselves at all times in such a way as to deserve and gain the respect of the juveniles, and to provide juveniles with a positive role model and perspective.

84. The administration should introduce forms of organization and management that facilitate communications between different categories of staff in each detention facility so as to enhance cooperation between the various services engaged in the care of juveniles, as well as between staff and the administration, with a view to ensuring that staff directly in contact with juveniles are able to function in conditions favorable to the efficient fulfilment of their duties.

85. The personnel should receive such training as will enable them to carry out their responsibilities effectively, in particular training in child psychology, child welfare and international standards and norms of human rights and the rights of the child, including the present Rules. The personnel should maintain and improve their knowledge and professional capacity by attending courses of in-service training, to be organized at suitable intervals throughout their career.

86. The director of a facility should be adequately qualified for his or her task, with administrative ability and suitable training and experience, and should carry out his or her duties on a full-time basis.

87. In the performance of their duties, personnel of detention facilities should respect and protect the human dignity and fundamental human rights of all juveniles, in particular, as follows:
(a) No member of the detention facility or institutional personnel may inflict, instigate or tolerate any act of torture or any form of harsh, cruel, inhuman or degrading treatment, punishment, correction or discipline under any pretext or circumstance whatsoever;
(b) All personnel should rigorously oppose and combat any act of corruption, reporting it without delay to the competent authorities;

(c) All personnel should respect the present Rules. Personnel who have reason to believe that a serious violation of the present Rules has occurred or is about to occur should report the matter to their superior authorities or organs vested with reviewing or remedial power;

(d) All personnel should ensure the full protection of the physical and mental health of juveniles, including protection from physical, sexual and emotional abuse and exploitation, and should take immediate action to secure medical attention whenever required;

(e) All personnel should respect the right of the juvenile to privacy, and, in particular, should safeguard all confidential matters concerning juveniles or their families learned as a result of their professional capacity;

(f) All personnel should seek to minimize any differences between life inside and outside the detention facility which tend to lessen due respect for the dignity of juveniles as human beings.

Principles for the Protection of Persons With Mental Illness and the Improvement of Mental Health Care

Principles for the protection of persons with mental illness and the improvement of mental health care, A/RES/46/119, 75th plenary meeting, 17 December 1991

Adopted by General Assembly resolution 46/119 of 17 December 1991

Application

These Principles shall be applied without discrimination of any kind such as on grounds of disability, race, colour, sex, language, religion, political or other opinion, national, ethnic or social origin, legal or social status, age, property or birth.

Definitions

In these Principles:

"Counsel" means a legal or other qualified representative;

"Independent authority" means a competent and independent authority prescribed by domestic law;

"Mental health care" includes analysis and diagnosis of a person's mental condition, and treatment, care and rehabilitation for a mental illness or suspected mental illness;

"Mental health facility" means any establishment, or any unit of an establishment, which as its primary function provides mental health care;

"Mental health practitioner" means a medical doctor, clinical psychologist, nurse, social worker or other appropriately trained and qualified person with specific skills relevant to mental health care;

"Patient" means a person receiving mental health care and includes all persons who are admitted to a mental health facility;

"Personal representative" means a person charged by law with the duty of representing a patient's interests in any specified respect or of exercising specified rights on the patient's behalf, and includes the parent or legal guardian of a minor unless otherwise provided by domestic law;

"The review body" means the body established in accordance with Principle 17 to review the involuntary admission or retention of a patient in a mental health facility.

General limitation clause

The exercise of the rights set forth in these Principles may be subject only to such limitations as are prescribed by law and are necessary to protect the health or safety of the person concerned or of others, or otherwise to protect public safety, order, health or morals or the fundamental rights and freedoms of others.

Principle 1

Fundamental freedoms and basic rights

1. All persons have the right to the best available mental health care, which shall be part of the health and social care system.

2. All persons with a mental illness, or who are being treated as such persons, shall be treated with humanity and respect for the inherent dignity of the human person.

3. All persons with a mental illness, or who are being treated as such persons, have the right to protection from economic, sexual and other forms of exploitation, physical or other abuse and degrading treatment.

4. There shall be no discrimination on the grounds of mental illness. "Discrimination" means any distinction, exclusion or preference that has the effect of nullifying or impairing equal enjoyment of rights. Special measures solely to protect the rights, or secure the advancement, of persons with mental illness shall not be deemed to be discriminatory. Discrimination does not include any distinction, exclusion or preference undertaken in accordance with the provisions of these Principles and necessary to protect the human rights of a person with a mental illness or of other individuals.

5. Every person with a mental illness shall have the right to exercise all civil, political, economic, social and cultural rights as recognized in the Universal Declaration of Human Rights, the International Covenant on Economic, Social and

Cultural Rights, the International Covenant on Civil and Political Rights, and in other relevant instruments, such as the Declaration on the Rights of Disabled Persons and the Body of Principles for the Protection of All Persons under Any Form of Detention or Imprisonment.

6. Any decision that, by reason of his or her mental illness, a person lacks legal capacity, and any decision that, in consequence of such incapacity, a personal representative shall be appointed, shall be made only after a fair hearing by an independent and impartial tribunal established by domestic law. The person whose capacity is at issue shall be entitled to be represented by a counsel. If the person whose capacity is at issue does not himself or herself secure such representation, it shall be made available without payment by that person to the extent that he or she does not have sufficient means to pay for it. The counsel shall not in the same proceedings represent a mental health facility or its personnel and shall not also represent a member of the family of the person whose capacity is at issue unless the tribunal is satisfied that there is no conflict of interest. Decisions regarding capacity and the need for a personal representative shall be reviewed at reasonable intervals prescribed by domestic law. The person whose capacity is at issue, his or her personal representative, if any, and any other interested person shall have the right to appeal to a higher court against any such decision.

7. Where a court or other competent tribunal finds that a person with mental illness is unable to manage his or her own affairs, measures shall be taken, so far as is necessary and appropriate to that person's condition, to ensure the protection of his or her interest.

Principle 2

Protection of minors

Special care should be given within the purposes of these Principles and within the context of domestic law relating to the protection of minors to protect the rights of minors, including, if necessary, the appointment of a personal representative other than a family member.

Principle 3

Life in the community

Every person with a mental illness shall have the right to live and work, as far as possible, in the community.

Principle 4

Determination of mental illness

1. A determination that a person has a mental illness shall be made in accordance with internationally accepted medical standards.

2. A determination of mental illness shall never be made on the basis of political, economic or social status, or membership of a cultural, racial or religious group, or any other reason not directly relevant to mental health status.

3. Family or professional conflict, or non-conformity with moral, social, cultural or political values or religious beliefs prevailing in a person's community, shall never be a determining factor in diagnosing mental illness.

4. A background of past treatment or hospitalization as a patient shall not of itself justify any present or future determination of mental illness.

5. No person or authority shall classify a person as having, or otherwise indicate that a person has, a mental illness except for purposes directly relating to mental illness or the consequences of mental illness.

Principle 5

Medical examination

No person shall be compelled to undergo medical examination with a view to determining whether or not he or she has a mental illness except in accordance with a procedure authorized by domestic law.

Principle 6

Confidentiality

The right of confidentiality of information concerning all persons to whom these Principles apply shall be respected.

Principle 7

Role of community and culture

1. Every patient shall have the right to be treated and cared for, as far as possible, in the community in which he or she lives.

2. Where treatment takes place in a mental health facility, a patient shall have the right, whenever possible, to be treated near his or her home or the home of his or her relatives or friends and shall have the right to return to the community as soon as possible.

3. Every patient shall have the right to treatment suited to his or her cultural background.

Principle 8

Standards of care

1. Every patient shall have the right to receive such health and social care as is appropriate to his or her health needs, and is entitled to care and treatment in accordance with the same standards as other ill persons.

2. Every patient shall be protected from harm, including unjustified medication, abuse by other patients, staff or others or other acts causing mental distress or physical discomfort.

Principle 9

Treatment

1. Every patient shall have the right to be treated in the least restrictive environment and with the least restrictive or intrusive treatment appropriate to the patient's health needs and the need to protect the physical safety of others.

2. The treatment and care of every patient shall be based on an individually prescribed plan, discussed with the patient, reviewed regularly, revised as necessary and provided by qualified professional staff.

3. Mental health care shall always be provided in accordance with applicable standards of ethics for mental health practitioners, including internationally accepted standards such as the Principles of Medical Ethics adopted by the United Nations General Assembly. Mental health knowledge and skills shall never be abused.

4. The treatment of every patient shall be directed towards preserving and enhancing personal autonomy.

Principle 10

Medication

1. Medication shall meet the best health needs of the patient, shall be given to a patient only for therapeutic or diagnostic purposes and shall never be administered as a punishment or for the convenience of others. Subject to the provisions of paragraph 15 of Principle 11, mental health practitioners shall only administer medication of known or demonstrated efficacy.

2. All medication shall be prescribed by a mental health practitioner authorized by law and shall be recorded in the patient's records.

Principle 11

Consent to treatment

1. No treatment shall be given to a patient without his or her informed consent, except as provided for in paragraphs 6, 7, 8, 13 and 15 below.

2. Informed consent is consent obtained freely, without threats or improper inducements, after appropriate disclosure to the patient of adequate and understandable information in a form and language understood by the patient on:
(a) The diagnostic assessment;
(b) The purpose, method, Likely duration and expected benefit of the proposed treatment;
(c) Alternative modes of treatment, including those less intrusive; and
(d) Possible pain or discomfort, risks and side-effects of the proposed treatment.

3. A patient may request the presence of a person or persons of the patient's choosing during the procedure for granting consent.

4. A patient has the right to refuse or stop treatment, except as provided for in paragraphs 6, 7, 8, 13 and 15 below. The consequences of refusing or stopping treatment must be explained to the patient.

5. A patient shall never be invited or induced to waive the right to informed consent. If the patient should seek to do so, it shall be explained to the patient that the treatment cannot be given without informed consent.

6. Except as provided in paragraphs 7, 8, 12, 13, 14 and 15 below, a proposed plan of treatment may be given to a patient without a patient's informed consent if the following conditions are satisfied:
(a) The patient is, at the relevant time, held as an involuntary patient;
(b) An independent authority, having in its possession all relevant information, including the information specified in paragraph 2 above, is satisfied that, at the relevant time, the patient lacks the capacity to give or withhold informed consent to the proposed plan of treatment or, if domestic legislation so provides, that, having regard to the patient's own safety or the safety of others, the patient unreasonably withholds such consent; and
(c) The independent authority is satisfied that the proposed plan of treatment is in the best interest of the patient's health needs.

7. Paragraph 6 above does not apply to a patient with a personal representative empowered by law to consent to treatment for the patient; but, except as provided in paragraphs 12, 13, 14 and 15 below, treatment may be given to such a patient without his or her informed consent if the personal representative, having been given the information described in paragraph 2 above, consents on the patient's behalf.

8. Except as provided in paragraphs 12, 13, 14 and 15 below, treatment may also be given to any patient without the patient's informed consent if a qualified mental health practitioner authorized by law determines that it is urgently necessary in order to prevent immediate or imminent harm to the patient or to other persons. Such treatment shall not be prolonged beyond the period that is strictly necessary for this purpose.

9. Where any treatment is authorized without the patient's informed consent, every effort shall nevertheless be made to inform the patient about the nature of the treatment and any possible alternatives and to involve the patient as far as practicable in the development of the treatment plan.

10. All treatment shall be immediately recorded in the patient's medical records, with an indication of whether involuntary or voluntary.

11. Physical restraint or involuntary seclusion of a patient shall not be employed except in accordance with the officially approved procedures of the mental health facility and only when it is the only means available to prevent immediate or imminent harm to the patient or others. It shall not be prolonged beyond the period which is strictly necessary for this purpose. All instances of physical restraint or involuntary seclusion, the reasons for them and their nature and extent shall be recorded in the patient's medical record. A patient who is restrained or secluded shall be kept under humane conditions and be under the care and close and regular supervision of qualified members of the staff. A personal representative, if any and if relevant, shall be given prompt notice of any physical restraint or involuntary seclusion of the patient.

12. Sterilization shall never be carried out as a treatment for mental illness.

13. A major medical or surgical procedure may be carried out on a person with mental illness only where it is permitted by domestic law, where it is considered that it would best serve the health needs of
(a) Recognition everywhere as a person before the law;
(b) Privacy;
(c) Freedom of communication, which includes freedom to communicate with other persons in the facility; freedom to send and receive uncensored private communications; freedom to receive, in private, visits from a counsel or personal representative and, at all reasonable times, from other visitors; and freedom of access to postal and telephone services and to newspapers, radio and television;
(d) Freedom of religion or belief.

2. The environment and living conditions in mental health facilities shall be as close as possible to those of the normal life of persons of similar age and in particular shall include:
(a) Facilities for recreational and leisure activities;
(b) Facilities for education;

(c) Facilities to purchase or receive items for daily living, recreation and communication;

(d) Facilities, and encouragement to use such facilities, for a patient's engagement in active occupation suited to his or her social and cultural background, and for appropriate vocational rehabilitation measures to promote reintegration in the community. These measures should include vocational guidance, vocational training and placement services to enable patients to secure or retain employment in the community.

3. In no circumstances shall a patient be subject to forced labour. Within the limits compatible with the needs of the patient and with the requirements of institutional administration, a patient shall be able to choose the type of work he or she wishes to perform.

4. The labour of a patient in a mental health facility shall not be exploited. Every such patient shall have the right to receive the same remuneration for any work which he or she does as would, according to domestic law or custom, be paid for such work to a non-patient. Every such patient shall, in any event, have the right to receive a fair share of any remuneration which is paid to the mental health facility for his or her work.

Principle 14

Resources for mental health facilities

1. A mental health facility shall have access to the same level of resources as any other health establishment, and in particular:

(a) Qualified medical and other appropriate professional staff in sufficient numbers and with adequate space to provide each patient with privacy and a programme of appropriate and active therapy;

(b) Diagnostic and therapeutic equipment for the patient;

(c) Appropriate professional care; and

(d) Adequate, regular and comprehensive treatment, including supplies of medication.

2. Every mental health facility shall be inspected by the competent authorities with sufficient frequency to ensure that the conditions, treatment and care of patients comply with these Principles.

Principle 15

Admission principles

1. Where a person needs treatment in a mental health facility, every effort shall be made to avoid involuntary admission.

2. Access to a mental health facility shall be administered in the same way as access to any other facility for any other illness.

3. Every patient not admitted involuntarily shall have the right to leave the mental health facility at any time unless the criteria for his or her retention as an involuntary patient, as set forth in Principle 16, apply, and he or she shall be informed of that right.

Principle 16

Involuntary admission

1. A person may (a) be admitted involuntarily to a mental health facility as a patient; or (b) having already been admitted voluntarily as a patient, be retained as an involuntary patient in the mental health facility if, and only if, a qualified mental health practitioner authorized by law for that purpose determines, in accordance with Principle 4, that person has a mental illness and considers:
(a) That, because of that mental illness, there is a serious likelihood of immediate or imminent harm to that person or to other persons; or
(b) That, in the case of a person whose mental illness is severe and whose judgement is impaired, failure to admit or retain that person is likely to lead to a serious deterioration in his or her condition or will prevent the giving of appropriate treatment that can only be given by admission to a mental health facility in accordance with the principle of the least restrictive alternative.

In the case referred to in subparagraph (b), a second such mental health practitioner, independent of the first, should be consulted where possible. If such consultation takes place, the involuntary admission or retention may not take place unless the second mental health practitioner concurs.

2. Involuntary admission or retention shall initially be for a short period as specified by domestic law for observation and preliminary treatment pending review of the admission or retention by the review body. The grounds of the admission shall be communicated to the patient without delay and the fact of the

admission and the grounds for it shall also be communicated promptly and in detail to the review body, to the patient's personal representative, if any, and, unless the patient objects, to the patient's family.

3. A mental health facility may receive involuntarily admitted patients only if the facility has been designated to do so by a competent authority prescribed by domestic law.

Principle 17

Review body

1. The review body shall be a judicial or other independent and impartial body established by domestic law and functioning in accordance with procedures laid down by domestic law. It shall, in formulating its decisions, have the assistance of one or more qualified and independent mental health practitioners and take their advice into account.

2. The review body's initial review, as required by paragraph 2 of Principle 16, of a decision to admit or retain a person as an involuntary patient shall take place as soon as possible after that decision and shall be conducted in accordance with simple and expeditious procedures as specified by domestic law.

3. The review body shall periodically review the cases of involuntary patients at reasonable intervals as specified by domestic law.

4. An involuntary patient may apply to the review body for release or voluntary status, at reasonable intervals as specified by domestic law.

5. At each review, the review body shall consider whether the criteria for involuntary admission set out in paragraph 1 of Principle 16 are still satisfied, and, if not, the patient shall be discharged as an involuntary patient.

6. If at any time the mental health practitioner responsible for the case is satisfied that the conditions for the retention of a person as an involuntary patient are no longer satisfied, he or she shall order the discharge of that person as such a patient.

7. A patient or his personal representative or any interested person shall have the right to appeal to a higher court against a decision that the patient be admitted to, or be retained in, a mental health facility.

Principle 18

Procedural safeguards

1. The patient shall be entitled to choose and appoint a counsel to represent the patient as such, including representation in any complaint procedure or appeal. If the patient does not secure such services, a counsel shall be made available without payment by the patient to the extent that the patient lacks sufficient means to pay.

2. The patient shall also be entitled to the assistance, if necessary, of the services of an interpreter. Where such services are necessary and the patient does not secure them, they shall be made available without payment by the patient to the extent that the patient lacks sufficient means to pay.

3. The patient and the patient's counsel may request and produce at any hearing an independent mental health report and any other reports and oral, written and other evidence that are relevant and admissible.

4. Copies of the patient's records and any reports and documents to be submitted shall be given to the patient and to the patient's counsel, except in special cases where it is determined that a specific disclosure to the patient would cause serious harm to the patient's health or put at risk the safety of others. As domestic law may provide, any document not given to the patient should, when this can be done in confidence, be given to the patient's personal representative and counsel. When any part of a document is withheld from a patient, the patient or the patient's counsel, if any, shall receive notice of the withholding and the reasons for it and shall be subject to judicial review.

5. The patient and the patient's personal representative and counsel shall be entitled to attend, participate and be heard personally in any hearing.

6. If the patient or the patient's personal representative or counsel requests that a particular person be present at a hearing, that person shall be admitted unless it is determined that the person's presence could cause serious harm to the patient's health or put at risk the safety of others.

7. Any decision whether the hearing or any part of it shall be in public or in private and may be publicly reported shall give full consideration to the patient's own wishes, to the need to respect the privacy of the patient and of other persons and to

the need to prevent serious harm to the patient's health or to avoid putting at risk the safety of others.

8. The decision arising out of the hearing and the reasons for it shall be expressed in writing. Copies shall be given to the patient and his or her personal representative and counsel. In deciding whether the decision shall be published in whole or in part, full consideration shall be given to the patient's own wishes, to the need to respect his or her privacy and that of other persons, to the public interest in the open administration of justice and to the need to prevent serious harm to the patient's health or to avoid putting at risk the safety of others.

Principle 19

Access to information

1. A patient (which term in this Principle includes a former patient) shall be entitled to have access to the information concerning the patient in his or her health and personal records maintained by a mental health facility. This right may be subject to restrictions in order to prevent serious harm to the patient's health and avoid putting at risk the safety of others. As domestic law may provide, any such information not given to the patient should, when this can be done in confidence, be given to the patient's personal representative and counsel. When any of the information is withheld from a patient, the patient or the patient's counsel, if any, shall receive notice of the withholding and the reasons for it and it shall be subject to judicial review.

2. Any written comments by the patient or the patient's personal representative or counsel shall, on request, be inserted in the patient's file.

Principle 20

Criminal offenders

1. This Principle applies to persons serving sentences of imprisonment for criminal offences, or who are otherwise detained in the course of criminal proceedings or investigations against them, and who are determined to have a mental illness or who it is believed may have such an illness.

2. All such persons should receive the best available mental health care as provided in Principle 1. These Principles shall apply to them to the fullest extent possible, with only such limited modifications and exceptions as are necessary in the circumstances. No such modifications and exceptions shall prejudice the persons' rights under the instruments noted in paragraph 5 of Principle 1.

3. Domestic law may authorize a court or other competent authority, acting on the basis of competent and independent medical advice, to order that such persons be admitted to a mental health facility.

4. Treatment of persons determined to have a mental illness shall in all circumstances be consistent with Principle 11.

Principle 21

Complaints

Every patient and former patient shall have the right to make a complaint through procedures as specified by domestic law.

Principle 22

Monitoring and remedies

States shall ensure that appropriate mechanisms are in force to promote compliance with these Principles, for the inspection of mental health facilities, for the submission, investigation and resolution of complaints and for the institution of appropriate disciplinary or judicial proceedings for professional misconduct or violation of the rights of a patient.

Principle 23

Implementation

1. States should implement these Principles through appropriate legislative, judicial, administrative, educational and other measures, which they shall review periodically.

2. States shall make these Principles widely known by appropriate and active means.

Principle 24

Scope of principles relating to mental health facilities

These Principles apply to all persons who are admitted to a mental health facility.

Principle 25

Saving of existing rights

There shall be no restriction upon or derogation from any existing rights of patients, including rights recognized in applicable international or domestic law, on the pretext that these Principles do not recognize such rights or that they recognize them to a lesser extent.

Excerpts from the Principles of Medical Ethics Relevant to the Role of Health Personnel

Principles of Medical Ethics relevant to the Role of Health Personnel, particularly Physicians, in the Protection of Prisoners and Detainees against Torture and Other Cruel, Inhuman or Degrading Treatment or Punishment, G.A. res. 37/194, annex, 37 U.N. GAOR Supp. (No. 51) at 211, U.N. Doc. A/37/51 (1982).

Adopted by General Assembly resolution 37/194 of 18 December 1982

Principle 2

It is a gross contravention of medical ethics, as well as an offence under applicable international instruments, for health personnel, particularly physicians, to engage, actively or passively, in acts which constitute participation in, complicity in, incitement to or attempts to commit torture or other cruel, inhuman or degrading treatment or punishment.[371]

Principle 5

It is a contravention of medical ethics for health personnel, particularly physicians, to participate in any procedure for restraining a prisoner or detainee unless such a procedure is determined in accordance with purely medical criteria as being necessary for the protection of the physical or mental health or the safety of the prisoner or detainee himself, of his fellow prisoners or detainees, or of his guardians, and presents no hazard to his physical or mental health.

---

[371] See the Declaration on the Protection of All Persons from Being Subjected to Torture and Other Cruel, Inhumane, or Degrading Treatment or Punishment (resolution 3452 (XXX), annex). [back to text]

APPENDIX B. RUSSIAN LAW

1. The Constitution of the Russian Federation
2. The Family Code of the Russian Federation
3. The Fundamentals of Legislation of the Russian Federation on Health
4. Protection (the Health Protection law)
5. The Federal Law on Education
6. U.N. Convention on the Rights of the Child
7. United Nations Declaration on the Rights of Mentally Retarded Persons
8. Law on Basic Guarantees of the Rights of the Child
9. The Law on Additional Guarantees for the Social Protection of Child-Orphans
10. Children without Parental Guardians
11. Law on Social Protection for Invalids in the Russian Federation
12. Criminal Code of the Russian Federation

APPENDIX C. COMMITTEE ON THE RIGHTS OF THE CHILD, COMMENTS ON THE RUSSIAN FEDERATION

U.N. Doc. CRC/C/15/Add.4 (1993). Distr. GENERAL, CRC/C/15/Add.4
18 February 1993, Original: ENGLISH

COMMITTEE ON THE RIGHTS OF THE CHILD
Third session

CONSIDERATION OF REPORTS SUBMITTED BY STATES PARTIES
UNDER ARTICLE 44 OF THE CONVENTION

Concluding observations of the Committee on the Rights of the Child:
Russian Federation

1. The Committee considered the initial report of the Russian Federation (CRC/C/3/Add.5) at its 62nd, 63rd and 64th meetings (CRC/C/SR.62 to 64), held on 21 and 22 January 1993, and adopted [*] the following concluding observations:

A. Introduction

2. The Committee expresses satisfaction at the timely submission of the Russian Federation's initial report and for the frank, self-critical and comprehensive manner in which it was prepared. The Committee notes with appreciation the high-level representation sent to discuss the report, which serves as an indication of the importance attached by the Government of the Russian Federation to its obligations under the Convention, and for the open, comprehensive and constructive approach which characterized the dialogue with the delegation.

B. Positive aspects

3. The Committee is encouraged by the Government's willingness to define and appreciate the problems impeding the implementation of the rights provided for in the Convention and to search for adequate solutions to face them. In this regard, the Committee notes with satisfaction the progress being made in introducing legislative measures to improve the application of the Convention as well as the proposed establishment of juvenile and family courts. Equally, it recognizes the importance of the steps being taken to develop: the involvement of local and regional authorities in taking responsibility for implementing the rights of the child; the participation of non-governmental organizations in programmes to implement the rights of the child; the training of social and other workers dealing directly with

209

children and family related problems; the awareness of the importance of the family and equal parental responsibilities; and the dissemination of information on the rights of the child.

4. The Committee also notes with satisfaction, in the light of article 4 of the Convention, the allocation of further resources for the benefit of children as a consequence of the economic effects of disarmament.

5. At a time of critical change in the State party and in view of the information provided by the delegation, the Committee recognizes the importance accorded by the State party to introducing positive changes for the benefit of children and to continuing to pursue policies that take into account the needs of children in a period of structural adjustment.

C. Factors and difficulties impeding the implementation of the Convention
6. The Committee recognizes the difficulties facing the Russian Federation in this period of political transition in a climate of social change and economic crisis. Similarly, the Committee recognizes the legacy of certain attitudes which hamper the implementation of the rights of the child. These relate to, inter alia, the institutionalization of child care, the disabled and family responsibilities.

7. While recognizing the importance of the various reforms mentioned by the delegation, the Committee notes, however, that it is unable at this stage to assess the impact of the new and proposed legislative and other changes on the situation of children.

D. Principal subjects of concern
8. The Committee is concerned about the effects on children of the economic crisis. In this connection, the Committee is particularly concerned as to whether adequate and appropriate measures are being taken to protect children from being the victims of economic reform in the light of articles 3 and 4 of the Convention.

9. The Committee is concerned that society is not sufficiently sensitive to the needs and situation of children from particularly vulnerable and disadvantaged groups, such as the disabled, in the light of article 2 of the Convention.

10. The Committee considers the serious problems of family life in the Russian Federation to be an area of priority concern. The Committee notes with particular concern the tendency towards the breakdown of family culture as regards

abandoned children, abortion, the divorce rate, the number of adoptions, the number of children born out of wedlock and recovery of maintenance obligations.

11. Similarly, the Committee is concerned about the practice of the institutionalization in boarding schools of children who are deprived of a family environment, particularly in cases of abandonment or where children are orphaned.

12. The Committee expresses its concern as to the problems encountered in the immunization programme, the level of antenatal care, family planning programmes and the training of local community health workers. The Committee also expresses its concern at the frequent recourse to abortion as what appears to be a method of family planning.

13. As regards the implementation of article 28 of the Convention, the Committee expresses its concern as to the situation of the girl child in rural areas.

14. The Committee expresses its concern as to the compatibility of juvenile justice and penitentiary institutions with article 37 of the Convention and how the rights of the child to leisure and contacts with the family and the best interests of the child are protected in such situations. The Committee also expresses concern at the present organization of the system of administration of justice and its compatibility with article 37 of the Convention and other standards relating to juvenile justice.

15. The Committee notes with concern the increasing crime rate among children and the vulnerability of children to sexual abuse, drug abuse and alcoholism.

E. Suggestions and recommendations
16. The Committee recommends that in a period of structural adjustment it is particularly important to monitor regularly the effects of economic change on children. The Committee also emphasizes the appropriateness of identifying and using indicators to follow the Government's progress in the implementation of legislative and other measures for the rights of the child.

17. The Committee proposes that the Government consider the establishment of a National State Committee or any similar structure with the purpose of coordinating the implementation of the Convention and the monitoring thereof. The Committee recommends that support should be given to local and other non-governmental organizations for the mobilization of work on the rights of the child. The Committee also recommends the active participation of non-governmental

organizations as well as children and youth groups in changing and influencing attitudes for the better implementation of the rights of the child.

18. The Committee considers that greater efforts should be made to provide family life education, to organize discussions on the role of the family in society and to develop awareness of the equal responsibilities of parents.

19. The Committee recommends that alternatives to institutionalization in boarding schools, such as foster care, should be actively sought. The Committee also recommends the further training of personnel in all institutions, such as social, legal or educational workers. An important part of such training should be to emphasize the promotion and protection of the child's sense of dignity and the issue of child neglect and maltreatment. Mechanisms to evaluate the ongoing training of personnel dealing with children are also required.

20. The Committee recommends that the primary health care system be improved regarding the effectiveness of, inter alia, antenatal care, health education, including sex education, family planning and immunization programmes. As regards problems relating specifically to the immunization programme, the Committee suggests that the Government should look to international cooperation for support in the procurement and manufacturing of vaccines.

21. The Committee is concerned about the occurrence of maltreatment and cruelty towards children in and outside the family and suggests that procedures and mechanisms be developed to deal with complaints by children of their maltreatment or of cruelty towards them.

22. Taking into account the positive steps being taken to revise the Penal Code and legislation in this field, the Committee recommends that the State party undertake comprehensive judicial reform as regards the administration of juvenile justice and that the international standards in this field, such as the "Beijing Rules", the "Riyadh Guidelines" and the Rules for the Protection of Juveniles Deprived of their Liberty, should serve as a guide in this revision. As regards alternative approaches to institutionalization, particular attention should be paid to rehabilitation measures, psychological recovery and social reintegration in line with article 39 of the Convention.

23. The Committee also suggests that part of the training of law enforcement officers, judges and other administration of justice officials be devoted to an understanding of international standards on juvenile justice.

24. The Committee emphasizes that more determined steps need to be taken to combat child prostitution; for example, the police forces should accord high priority to the investigation of such cases and the development of programmes to implement the provisions contained in article 39 of the Convention.

* At the 73rd meeting, held on 28 January 1993.

Life of an Orphan in the Russian Federation 1998

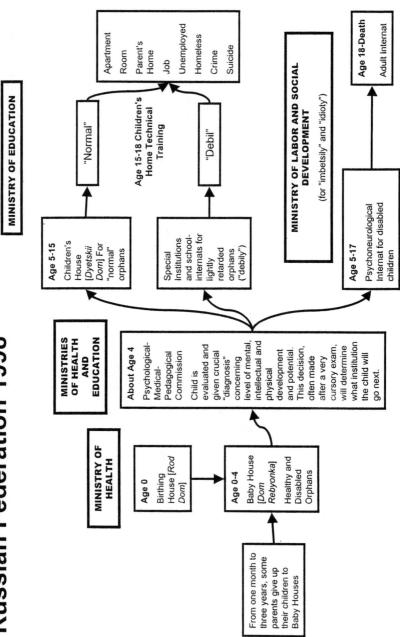

MINISTRY OF EDUCATION

"Normal"

Age 15-18 Children's Home Technical Training

"Debil"

Apartment
Room
Parent's Home
Job
Unemployed
Homeless
Crime
Suicide

Age 5-15
Children's House [Dyetskii Dom] For "normal" orphans

Special Institutions and school-internats for lightly retarded orphans ("debily")

MINISTRY OF LABOR AND SOCIAL DEVELOPMENT
(for "imbetsily" and "idioty")

Age 18-Death
Adult Internat

MINISTRIES OF HEALTH AND EDUCATION

About Age 4
Psychological-Medical-Pedagogical Commission

Child is evaluated and given crucial "diagnosis" concerning level of mental, intellectual and physical development and potential. This decision, often made after a very cursory exam, will determine what institution the child will go next.

Age 5-17
Psychoneurological Internat for disabled children

MINISTRY OF HEALTH

Age 0
Birthing House [Rod Dom]

Age 0-4
Baby House [Dom Rebyonka] Healthy and Disabled Orphans

From one month to three years, some parents give up their children to Baby Houses